Journey to a War

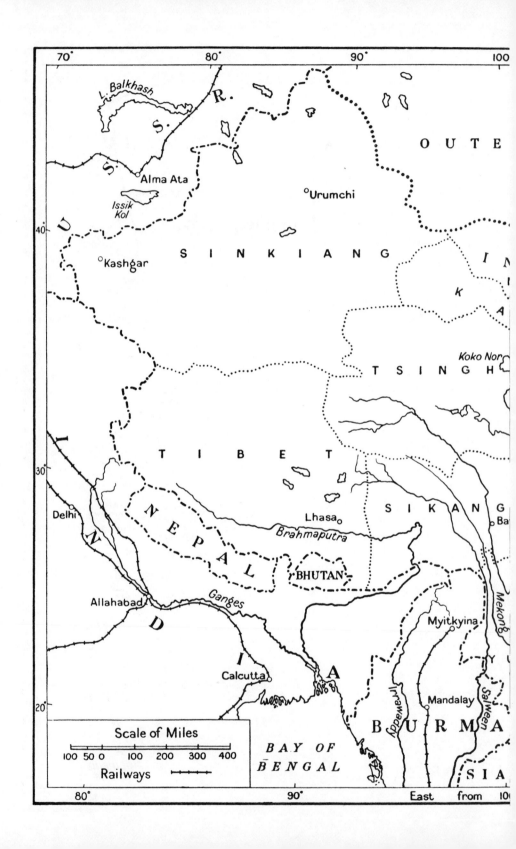

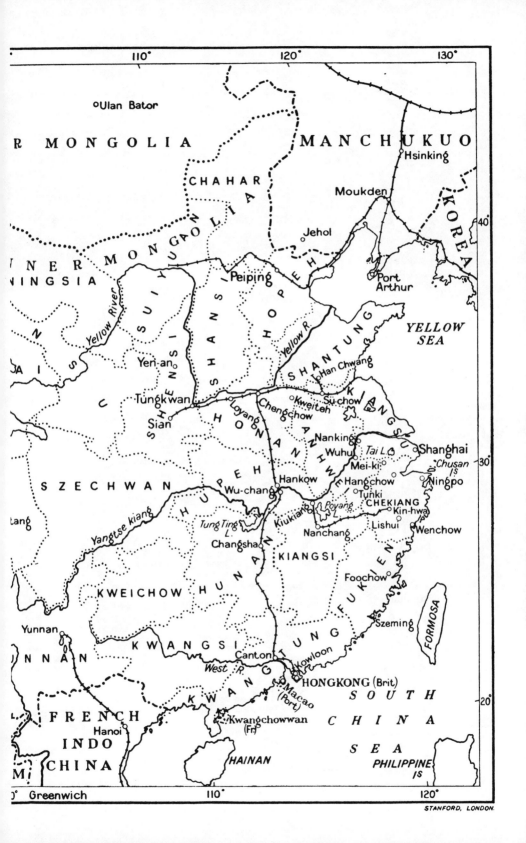

OUTER MONGOLIA

OUTER MONGOLIA

MANCHUKUO

oUlan Bator

Hsinking

CHAHAR

Moukden

KOREA

Jehol

40°

NINGSIA

INNER MONGOLIA

Peiping

HOPEH

Port
Arthur

YELLOW
SEA

SUIYUAN

SHANSI

Yellow River

Yellow R.

SHANTUNG

Yen-an

oHan Chwang

Tungkwan

Kweiteh

Su-chow

KIANGSU

Sian

Loyang

Chengchow

SHENSI

HONAN

Nanking

Wuhu

Tai L.

Shanghai

ANHWEI

Mei-ki

Chusan Is.

30°

SZECHWAN

HUPEH

Hankow

Wu-chang

Hangchow

Ningpo

Tunki

CHEKIANG

Yangtse kiang

Tung Ting
L.

Kiukiang

Poyang

Kin-hwa

Lishui

Wenchow

Changsha

Nanchang

KIANGSI

KWEICHOW

HUNAN

Foochow

FUKIEN

Yunnan

KWANGSI

Szeming

FORMOSA

YUNNAN

Canton

Kowloon

KWANGTUNG

West R.

HONGKONG (Brit)

Macao
(Port)

SOUTH

FRENCH

Kwangchowwan
(Fr)

CHINA

Hanoi

INDO

HAINAN

SEA

CHINA

PHILIPPINE
IS

20°

Greenwich

110°

120°

STANFORD, LONDON.

為仇恨而生

葉淺予作

Terror Bequeathed

Cartoon by Yet Chian-yu from the magazine 'War-time Cartoons'

JOURNEY
TO A
WAR

By

W. H. AUDEN

&

CHRISTOPHER ISHERWOOD

PARAGON HOUSE

New York

First Paragon House edition, 1990

Published in the United States by

Paragon House
90 Fifth Avenue, NY 10011

Published by arrangement with
Random House, Inc.
Library of Congress Cataloging-in-Publication
Data
Auden, W. H. (Wystan Hugh), 1907-1973.
Journey to a war / by W.H. Auden &
Christopher Isherwood.—1st Paragon House
ed. p. cm.
Reprint. Originally published: New York :
Random House, c1939.
ISBN 1-55778-328-4
1. China—Description and travel—
1901-1948. 2. Sino-Japanese Conflict,
1937-1945. 3. Auden, W.H. (Wystan Hugh),
1907-1973—Journeys—China.
I. Isherwood, Christopher, 1904-. II. Title.
DS710.A93   1990
915.104'42—dc20   89-38303
                                   CIP

Manufactured in the United States of America

This book is printed on acid-free paper

To E. M. FORSTER

Here, though the bombs are real and dangerous,
And Italy and King's are far away,
And we're afraid that you will speak to us,
You promise still the inner life shall pay.

As we run down the slope of Hate with gladness
You trip us up like an unnoticed stone,
And just as we are closeted with Madness
You interrupt us like the telephone.

For we are Lucy, Turton, Philip, we
Wish international evil, are excited
To join the jolly ranks of the benighted

Where Reason is denied and Love ignored:
But, as we swear our lie, Miss Avery
Comes out into the garden with the sword.

FOREWORD

Early in the summer of 1937, we were commissioned by Messrs. Faber and Faber of London and by Random House of New York to write a travel book about the East. The choice of itinerary was left to our own discretion. The outbreak of the Sino-Japanese War in August decided us to go to China. We left England in January 1938, returning at the end of July.

This was our first journey to any place east of Suez. We spoke no Chinese, and possessed no special knowledge of Far Eastern affairs. It is hardly necessary, therefore, to point out that we cannot vouch for the accuracy of many statements made in this book. Some of our informants may have been unreliable, some merely polite, some deliberately pulling our leg. We can only record, for the benefit of the reader who has never been to China, some impression of what he would be likely to see, and of what kind of stories he would be likely to hear.

It would take too long to mention all those to whom we are indebted, but we should like particularly to thank:

Mr. Sloss (Vice-Chancellor of Hongkong University), the Rev. and Mrs. Geoffrey Allen, Mr. Basil Boothby, Mr. William Spring, the Military Governor of Che-kiang, the Provincial Government of Kinhwa, Dr. Ayres, Dr.

FOREWORD

Brown, Dr. Gilbert, Dr. MacFadyen, Sir Archibald and Lady Clark Kerr—for their hospitality;

Mr. Blunt (H.M. Consul-General at Canton), Mr. Moss (H.M. Consul-General at Hankow), the Governor of Kwantung, Mr. Wu Teh-chen, Mr. Hollington Tong, Dr. Han Li-wu, Miss Agnes Smedley, Mr. France, Mr. Edgar Snow, Mr. Freddy Kaufmann, and Mr. Rewi Alley—for information and introductions;

The Hankow Film Studios, for two stills from *Fight to the Last*;

Mr. C. C. Yeh, for the cartoon used as our frontispiece;

Major Yang and Mr. Zinmay Zau, for Chinese poems;

Mr. Hughes of Oxford, for assistance in translation; and, last but not least, our Boy, Chiang, for his faithful and efficient service.

W. H. A.
C. I.

December 1938.

LONDON TO HONGKONG

The Voyage

Where does the journey look which the watcher upon the
    quay,
Standing under his evil star, so bitterly envies?
When the mountains swim away with slow calm strokes,
    and the gulls
Abandon their vow? Does it still promise the Juster Life?

And, alone with his heart at last, does the traveller find
In the vaguer touch of the wind and the fickle flash of the
    sea
Proofs that somewhere there exists, really, the Good
    Place,
As certain as those the children find in stones and holes?

No, he discovers nothing: he does not want to arrive.
The journey is false; the false journey really an illness
On the false island where the heart cannot act and will
    not suffer:
He condones the fever; he is weaker than he thought; his
    weakness is real.

But at moments, as when the real dolphins with leap and
    abandon
Cajole for recognition, or, far away, a real island
Gets up to catch his eye, the trance is broken: he remem-
    bers
The hours, the places where he was well; he believes in joy.

And maybe the fever shall have a cure, the true journey
    an end
Where hearts meet and are really true: and away this sea
    that parts
The hearts that alter, but is the same, always; and goes
Everywhere, joining the false and the true, but cannot
    suffer.

The Sphinx

Did it once issue from the carver's hand
Healthy? Even the earliest conquerors saw
The face of a sick ape, a bandaged paw,
A Presence in the hot invaded land.

The lion of a tortured stubborn star,
It does not like the young, nor love, nor learning:
Time hurt it like a person; it lies, turning
A vast behind on shrill America,

And witnesses. The huge hurt face accuses,
And pardons nothing, least of all success.
The answers that it utters have no uses

To those who face akimbo its distress:
'Do people like me?' No. The slave amuses
The lion: 'Am I to suffer always?' Yes.

LONDON TO HONGKONG

The Ship

The streets are brightly lit; our city is kept clean:
The third class have the greasiest cards, the first play high;
The beggars sleeping in the bows have never seen
What can be done in staterooms; no one asks why.

Lovers are writing letters, sportsmen playing ball;
One doubts the honour, one the beauty, of his wife;
A boy's ambitious; perhaps the captain hates us all;
Someone perhaps is leading the civilized life.

It is our culture that with such calm progresses
Over the barren plains of a sea; somewhere ahead
The septic East, a war, new flowers and new dresses.

Somewhere a strange and shrewd To-morrow goes to bed
Planning the test for men from Europe; no one guesses
Who will be most ashamed, who richer, and who dead.

The Traveller

Holding the distance up before his face
And standing under the peculiar tree,
He seeks the hostile unfamiliar place,
It is the strangeness that he tries to see

Of lands where he will not be asked to stay;
And fights with all his powers to be the same,
The One who loves Another far away,
And has a home, and wears his father's name.

Yet he and his are always the Expected:
The harbours touch him as he leaves the steamer,
The Soft, the Sweet, the Easily-Accepted;

The cities hold his feeling like a fan;
And crowds make room for him without a murmur,
As the earth has patience with the life of man.

Macao

A weed from Catholic Europe, it took root
Between the yellow mountains and the sea,
And bore these gay stone houses like a fruit,
And grew on China imperceptibly.

Rococo images of Saint and Saviour
Promise her gamblers fortunes when they die;
Churches beside the brothels testify
That faith can pardon natural behaviour.

This city of indulgence need not fear
The major sins by which the heart is killed,
And governments and men are torn to pieces:

Religious clocks will strike; the childish vices
Will safeguard the low virtues of the child;
And nothing serious can happen here.

LONDON TO HONGKONG

Hongkong

The leading characters are wise and witty;
Substantial men of birth and education
With wide experience of administration,
They know the manners of a modern city.

Only the servants enter unexpected;
Their silence has a fresh dramatic use:
Here in the East the bankers have erected
A worthy temple to the Comic Muse.

Ten thousand miles from home and What's-her-name,
The bugle on the Late Victorian hill
Puts out the soldier's light; off-stage, a war

Thuds like the slamming of a distant door:
We cannot postulate a General Will;
For what we are, we have ourselves to blame.

TRAVEL-DIARY

1

On February 28th, 1938, we left Hongkong in the *Tai-Shan*, a river-boat, bound for Canton.

At this time, Canton could be reached by two alternative routes: the river-line or the Kowloon–Canton railway. The railway was being bombed, almost daily, by Japanese planes operating from an aircraft-carrier anchored somewhere off Macao; but these attacks did very little to disturb traffic. Most of the bombs fell wide of their mark. If the track was hit, gangs of coolies, working at amazing speed, could repair it within a few hours. The river-boats, which were British-owned, had never been bombed at all.

It was a fine, hot, steamy morning. We breakfasted on board, and hurried out on to the deck, eager to miss none of the sensational sights which had been promised us. Friends in Hongkong, who had made the trip, had described how Japanese planes, returning from a raid, might swoop low over the *Tai-Shan*, playfully aiming their machine-guns at our heads. Or perhaps we should actually see the Japanese warships engaged in an artillery duel with the Bocca Tigris forts. If only we could get some photographs! We were secretly determined to try, despite the printed warning against cameras which we had read in the dining-saloon: 'During the critical time of the coun-

27

try, anything might be considered as a wrong deed or sub-
jected to a guilty movement. . . .'

One's first entry into a war-stricken country as a neutral observer is bound to be dream-like, unreal. And, indeed, this whole enormous voyage, from January London
to tropical February Hongkong had had the quality—
now boring, now extraordinary and beautiful—of a dream.
At Hongkong, we had said to each other, we shall wake
up, everything will come true. But we hadn't woken; only
the dream had changed. The new dream was more con-
fused than the old, less soothing, even slightly apprehensive. It was all about dinner-parties at very long tables,
and meetings with grotesquely famous newspaper-charac-
ters—the British Ambassador, the Governor, Sir Victor
Sassoon. We seemed to be in a perpetual hurry, struggling
into our dinner-jackets, racing off in taxis to keep appoint-
ments for which we were already hopelessly late. And always, like dreamers, we were worried—listening in a daze
to instructions or advice which we knew, only too well,
we should never be able to remember in the morning.
There were warnings, too; some of them as fantastic as
any nightmare: 'Never mix with a Chinese crowd, or you'll
get typhus.' 'Never go for a walk alone, or they may shoot
you as a spy.'

Now, as the *Tai-Shan* steered out of the harbour, towards the big whitewashed rock which marks the passage
into the mouth of the West River, we made another effort
to shake ourselves free from the dream. 'Well', Auden said,
'here we are. Now it's going to start.'

Here we were, steaming smoothly into the estuary of
the broad, softly-swimming river, steaming away from the
dinner-tables, the American movies, the statue of Queen
Victoria on the guarded British island, steaming west into

dangerous, unpredictable war-time China. Now *it*—whatever it was—was going to start. This wasn't a dream, or a boys' game of Indians. We were adult, if amateur, war-correspondents entering upon the scene of our duties. But, for the moment, I could experience only an irresponsible, schoolboyish feeling of excitement. We scanned the river-banks eagerly, half-expecting to see them bristle with enemy bayonets.

'Look! A Japanese gunboat!'

There she lay, murderously quiet, anchored right across our path. We passed very close. You could see the faces of her crew, as they moved about the deck, or polished the sights of a gun. Their utter isolation, on their deadly little steel island, was almost pathetic. Self-quarantined in hatred, like sufferers from a fatally infectious disease, they lay outcast and apart, disowned by the calm healthy river and the pure sanity of the sky. They were like something outside nature, perverse, a freak. Absorbed in their duties, they scarcely gave us a glance—and this seemed strangest, most unnatural of all. That is what War is, I thought: two ships pass each other, and nobody waves his hand.

The river narrowed in. Here were the Bocca Tigris forts. Ranged along the fertile shore, and rising out of the shallow golden water on their leafy islands, they looked utterly deserted, harmless and picturesque as the ruins of a hundred-year-old campaign. It was hard to believe that they were equipped with modern weapons which had actually inflicted considerable damage upon the Japanese ships. Behind them, in the middle of the river, stood a small grey mountain shaped like a swimming turtle. The sailors began to take soundings. A young American journalist told us that river-boats sometimes ran aground here. In the course

29

of our conversation, he mentioned casually that he had been on the *Panay* at the time of the incident. Thrilled and goggling, we were prepared to hang upon his words; but he was bored and tired—homesick, weary of China and the war. He was giving Canton its last chance. If a real story didn't break within a fortnight, he'd do his best, he said, to get sent back to the States. We retired, not wishing to bother him further, and viewed him from a respectful distance, with awe. A disillusioned journalist is the Byron, the romantic Hamlet of our modern world.

It was very hot. As we approached Canton, the scenery reminded us of the Severn Valley—there were willows and fruit-trees; an old country house standing within a walled garden had the sadness and charm of a mortgaged English estate. Great junks passed us. They resembled Elizabethan galleons, towering up sheer out of the water, architectural, richly carved, top-heavy. They were dangerously crowded with passengers, and, apparently, sailing backwards. Even a little green gunboat seemed uniquely Chinese, with its slender, quaintly tall funnels—less like a warship than some exotic sort of water-beetle. On the deck of a British steamer, a man in white ducks was practising drives with a golf-club. Warehouses began to crowd along the banks; many of them had Union Jacks, swastikas, or Stars and Stripes painted upon their roofs. We imagined a comic drawing of a conscientious Japanese observer looking down in perplexity from a bombing-plane upon a wilderness of neutral flags, and finally espying a tiny, unprotected Chinese patch: 'Don't you think', he says, 'we might be able to fit a little one in, just there?'

Canton has two semi-skyscrapers which first appear, at some distance, rising above the fields. The river near the landing-stages was infested with launches, sampans, and skiffs, creaking and bumping together in an apparently hopeless traffic-jam. Our steamer barged its way patiently through them towards the shore. The sampans were often navigated by a whole family of men, women, and children, each punting or rowing furiously in a different direction, and screaming all the time. Somehow or other, we elbowed our way down the gang-plank, and out through a quay-side mob of police, customs officials, travellers, porters, and onlookers, to the waiting car which the British Consul-General had most kindly sent to meet us.

The British Consulate is in the foreign concession, on the river-island of Shameen. For once, we had to admit—remembering the horrors of Colombo, Singapore, Hong-kong—the British had shown some good taste. Shameen is delightful: its houses are well-proportioned and unpretentious, with large airy verandahs and balconies, and there is a wide central avenue of lawns and trees. You cross to the island over a narrow sandbagged bridge; strongly guarded, for the foreigners fear a stampede of Chinese into the concession, in the event of a large-scale air-raid or a Japanese attack. British and American gun-boats were moored alongside the outer shore. Their crews were playing football—hairy, meat-pink men with power-ful buttocks, they must have seemed ferocious, uncouth giants to the slender, wasp-waisted Cantonese spectators, with their drooping, flowerlike stance and shy brilliant smiles.

We were to stay at Paak Hok Tung, a village half a mile down the river. American and English missionaries have made a settlement there. Walking up the tidy path be-tween playing-fields, college buildings, and villa gar-dens, you might fancy yourself at home in one of the pleasanter London suburbs. And it was in a pleasant, cul-

31

tured suburban drawing-room that our missionary host
and hostess gave us tea. Had we had a nice journey? Yes,
thank you, very nice. Any trouble at the customs? Well,
unfortunately, yes: Auden had had to pay thirty dollars
duty on his camera. Oh, how tiresome; but you'll get it
back. Was it usually so hot in Canton at this time of year?
No, it wasn't. Five days ago, it had been quite chilly.

Somewhere, from far away across the river, came a succession of dull, heavy thuds; felt rather than heard. And
then, thin and distinct, the whine which a mosquito makes,
when it dives for your face in the dark. Only this wasn't
a mosquito. More thuds. I looked round at the others. Was
it possible that they hadn't noticed? Clearing my throat,
I said as conversationally as I could manage: 'Isn't that
an air-raid?'

Our hostess glanced up, smiling, from the tea-tray: 'Yes,
I expect it is. They come over about this time, most after-
noons. . . . Do you take sugar and milk?'

Yes, I took both; and a piece of home-made sultana cake
as well, to cover my ill-bred emotion. It was all very well
for Auden to sit there so calmly, arguing about the Group
Movement. He had been in Spain. My eyes moved over
this charming room, taking in the tea-cups, the dish of
scones, the book-case with Chesterton's essays and Kip-
ling's poems, the framed photograph of an Oxford college.
My brain tried to relate these images to the sounds outside; the whine of the power-diving bomber, the distant
thump of the explosions. Understand, I told myself, that
those noises, these objects are part of a single, integrated
scene. Wake up. It's all quite real. And, at that moment, I
really did wake up. At that moment, suddenly, I arrived
in China.

'They're moving off now,' our hostess told me. She had

the kindly air of one who wishes to reassure a slightly nervous child about a thunderstorm. 'They never stay very long.'

After tea, she and I went for a walk. It was already beginning to get dark. We climbed a small hill behind the village, overlooking the Canton valley. Beneath us lay the great sprawling city, and, all around it, in the dusk, the mysterious, wooded Kwantung plains. Along the horizon, miniature mountains poked up their little hat-like peaks. It was the landscape of *Alice through the Looking-Glass*. Here you might make a Lewis Carroll walking-tour, coming unexpectedly upon the strangest of people engaged in the queerest of tasks—two old men trying to put a rat into a bottle, a woman pouring water through a sieve. And yet all these topsy-turvy occupations, when one came to inquire into their purpose, would prove, no doubt, to be eminently practical and sane. The Chinese, we had been told, do nothing without an excellent reason.

As we walked home, our hostess discussed the students at the Paak Hok Tung theological college. The teaching of Christian theology, she said (and we were to hear this repeated by many other mission-workers), is a difficult problem in China. The motives which bring the Chinese student into the western mission-school are likely to be mixed. On the material side, he has much to gain: knowledge of a European language, initiation into Occidental ways, the possibility of a good job. Christianity, since the conversion of Chiang Kai-shek, is politically fashionable, and is likely to become even more so in the future, if the present régime survives this war.

And, even supposing that the student is earnest in his intentions, he will find Christian theology hard to digest. The Chinese mind is not naturally attracted to the Myth.

33

It is preoccupied with practical ethics. It asks to be given
the seven rules for the Good Life. It is far more interested
in this world than in the possibilities of the next. And so
these young men—however quickly they may acquire the
theological technique, however cleverly they answer their
teacher's questions—are apt, in later life, to backslide into
philosophical paganism.

Our hosts had been disappointed in the attitude of the
young Cantonese intellectuals towards the war. Before the
fighting began, they had taken the lead in anti-Japanese
propaganda, and demanded the use of force. But now few
of them seemed inclined to go into the trenches. 'This',
they said, 'is a coolies' war. Our job is to educate ourselves
for the task of reconstruction which will come later.'
Nevertheless, there is a good deal to be said on the students' side. China can ill afford to sacrifice her comparatively small educated class. And it must be remembered
that, for the Cantonese, the land warfare was taking place
in an area hundreds of miles distant, inhabited by a people
whose language they could not even understand.

Next day, we were woken by mixed noises—the far-off
explosions of the morning air-raid and the strains of our
host's harmonium from the neighbouring chapel. Directly
after breakfast we left by launch for the city. The Consul-
General had lent us his car to pay an official visit to the
Mayor, Mr. Tsang Yan-fu. This was our first attempt at a
professional interview, and we were anxious not to disgrace ourselves. Seated proud but nervous behind the consular chauffeur, and the fluttering Union Jack on the bon-
net, we wondered what questions we should ask him. The
streets swept past, some westernized, some purely Chinese,
all hung with the long inscribed shop-banners, golden,

scarlet, and white, which make every town in this country seem permanently *en fête*. The crowds were enormous; every road was blocked with foot-passengers, rickshaws, carts. We saw few signs of air-raid damage. For several months now, the Japanese had dropped no bombs on the centre of the city—attacking only the railway-stations, the flying-field, and the suburbs. There were piles of sand-bags at the entrances of the larger hotels.

The Mayor's office was a huge building, guarded by boys with automatic pistols. The sentries returned our tentative smiles with the blank glare of armed idiocy peculiar to very young troops. Like most of the soldiers we had seen in the streets, they looked about fifteen years old.

Mr. Tsang Yan-fu received us in his private bureau, alone. He was dressed in the simple, becoming blue uniform of a government official, without medals or gold braid, which resembles the costume of an English chauffeur. The Mayor's smooth round face was split permanently, it seemed, by an immense grin; like a melon from which a slice has been cut. It was hardly necessary for us to interview him: he interviewed himself, laughing all the time:

'We not wan' to fight Japan. Japan wan' to fight *us*! Ha, ha, ha! Japan velly foolish. First she wan' to be number *tree* power. Then number *two*. Then number *one*. Japan industrial country, you see. Suppose we go Japan, dlop bomb —woo-er, boom! Velly bad for Japanese, I tink? Japanese come to China. China aglicultural country. Japanese dlop bomb—woo-er, boom! Only break up earth, make easier for Chinese plough land! Much people is killed of course. Velly cruel. But we have lots more, yes? Ha, ha, ha, ha!'

At this moment, we were deafeningly interrupted by the air-raid sirens. They were just outside the window. Mr.

35

Tsang became almost unintelligible with amusement; he shook violently in his chair: 'You see? The Japanese come to dlop bombs on our heads! We sit here. We smoke our cigarettes. We are not afraid! Let us have some tea!'

But the raiders didn't, on this occasion, reach Canton after all. We were disappointed, for we had been hoping to see the Mayor's luxury dugout, said to be one of the wonders of the city. Auden took some photographs, for which Mr. Tsang obligingly posed; and we bowed ourselves out of the room.

We both liked Mr. Tsang. If this was typical of China's attitude towards the Japanese, it was certainly an example to the West—with its dreary hymns of hate, and screams of 'Baby-killer', 'Hun', 'sub-human fiends'. This scornful, good-natured amusement was, we agreed, exactly the note which a cultured, pacific country should strike in its propaganda against a brutal, upstart enemy. Mr. Tsang's kind of humour, if properly exploited, should win China many friends abroad.

That evening there were guests at dinner—among them a Chinese colonel and his wife. The Colonel was a somewhat enigmatic figure; his communicative manner and fluent American English may have hidden as many secrets as the traditional reticence of the Orient: 'You have a nice place here, Reverend. It's simple but it's good. . . . How much you pay for that cabinet, excuse?' He was perfectly willing to discuss anything—Chinese music, the war, his wife. They had been affianced to each other at the age of two; for their respective fathers were friends, and wished to perpetuate the memory of their affection. Since childhood, the Colonel hadn't seen his fiancée until the age of twenty-six. Then he returned from Russia, and they were married immediately. 'So you don't have any marriages for love?' a lady in the party asked, with less than English tact. And: 'But you have been very lucky, Colonel,' our hostess put in hastily. The Colonel bowed: 'Thank you, Madam.'

He then informed us that Canton now had a considerable force of chaser planes. During the past fortnight, eleven Japanese had been brought down. The Government had offered a reward to anybody who could bring down a plane; as a result, anti-aircraft defence had become a local sport, like duck-shooting. When the planes came over, everybody blazed away—even the farmers with their blunderbusses in the fields. One Japanese pilot, flying incautiously low, had been wrecked by a hundred-year-old mortar in a junk. On another occasion, when two Japs had made a forced landing, the peasants ambushed them, and would even have succeeded in capturing one of the planes in perfect working-order, if a third Jap hadn't swooped down and destroyed it with a bomb.

At dinner, the Colonel entertained us single-handed. He told us how, during a visit to London, he had walked through Limehouse, and seen a Chinese notice: 'Best opium fresh from Yun-nan', prominently displayed in a doorway, under the nose of a patrolling bobby. He knew all about cooking, and showed our hostess how to prepare a fish. Certainly, he assured us, you could get roast dog. Snake wine was good for rheumatism. He invited us all to his house to eat ancient eggs.

The Colonel, it appeared, was a noted singer. After dinner, he was persuaded, without much difficulty, to oblige. In Chinese opera, he explained, there are various styles of singing, adapted to the different stock characters; and he undertook to give us samples of each. The romantic hero emits sounds like a midnight cat, the heroine a thin nasal

37

falsetto; the bandit is quite terrifying—the volume is small, but the effort involved would have put Caruso to shame. Before our fascinated eyes the Colonel's face turned from yellow to purple, from purple to black; his veins bulged like ropes. But just when it seemed that he would injure himself seriously and permanently, he burst out laughing —with a gesture of comic indignation towards his placid, bespectacled wife: 'How shall I sing', he exclaimed, 'when she looks at me like that?'

We had been invited to lunch, next day, with General Wu Teh-chen, the ex-mayor of Shanghai, now Governor of Kwantung Province.

General Wu lived on the outskirts of the city, in a comfortable but unpretentious concrete villa. Mr. Tong, the Governor's secretary, welcomed us in the hall—a smiling, moon-faced man, so soft and gentle that one could barely resist the impulse to stroke his cheek and offer him a lump of sugar. He told us that the Governor would soon be down, and introduced us to the half-dozen other guests; both English and Chinese. A swarthy, efficient-looking young man in blue uniform proved to be Mr. Percy Chen, whose book on the first phases of the present war we had read during our stay in Hongkong. (One sentence in it had particularly pleased us: the author is speaking of the incident at the Marco Polo bridge—'Shortly before midnight, the manœuvres developed towards realism, and live ammunition was used on both sides.' Surely, the outbreak of a war has never been more tactfully described?)

Mr. Chen spoke English perfectly. He had been a barrister of the Middle Temple, and had spent eight years in Russia. Indeed, as he himself confessed, his life had been lived so much abroad that he felt himself to be almost a foreigner in China. He was very critical of the Japanese strategy. There was no co-ordination, he said, between the various commands: whole divisions would often advance without orders. All the Chinese present were anxious to know what we thought of Mr. Eden's resignation and its possible effect on British foreign policy in the Far East.

General Wu now came into the room, and we were introduced. The Governor was a strongly-built man, in a loosely-fitting brown uniform, with talkative, informal manners. His eyes, behind thick horn-rimmed glasses, were earnest and sometimes puzzled. He spoke with hesitation, feeling for his words, and looking round the whole company, as if for support: 'The war is the biggest disconception China has ever suffered. The peoples lose their homes and walk. But it makes them a nation. This is the one thing China gets from the war. . . . After the war, the bankers spend the money on the countries.'

We began to move into the dining-room, still talking; there seemed to be no special order of precedence. All this informality, admirable as it was, disappointed us a little. Both Auden and myself were still steeped in the traditions of *The Chinese Bungalow*. We had even rehearsed the scene beforehand, and prepared suitable compliments and speeches. The Governor should have said: 'My poor house is honoured.' And we should have replied: 'Our feet are quite unworthy to rest upon your honourable doorstep.' On which, the Governor, had he known his stuff, would have cracked back: 'If my doorstep were gold, it would hardly be fit for your distinguished shoes.' And so on. Perhaps, after all, it was a good thing that General Wu was unacquainted with the subtleties of European stage-Chinese, or we might never have reached the lunch-table.

One's first sight of a table prepared for a Chinese meal hardly suggests the idea of eating, at all. It looks rather as if you were sitting down to a competition in water-colour painting. The chopsticks, lying side by side, resemble paint-brushes. The paints are represented by little dishes of sauces, red, green, and brown. The tea-bowls, with their lids, might well contain paint-water. There is even a kind of tiny paint-rag, on which the chopsticks can be wiped.

You begin the meal by wiping hands and face with hot moistened towels. (These towels are, perhaps, China's most brilliant contribution to the technique of material comfort; they should certainly be introduced into the West.) Then comes the food. It is served in no recognizable order of progression—fish does not necessarily follow soup, nor meat fish. Nor can the length of the meal be foreseen by the guest. His favourite dish may well appear at the very end, when he is too bloated even to taste it. *Hors-d'œuvre* delicacies remain in presence throughout—and this, too, is like painting; for the diners are perpetually mixing them in with their food, to obtain varying combinations of taste.

To-day we had shark's fin soup (one of the great soups of the world; quite equal to minestrone or borsch), lobster, chicken, rice, and fish. The drink, which was served in small metal teapots, resembled Korn or Bols. It was made from rose-petals and maize. The Governor had considerately provided us with knives and forks, but these we declined to use. We had eaten already with chopsticks in Hongkong, and were anxious for more practice. In China, it is no social crime to drop your food on the table. When a new dish comes in, the host makes a gesture towards it with his chopsticks, like a cavalry-commander pointing with his sabre to an enemy position, and the attack begins. This scramble, so informal yet so scrupulously polite, is the greatest charm of a Chinese meal; and even the most expert eater can hardly avoid making a certain amount of mess. One of the English guests was showing me how to pick up a shrimp patty, when he let it fall on to the carpet. His face was promptly saved by Mr. Tong, who exclaimed: 'Ah, that shrimp must be alive!'

Hot brown rice-wine followed the rose-petal gin. The Governor raised his glass to us: 'Welcome to China!' The Minister of Agriculture, who was sitting next to Auden, began to discuss the rice-problem. Before the war, much of the rice consumed in Kwantung Province was imported. Now there was a shortage, because these areas had been occupied by the Japanese. The Government was therefore encouraging the Cantonese to use sweet potatoes as a substitute. It had issued a wartime cookery-book, explaining what could be done with the available foodstuffs. Remembrance-days had been instituted, on which no rice might be eaten. Originally, these days were to commemorate certain important dates in the Sino-Japanese dispute—beginning with the invasion of Manchuria; but the Governor had decided that these would be too difficult to remember. Now the no-rice rule came into force simply on every fifth day. To check the spread of beri-beri, the sale of polished rice had been prohibited altogether.

Both the Governor and the Minister were interested in rural education. The country schools, said General Wu, were not designed to make their pupils eager to migrate into the towns; they aimed at producing good and contented farmers. Auden, who had read in a local paper that morning that the farmers had rioted against a new agricultural station, asked if the peasants, in general, resented the introduction of scientific farming methods. The Governor denied this: 'But we must not expect them to come to us,' he said. 'We must go to them.'

Somebody mentioned Hitler's Reichstag speech. 'I think Germany is very silly,' said General Wu. 'She says that Japan defends against Bolshevism; unless Japan would fight, China goes Communist. But Germany is wrong. China will not go Communist; but if war continues a long time, Japan she goes Bolshevist. China has four hundred million peoples, Japan one hundred million; but there are more Communist agitators in Japan than in whole of China.'

'So you think Communism's impossible in China?' Auden asked.

'China agricultural country. I have thousand acres. I have ten sons. They have only hundred acres. In China there are no big landlords. Every Chinese man must have a house, he must marry; then he has credit with society.'

Here General Wu was interrupted by a servant, who brought a message to say that the Japanese were raiding the railway, near the frontier between Kwantung and the New Territories. 'The Japanese mind', he observed, 'is funny. It can get everything without war, but it must make war. Japan doesn't think like other nations. . . . But Great Britain', he appealed suddenly to us, 'she can stop this war?'

Yes, we agreed, she could stop it. But would she? Ah. . . . There was a moment's embarrassed silence. Then the Governor tactfully indicated that lunch was over.

We spent the next two days chiefly in shopping and wandering about the city. Neither of us could ever tire of walking the streets: there was so much to see. The commonest shops seemed to be barbers and apothecaries, whose windows exhibited deer-horn (to cure impotence) and strange, twisted roots, like mandrakes, in glass cases. There were bizarre placards, in English: 'New Life Cars.' 'Street-Sleepers' Association.' 'Blood Protection Co. Ltd.' The food-shops were fascinating, too. Auden gazed in horror at the edible black-beetles, I at the tubs of live swimming snakes. If I had to eat snake, I said, I thought I should really go mad. Auden determined to trick me into doing so at the first possible opportunity.

All around us crowded and jostled the Cantonese, in their light pyjama-clothes—a small, gay, elegant people, of great physical beauty. The more fashionable girls had had their hair curled and permanently waved, which didn't suit them, however. Some of the very young children wore brilliant scarlet jackets and parti-coloured jockey-caps; their naked buttocks, pushing out through the divided breeches, were smeared with dirt from the road. We noticed a few whose faces were powdered and rouged; this is sometimes done, we were told, on the child's birthday.

On the advice of our hosts, we bought two camp-beds, complete with mosquito-nets, which folded neatly into canvas sacks. Another big sack would hold the bedding, and could be used, later on, for our necessary clothes as well. These beds proved, later, to be invaluable. (At the present moment, they are ornamenting a doss-house, somewhere in New York.)

We had also to provide ourselves with visiting-cards, in English and Chinese. Without cards, travel in China would be difficult in the extreme. A friend in Hongkong had supplied us already with phonetic Chinese names—Au Dung and Y Hsiao Wu: in Canton, we got them printed.

On our last evening we were invited to dine with the captain of a British gunboat, anchored off Shameen. The captain was fond of flowers; there were plenty of them in

43

his tiny cabin, and orange-trees in tubs stood on the few square feet of deck around the gun. You had to be careful, he told us, when buying flowers in the Canton markets; the blossoms are often wired on, so are the roots. On the whole, his opinion of Chinese honesty was low.

The chief function of the gunboats, in peace time, is the protection from pirates of British-owned ships. The gunboats are flat-bottomed, drawing only five feet of water, and they can steam far up the river. They are capable of doing fourteen knots; but this speed is inadvisable, for it washes away the banks, and they are likely to be fired on, in retaliation, by angry farmers. They are built in England, and their voyage to the East is something of an adventure; if the sea is rough, they are towed, with all hatches battened down; if smooth, they proceed under their own steam.

The dinner was excellent, with caviare and French wines. We caught a glimpse of a lonely, formal, self-contained existence; and wondered what an American or a French naval officer would make of the captain—he was so much more subtle, more intelligent than his cultivated Bertie Wooster drawl. ('The shooting-season opened with a fine bag. We got five pirates; two of 'em in the water.') When it was time for us to go, the ship's private sampan rowed us ashore. The old lady, its owner, had decorated the basket-work roof with photographs of football teams and British crews.

We were to leave Canton next day, March 4th, by rail for Hankow. The train was scheduled to start at 6 p.m. Earlier in the afternoon we went round to the British Consulate to say goodbye. The Consul wasn't particularly cheerful. Yesterday, he told us, the line had been heavily bombed and cut by the Japanese. Trains took anything from five to seven days to make the journey; you might even be turned out of them altogether and compelled to spend the night in an obscure provincial village. A lady who had just arrived from Hankow had assured him that she wouldn't make the trip again for ten thousand pounds. 'Not, of course', the Consul added, smiling, 'that I want to discourage you.'

We protested that we weren't discouraged—that the air-raids would help to pass the time, and a night in the paddy-fields would provide excellent copy. Nevertheless, as we approached the Canton railway station, I began to cast nervous glances at the sky. It was a warm, windless evening—perfect weather for the Japs.

Along the road near the line hundreds of coolies squatted humbly in the dust: these, it appeared, never aspired to get on to the platform at all. Only, at the very last moment, when everybody of any consequence was already on board, they might be allowed to scramble over the fence and mingle in one desperate fighting rush for the few remaining places in a cattle-truck. Many of them, obviously, would be left behind. Several would very likely break an arm or a leg.

The station building was small, shabby, and crammed with soldiers. It smelt very bad indeed. A group of police officers in smart black-and-silver uniforms challenged us smilingly. But they didn't want to see our tickets, or even our passports; they merely demanded from each of us a visiting-card. These cards, somebody told us later, are the perquisites of the officials who collect them; they like to show them to their wives, and boast about the interesting people they have met.

Thanks to the influence of Governor Wu, our reservations were the best obtainable on the train: a two-berth coupé in the first-class coach. This coach was almost the only one in the immensely long train whose roof was painted with camouflage: we speculated on the advantages and disadvantages of our presumed invisibility from the air. The station officials were nervous too, perhaps; for our departure was punctual to the minute. As we drew slowly down the platform, soldiers and police stood to attention and saluted. One of the passengers—a pale, calm young man, with a long whippet-nose and protruding under-lip —bowed in silent acknowledgment; he was evidently an important Government official. The whole effect was slightly sinister—like watching your own military funeral from the gun-carriage itself.

Our train puffed leisurely out through the suburbs, into the open country. At this stage of the journey I blessed the driver's caution; for the Consul had added to my nervousness by tales of bombed bridges imperfectly repaired with bamboo stakes. Besides, if the Japanese came over, you could jump out of the window without the slightest risk. Standing in the corridor we made friends with a Chinese bank-director who assured us that, all being well, we should reach Hankow in two days and three nights only. Our spirits rose considerably.

Actually we saw the traces of only one air-raid, at a small station where we stopped soon after dark. A bomb had landed right beside the track; the ruins of the waiting-room were scattered around its crater. If there were other such ruins we must have passed them after we had gone to bed. There were many hold-ups and long waits. By night we travelled much more slowly than by day.

There was no restaurant on this train, but the stewards provided plenty of food. There was even a special Euro-

pean menu. This we rejected, after one trial, as too nasty
—until the boredom of the Chinese dishes drove us back to
it, later on. In any case, we weren't particularly hungry.

About breakfast-time we stopped at a mountain station
near the Kwantung-Hu-nan provincial border. A big
crag, wrapped in mist, towered above the track. Peasants
brought baskets of fruit for sale—they looked like miniature oranges. In defiance of Hongkong's warnings against
dysentery we ate them skin and all.

All that day, we rumbled through the fertile, blood-
coloured valleys of southern Hu-nan, bathed in hot sunshine. Charming, compact villages of grey and white
houses clustered round their square watch-towers, which
resembled the towers of English country churches. There
were rookeries in the copses, and haystacks built round
the tree-trunks. The paddy-fields mounted the gentle hill-
slopes, terrace by terrace, like tarnished mirrors reflecting
the sky. Here and there big gangs of coolies were working
on the track. As we passed, one of them forcibly pulled
down his friend's trousers, exhibiting him, grinning, to
the entire train.

The stewards hurried up and down the corridor with hot
face-towels, bowls of rice, cups of tea. As the journey progressed the tea grew nastier, tasting increasingly of fish.
The two armed guards in the corridor—one of them surely
not more than twelve years old—peered into our compartment to watch the foreign devils screaming with laughter at mysterious jokes, singing in high falsetto or mock
operatic voices, swaying rhythmically backwards and forwards on their seats, reading aloud to each other from
small crimson-bound books. The swaying was an exercise
which we had invented, in a vain effort to ward off consti-
pation; the books were *Framley Parsonage* and *Guy Man-*

47

nering. Neither was a great success. We admired Scott's skill in spinning out the story; Trollope we found merely dull. He seemed interested exclusively in money, and the appalling consequences of signing your name on a bill. By the middle of the second day we had finished them both. We had nothing else to read, and our voices were too hoarse for any more singing. The journey ceased to amuse.

After Changsha the weather turned cloudy and much cooler. The peasants on the stations wore huge turbans, like figures in a Rembrandt biblical painting. Soldiers toiled past, in their heavy equipment, patiently clutching paper umbrellas. We had rain-swept glimpses of the vast Tung-ting Lake. (How strange to remember that in London, only three months ago, I had placed my finger on it in the atlas, and said, 'I wonder if we shall ever get as far as *here?*')

Early next morning we arrived at Wuchang. The thermometer had dropped during the night, and we staggered out of the station into a driving blizzard. The causeway and the stone stairs down to the ferry were slippery with ice. Coolies jostled blindly against us, with the averted, snot-smeared, animal faces of the very humble, the dwellers in Society's smallest crevices, the Insulted and Injured. Auden's paper umbrella had broken in the storm; it wrapped itself round his head like a grotesque kind of hat. Slithering and cursing, we crowded into the hold of the listing steamer and stood, jammed too tight to move, amidst straw baskets, rifles, soldiers, peasants, and sacks. This was not the moment to fuss about infection or lice. On the distant shore, the buildings of Hankow stood grim and black against the low clouds; before us swept the Yangtze, a terrible race of yellow waves and tearing snow. We had arrived, it seemed, at the very end of the world.

2

March 8

Today Auden and I agreed that we would rather be in Hankow at this moment than anywhere else on earth.

Stark and blank along the northern shore, the buildings of the old treaty port present their European façades to the winter river. (Only the French Concession still officially exists; and the authorities are preparing to barricade it with barbed wire and big wooden gates in the event of a Japanese attack.) There are consulates, warehouses, offices, and banks; British and American drug-stores, cinemas, churches, clubs; there is a good lending library, a Y.M.C.A., a red-light street of cafés—Mary's, the Navy Bar, The Last Chance. Around all this the Chinese city stretches for miles, a warren of ramshackle, congested streets, out to the race-track, the air-field, and the snow-covered Hu-Peh plains.

The clothing-shops, the cafés, and the restaurants are kept by White Russian emigrants. You see two or three of them behind nearly every bar—a fat, defeated tribe who lead a melancholy indoor life of gossip, mah-jongg, drink, and bridge. They have all drifted here somehow—by way of Mongolia, Hongkong, or the United States—and here they must stop; nobody else will receive them. They have established an insecure right to exist—on

49

Nansen passports, Chinese nationality-papers of doubt-
ful validity, obsolete Tsarist identity-certificates as big as
table-cloths, or simply their mere impoverished presence.
Their great pallid faces look out into the future, above
innumerable cigarettes and tea-glasses, without pity or
hope. 'Their clocks', says Auden, 'stopped in 1917. It has
been tea-time ever since.'

In the slushy streets the raw Siberian wind stings the
cheeks of the hurrying crowd—Europeans in fur-lined
coats, Chinese in skin caps with ear-guards like airmen's
helmets. The rickshaws are fitted with hoods and carriage-
lamps—as though, by some process of age and desiccation,
hansom-cabs had shrunk to the size of prams. Coolies
stagger in and out of doorways, balancing cases slung on
springy bamboo poles. They encourage each other with
sharp rhythmical cries: 'Hoo, ha, ah, hoo, hi, ha!' Soldiers
in uniforms of blue quilt pad silently by, splashed with
mud from passing cars, their thin sandals sodden in the
melting snow.

This is the real capital of war-time China. All kinds
of people live in this town—Chiang Kai-shek, Agnes
Smedley, Chou En-lai; generals, ambassadors, journalists,
foreign naval officers, soldiers of fortune, airmen, missionaries, spies. Hidden here are all the clues which would
enable an expert, if he could only find them, to predict
the events of the next fifty years. History, grown weary
of Shanghai, bored with Barcelona, has fixed her capri-
cious interest upon Hankow. But where is she staying?
Everybody boasts that he has met her, but nobody can
exactly say. Shall we find her at the big hotel, drinking
whisky with the journalists in the bar? Is she the guest of
the Generalissimo, or the Soviet Ambassador? Does she
prefer the headquarters of the Eighth Route Army, or the

German military advisers? Is she content with a rickshaw-coolie's hut?

Perhaps she is nearer than we think—at the neighbouring house in the compound of the British Consulate-General, where T. V. Soong sometimes confers far into the night on the problematical future of the Chinese Dollar. The Consul has offered us the hospitality of a big empty room, in which we can pitch our camp-beds. Downstairs, in an atmosphere of Winchester, Racine, service gossip, and Chinese vases—all of them museum-pieces; a few disconcertingly ugly—we discuss our future plans. We have decided to go north: first to Cheng-chow, and thence to some point on the Yellow River front. To do this, we shall need a servant-interpreter. The Consul has found us one already, a friend of his own Number One Boy. His name is Chiang.

Chiang is one of the few Chinese we have seen whose appearance could be described as middle-aged. He has the manners of a perfect butler. His English leaves much to be desired, and he does not even pretend to be able to cook. Nevertheless, we have engaged him, for expenses and forty dollars a month. Before the deal was concluded, the Consul warned him, at our request, that we were going into the war area. Would he be frightened? 'A servant', Chiang replied, 'cannot afford to be frightened.'

This afternoon we paid a visit to Bishop Roots, the American bishop of Hankow. Bishop Roots has spent a lifetime in China. Within a few weeks he is going to retire. Lately the bishop's ideas have moved sharply towards the Left; he describes himself as a 'Christian revolutionary'. A short time ago his daughter caused a local sensation by journeying to the north-west to visit the red Eighth Route

Army, now officially incorporated into the Chinese forces. Since Miss Agnes Smedley came to stay with the bishop his house has been nicknamed 'The Moscow–Heaven Axis'.

Bishop Roots is bald, sententious, and oracular in the grand American manner. He reproved us gently for our interest in the immediate outcome of the war. 'You've got to think in terms of five hundred years. . . . This country has an historic part to play in the future of the world. Here the great stream of western culture which sprang from Greece and Rome, was modified by Judah and absorbed technics, will meet that other great humanist stream which sprang from Confucius, was modified by India and did not absorb technics. This will be the birthplace of the new world-civilization, and the Chinese realize it. . . . Only a revolution in men's hearts, a new idealism —such as the Oxford Group Movement is attempting— can save the world from destruction. I believe it must come. . . . Thank you for visiting me. I like to have a talk with newcomers, before any one else gets hold of them. . . . Miss Smedley, I'm afraid, is out.'

March 9

This afternoon we attended the press conference. It is held daily, at five o'clock, in the offices of Mr. Hollington Tong, Hankow's publicity chief.

The narrow stuffy room was crowded with camp-stools, and half-filled by a long table, on which stood tea-cups, chocolates, and cigarettes. The correspondents of the various foreign newspapers lounged or chatted in groups, frowning as they puffed disgustedly at their pipes. Nearly all of them were American or Australian; we were the only English present. And there was a pale, worried-looking boy from Berlin, in a black shirt, breeches, and dispatch-rider's boots.

The first two or three minutes were embarrassing. The old hands viewed us with inquisitively hostile eyes. We hastened to explain that we were not real journalists, but mere trippers, who had come to China to write a book. The hearty, square-shouldered, military-looking man to whom we had addressed ourselves slapped us both on the back: 'These young fellows', he shouted to the others, 'are desperate to go to the front at once.' The great news-men smiled, weary but indulgent. 'Why, isn't that just fine?' some one drily observed. 'I don't mind telling you', the military-looking man continued, 'I haven't been to the front myself. But I've been darn near death several times.' We flattered him with timid grins.

Presently, to our delight, two friends walked in—Capa and Fernhout (we had got to know them both during the voyage from Marseilles to Hongkong. Indeed, with their horse-play, bottom-pinching, exclamations of 'Eh, quoi! Salop!' and endless jokes about *les poules*, they had been the life and soul of the second class.) Capa is Hungarian, but more French than the French; stocky and swarthy, with drooping black comedian's eyes. He is only twenty-three, but already a famous press-photographer. He has been through most of the civil war in Spain. Fernhout is a tall, blonde young Dutchman—as wild as Capa, but slightly less noisy. He worked with Ivens and Hemingway as a camera-man on the film *Spanish Earth*. Ivens was with them now. We hadn't met him before. He is a good deal older than the others, small, dark, with sparkling little eyes. The three of them have just arrived in Hankow direct from Hongkong, by air.

They are waiting here for their equipment, which is

53

being sent by rail, before starting for the north-west. They are going to make a film about the life of a child soldier, a 'little red devil', in one of the mobile units of the Eighth Route Army. They hope to leave Hankow sometime next week.

The daily news-bulletin was read by Mr. T. T. Li, the official mouth-piece of the Government. He resembles the most optimistic of Walt Disney's Three Little Pigs. The word 'defeat' has no place in his mouth. Every Japanese advance is a Chinese strategic withdrawal. Towns pass into Japanese hands in the most tactful manner possible —they simply cease to be mentioned. He reads very fast, and keeps losing the place in his papers: 'Of seven planes brought down by Chinese ground forces, fifteen were destroyed by infantry.' Nobody bothered to question the arithmetic, or, indeed, to pretend any interest whatsoever. Any scraps of genuine news would be circulated later, when the journalists had dispersed to the bars for a pre-dinner drink.

The lecture over, we approached Mr. Tong himself, with a request for the Government passes which are necessary for any journey to the north. Mr. Tong listened gravely; his eyes tired and calm behind his tinted, rimless spectacles. Yes, everything should be arranged; though he doubted whether we should get permission to visit Sian. It would be several days, in any case, before the passes were ready.

An immediate consequence of our visit to the press conference has been the arrival at the Consulate, during dinner, of an enormous packet. It contains all the press bulletins of the China Information Committee for the past three months. We are supposed, apparently, to study them before tomorrow afternoon. Auden calls them 'our lessons'.

March 10

This morning we went to interview Mr. Donald, friend and adviser to the Generalissimo and Madame Chiang Kai-shek. Mr. Donald is living, at present, in a flat on the Bund—a large, ramshackle place, guarded by quantities of slightly conspiratorial secretaries, menservants, and messenger-boys. He received us in his bedroom. He was just recovering from a bad cold, and a whole chemist's shop of bottles was laid out on the table by the bed. Donald is a red-faced, serious man, with an Australian accent and a large, sensible nose—a pleasant surprise; for most of our informants had led us to expect an oily, iron-grey, evangelical figure, with a highly developed manner. He neither boomed nor snapped; but lectured us, as we desired, on the war-situation, clearly and concisely, with the aid of a big map. We talked chiefly about the possibilities of Russia giving military assistance to the Chinese. Donald said that the extent of this assistance has been much exaggerated. Nevertheless, he thinks that the Japanese are likely to make a drive on Sian, in order to prevent possible Russian supplies coming into China. If the Sian–Lanchow road were cut, these supplies would be obliged to take an interior route of extreme difficulty, over the mountains.

We asked him what part the Communists are likely to play after the war. He counter-questioned: 'What do the Communists stand for? Can they, in fact, be called Communists at all?' In his view, Communism ceased to exist in China after the withdrawal of Borodin.

Donald's own career has been extraordinary. He was a *Times* correspondent in Harbin. Then he became adviser to Chang Hsueh-liang, the 'Young Marshal'; and later the 'foreign friend' of Chiang Kai-shek himself. He says habitually: 'We think this,' 'we decided that,' and 'I said to the Generalissimo,' 'the Generalissimo said to me,' although neither can speak the other's language. Donald's well-known ignorance of Chinese has, no doubt, been a great protection to him in this country of plots and secrets. He hears no more than is good for him to hear. He is the man whom everybody can trust.

As we were going he asked us about our plans. We told him of our proposed journey to the north. Donald looked dubious and shook his head: 'Well, I wish you luck. But it's a hard road. A hard road.' He paused, then added, in a lower, dramatic tone: 'You may have to eat Chinese food.'

We laughed. He might have been about to warn us against nameless horrors. 'But surely', asked Auden, 'you eat it yourself?'

'*Chinese* food!' Donald's face contracted with disgust. 'Never touch the stuff! It ruins my stomach.'

March 11

Mr. Donald has given us an introduction to General von Falkenhausen, the chief of Chiang Kai-shek's German military advisers. This afternoon I took a rickshaw and started out to look for his headquarters.

They were somewhere out in the old Japanese Concession, at the far end of the Bund. But the address had been mis-spelt, and we wandered backwards and forwards for a long time. Many of the houses in this part of the city have been commandeered by the Chinese Army since their owners fled to Japan. Soon after the outbreak of war, the police made a raid and discovered that the Concession had been the centre of a big illicit drug-traffic.

All along the streets raw recruits were being drilled. They were mere boys, awkward-looking and unnaturally stout in their quilted uniforms, their poor yellow hands turned rubber-grey by the cold. They seemed to be performing all kinds of outlandish physical exercises. A single recruit knelt on one knee opposite his N.C.O., and the two regarded each other in silence for minutes on end, as though the private were being hypnotized. A little further on another N.C.O. barked out an order, and his whole squad slightly and elegantly advanced one foot, in an attitude which suggested ballet-dancing, combined with a sort of stolid ferocity. My coolie rambled this way and that, stopping frequently to ask the way, which everybody told him and no one knew. We kept passing and repassing the same platoon. In my newly-made riding-boots I tried, unsuccessfully, to look very stern and official. Presently I had to laugh; the recruits grinned back. I gave them a mock salute, which they returned. Their officers shouted at them, but they were smiling, too. Just when discipline threatened to become seriously disorganized I noticed that we were passing the General's house for the third time.

The General was out, but his A.D.C. received me—a mountainous figure, with clipped silver hair, a gold bracelet as thick as a bicycle-chain, and a monocle screwed several inches into his face. Even in his tweed jacket and flannel trousers he was unmistakably the Reichswehr officer. And his office, despite its thick Japanese matting, was a bit of old Potsdam, with secretaries coming in and out, heel-clicking, jerking forward their bodies in stiff, formal bows.

Most of the Germans have been in China for several years. They belong to the pre-Hitler emigration period, when an ambitious officer could foresee no adventurous military career in his own country, and often preferred to go abroad. Between them they have built up all the more modern units of the Chinese Army, and it is only natural that they should want to remain to see it in action. Nobody we have so far met has ever seriously suggested that they could be suspected of disloyalty to China, despite the Anti-Comintern Pact. Nevertheless, their position at the present moment, amidst this weird collection of helpers and allies, is certainly ambiguous. What does Berlin think of their activities? What does Moscow? Does Chiang himself entirely trust them? Perhaps not. At any rate their advice is not always taken; but this may be due to the jealousy which native generals invariably display towards their foreign colleagues—as in Franco's army in Spain.

The A.D.C. thought that China could certainly win this war—if only her troops would 'stand up straight and do as they're told'. But he sometimes sighed, one suspected, for three or four crack German divisions to put some stiffening into the Chinese resistance. From military matters our talk wandered back to the Harz Mountains. Wernigerode, which we both knew, was the A.D.C.'s native town.

Auden and I are to come back and see General von Falkenhausen tomorrow morning.

March 12

When we arrived at headquarters the A.D.C. greeted us: 'Well, gentlemen; you've heard the news?'

No, we said, we hadn't.

'Last night the German Army marched into Austria.'

The bottom seemed to drop out of the world. But the A.D.C. was taking it very calmly. 'Of course', he said, 'it had to happen. And now I hope that England and Germany will be friends. That's what we Germans have always wanted. Austria was only causing trouble between us. A good thing the whole business is settled, once and for all.'

He led us, still rather dazed, into another room, where General von Falkenhausen was sitting. 'Here they are, Excellency.' He bowed and left us alone.

The General looks more like a university professor than a Prussian officer. He wears pince-nez; a gaunt, grizzled man of about fifty-five. We asked him the routine question: could China win?

'Well,' said the General, 'I am an optimist. I am an optimist for three reasons. First, because I am a soldier. A soldier is a professional optimist. Secondly, because, if I were not optimistic, I could not give confidence to those around me. Thirdly, because the present situation really affords grounds for optimism.' He thinks that the Yellow River line is strong; and that Hankow can be easily defended—there are plenty of troops. When I asked him (more for the sake of saying something than because I really wanted to know) where he had been during the battle for Shanghai, he smilingly refused to answer. Why, neither of us can imagine.

As we walked home the whole weight of the news from Austria descended upon us, crushing out everything else. By this evening a European war may have broken out. And here we are, eight thousand miles away. Shall we change our plans? Shall we go back? What does China matter to us in comparison with this? Bad news of this sort has a curious psychological effect: all the guns and bombs of the Japanese seem suddenly as harmless as gnats. If we are killed on the Yellow River front our deaths will be as provincial and meaningless as a motor-bus accident in Burton-on-Trent.

Meanwhile our daily round had to continue. We had got an appointment with Miss Agnes Smedley.

We found her in an upstairs bed-sitting-room at Bishop Roots's house, staring dejectedly into the fire. She is really not unlike Bismarck, with her close-cropped grey hair, masculine jaw, deeply-lined cheeks and bulging, luminous eyes. 'Hullo,' she greeted us, listlessly: 'What do you two want?'

We introduced ourselves, and she began to cross-examine us, mockingly rather than aggressively: 'What's your background?' 'Are you a leftist?' 'Do you poetize?' Our answers seemed to amuse her. She shook a little, unsmiling, with the faintest kind of laughter; but all the time she held us, suspiciously, with her fearless, bitter grey eyes. We got a bad mark, I could see, when we admitted that we were staying at the British Consulate; and another when we told her that we had just been visiting the German military advisers. 'What are they plotting now?' she asked. We protested that General von Falkenhausen was certainly quite above suspicion. 'I don't trust any German!' exclaimed Miss Smedley, passionately.

It is impossible not to like and respect her, so grim and sour and passionate; so mercilessly critical of every one, herself included—as she sits before the fire, huddled together, as if all the suffering, all the injustice of the world were torturing her bones like rheumatism. She has just suffered a great personal disaster. Her notes and photographs, taken during her latest visit to the Eighth Route Army, have all disappeared in the Chinese post. 'There's plenty of people here', she commented, darkly, 'who didn't want them to arrive.'

Towards the end of our interview she appeared to soften a little. Auden's untidiness pleased her, I think. 'After all', one could see her reflecting, 'they're probably quite harmless.' 'Do you always', she asked ironically, 'throw your coats on the floor?' Before we left she wrote us an introduction to the Hankow office of the Eighth Route Army.

The press conference this afternoon was particularly dreary. Austria cast its shadow over us all, and the glib evasions of the official war-bulletin made our hearts sink with boredom and apprehensive despair. We sneaked out early in the middle of an immense tactical lecture by a Chinese correspondent lately returned from the front.

This evening we called at the offices of the Eighth Route Army. They, too, are in the former Japanese Concession, not far from the German headquarters. Everything seemed very friendly and informal. We spent a quarter of an hour with Comrade Po Ku, the Army's Hankow representative, sitting on stools in a bare little room, and drinking glasses of hot water into which a few tea-leaves had been dropped. Po Ku himself took part in the Long March across the Grasslands to the North-West. He is frail-looking, gentle-voiced, and gay, with a slight squint. His movements appear somewhat numbed, as though he had stayed far too long out in the snow.

Po Ku asked if we were thinking of visiting the Eighth Route Army. We said, 'No—so many journalists have been up there already, and written about it so well. Besides, the journey requires more time than we could possibly allow.' Po Ku agreed, but suggested that after we return to Hankow we might travel down to the south-eastern front. Another Communist army (the new Fourth Army) is being formed at Nanchang. If we cared to, he would give us the necessary letters. We agreed that this might be a very good idea.

March 13

This evening we have seen our first Chinese opera. We were the guests of Mr. Hsiao Tung-tze, managing director of the Central News Agency. Mr. Hsiao has been more than kind to us already: he has promised to present each of us with an album of Chinese operatic records to take home to England.

Tonight they were performing the original Chinese version of the westernized play called *Lady Precious Stream.* We arrived late, during the big scene in which Lady Precious Stream recognizes her husband on his return from fighting the barbarians of the west.

The theatre was packed. Every one in the audience was laughing, talking, shouting across the auditorium to greet his friends. People kept coming in and going out. Attendants ran round with hot face-towels and glasses of tea. It seemed nearly impossible to hear a single word from the stage: but no doubt this didn't matter, because the public knew the whole play by heart. As Auden remarked, it was like hearing Mass in an Italian church.

The performance was highly artificial and ritualistic— a mixture of song, ballet, fairy-story, and knock-about. The dresses were gorgeous: scarlet, orange, or green silk, embroidered with fantastic flowers and dragons. The head-dress is symbolically important: Generals in command of armies wear four flags planted on their heads, like the regimental colours in a military chapel; the hero has a kind of pin-cushion crown, stuck with flowers; the barbarian princess trails two enormously long peacock feathers from her hair, like an insect's antennae. The female roles are played by men—their faces transformed by make-up into pink and white masks. The sleeves of their robes are cut so that they fall almost to the floor. The gestures made by the actors in flapping these sleeves, to express anger or contempt, are an important technical feature of the drama, and are closely watched by connoisseurs in the audience. Emperors wear long beards, villains comic masks. There is hardly any attempt at scenery; only a single back-drop, some cushions, and a few chairs. The stage-hands lounge at the back of the stage, in full view of the spectators, occasionally coming forward to place a cushion, adjust the folds in an actor's robe, or offer a bowl of tea to refresh one of the singers after a difficult passage. This tea-drinking has become, in the course of centuries, an integral part of the performance. It is said of an actor: 'He drinks his tea beautifully.' The actors also show great dexterity in handling the cushions on which they kneel in moments of supplication or despair; when they have finished with them they skim them nonchalantly back to the stage-hands, with a flick of the wrist, like quoits.

There is a certain amount of spoken dialogue, but the opera consists chiefly of sung recitative, within a five-note compass. The orchestra is seated upon the stage itself: there are several percussion instruments, a violin, and a sort of bagpipe. The singing is thin, reedy, nasalized; to western ears it startlingly resembles Donald Duck. We were quite unable to distinguish the gay from the tragic, or the bridge-passage from the climax. But the audience, despite its chatter, was evidently following the music with critical attention; for, at certain points, it broke into the kind of applause which, in Europe, greets a very pretty high C.

Our Chinese hosts did their best to explain the story. Some women flap their sleeves. 'The wives are despising her for not having a husband.' Lady Precious Stream utters some piercing, Disneyesque sounds. 'Now she is

63

reconciling filial piety with her wifely duty.' A general is sent to kill the hero; they engage in a ballet-fight. The hero, to our surprise, is beaten. But he has won a moral victory, for the general repents and begs his forgiveness. The old Emperor, father of Lady Precious Stream, is deposed, and the hero takes the throne. His frumpish old mother is honoured; the villain is led out to execution. The old Emperor sulks a bit, but gives in at last with a good grace. Lady Precious Stream receives a little flag to show that she is now Wife Number One.

March 14

This afternoon Mr. Donald took us to have tea with Madame Chiang Kai-shek.

We crossed the river to Wuchang in the lace-curtained cabin of a private Government launch. The guards all sprang to attention and saluted as we stepped on board; Donald leading the way, looking very grand and ministerial in his fur coat with its black astrakhan collar. His cold was still bothering him, he told us.

The Generalissimo and Madame are living, at present, in the old provincial army headquarters. Our car passed under a stone gateway, flanked by painted lions, circled a lawn beneath which a solid-looking dug-out had been built, and stopped before the guarded doors of the villa. Donald took us straight upstairs to wait in a small sitting-room, furnished in sham walnut, like the interior of an English road-house. From the bare wall the photograph of Dr. Sun Yat-sen looked down, decorated with the crossed flags of the Republic and the Kuomintang. In the corner stood a cabinet full of cutlery and dusty champagne-glasses; on a table a cellophane box enclosed a huge birthday-cake, at least two feet high. Yesterday, Donald told us, was Madame's birthday. The cake was a present from the ladies of Hankow. Madame was going to send it to a home for refugee children.

A servant brought in the tea-things and, a few moments later, Madame herself appeared. She is a small, round-faced lady, exquisitely dressed, vivacious rather than pretty, and possessed of an almost terrifying charm and poise. Obviously she knows just how to deal with any conceivable type of visitor. She can become at will the cultivated, westernized woman with a knowledge of literature and art; the technical expert, discussing aeroplane-engines and machine-guns; the inspector of hospitals; the president of a mothers' union; or the simple, affectionate, clinging Chinese wife. She could be terrible, she could be gracious, she could be businesslike, she could be ruthless; it is said that she sometimes signs death-warrants with her own hand. She speaks excellent English, with an intonation which faintly recalls her American college-training. Strangely enough, I have never heard anybody comment on her perfume. It is the most delicious either of us has ever smelt.

We began by congratulating her upon her birthday.

'Ah . . .' she smiled and shook her head, with a simplicity which was none the less attractive for being artificial: 'I hoped no one would know. . . . A man likes to have birthdays. A lady not. It reminds her that she is getting old.'

We sat down at the tea-table. 'Please tell me,' said Madame, 'do poets like cake?'

'Yes,' replied Auden. 'Very much indeed.'

'Oh. I am glad to hear it. I thought perhaps they preferred only spiritual food.'

The cakes were extremely good. (Had Donald chosen

65

them, we wondered?) Madame herself ate nothing. Behind her mask of vivacity she looked tired and far from well. We chatted about England, about our journey, about our impressions of China. When we had finished she said: 'And now perhaps you would like to ask me some questions?'

We answered that we should like her to tell us something about the New Life Movement.

In Hongkong we had heard our first reports of this curious moral crusade, launched by the Generalissimo and his wife, four years ago—and they had been most unfavourable. Priggery and hypocrisy, it seemed, were flavoured unpleasantly with police bullying. A specimen frock, showing the correct length of sleeve for a chaste woman, had been exhibited in Peking. A young English traveller had been reprimanded in the streets of Sian for smoking a pipe out of doors. Some people even had had their teeth compulsorily scrubbed. Mixed walking, it was rumoured, was forbidden in the cities of the interior.

(This public segregation of the sexes is, of course, nothing new in China. As the essay of a modern Hongkong student so charmingly put it: 'In the days of Confucius everything was well managed in the Land of Loo. The coffin-cloths were fine and thick. Men and women walked on opposite sides of the street.')

Mr. Tsang, the Mayor of Canton, had been more reassuring: 'New Life is not *under* and not *over* human nature.' But, so far, every one we had met, Chinese and European alike, had seemed slightly vague about the exact character of the Movement itself.

Folding her hands and lowering her eyes to the table Madame now began to deliver what was evidently, to her, a familiar lecture. For centuries, she told us, the Chinese people had been ruled by a despotic governing class. Therefore, when China became a republic, they had very little idea of how to govern themselves. The officials of the old imperial order had possessed a definite moral code which, in theory at least, they acknowledged as binding —however often they may have failed to put it into practice. But this moral code died with them, and a period of chaos ensued, which was a fertile breeding-ground for Communist propaganda. And so the New Life Movement was inaugurated in a speech by the Generalissimo himself at Nanchang, in 1934. According to Madame, it was the sight of the desolation wrought by the Communists in Kiangsi Province and the feeling that something must be done for the peasants which roused the Generalissimo to action.

(Elsewhere we have heard a different and more convincing explanation. When the Nanking Government suppressed the Communists it still had to reckon with the effects of their propaganda amongst the common people, who had come to respect them and to learn from them a different way of life. The New Life Movement was therefore, according to this view, a direct attempt to compete with the Communist platform of economic and social reform, substituting a retreat to Confucius for an advance to Marx. In a sense Madame herself admitted this when she said: 'We are giving the people what the Communists promised but couldn't perform.')

The New Life Movement is based on the practice of four moral virtues: *Li* or Reason, *I* or Propriety of the Outward Man, *Lien* or Moral Judgment, and *Chih* or Conscience. It aims at instilling into the people ideals of civic responsibility and social service. Volunteers have been sent out to check administrative corruption, clean

67

city streets, and generally raise the standard of public health. Hospitals and relief-works have been established. Mah-jongg and opium-smoking have been forbidden. Government officials are not allowed to visit brothels.

Madame, we were bound to admit, made all this sound eminently practical and sensible: 'To Europeans, our virtue of Outward Propriety may seem rather silly. But China has forgotten these things, and so they are important.' We repeated some of the stories we had heard of reformist extravagance, and she agreed that they were probably quite true. Some of the followers of the Movement had been stupid, over-zealous, dizzy with success; but the Government certainly did not encourage them.

We asked her whether, after the war was over, the Government would be prepared to co-operate with the Communists. 'It is not a question', Madame replied, 'of our co-operating with the Communists. The question is: Will the Communists co-operate with *us*?' 'I had two Communist women to tiffin today,' she added. 'I told them: "As long as the Communists want to fight for China we are all friends."'

Just as we had said good-bye and were leaving the room, an officer came up the stairs. It was the Generalissimo himself. We should hardly have recognized in this bald, mild-looking, brown-eyed man, the cloaked, poker-stiff figure of the news-reels. In public and on official occasions, Chiang is an almost sinister presence; he has the fragile impassivity of a spectre. Here in private he seemed gentle and shy. Madame led him out on to the balcony to pose, arm-in-arm, for yet another photograph. Under the camera's eye he stiffened visibly, like a schoolboy who is warned to hold himself upright.

On the way back to Hankow we discussed the Movement and the Chiang régime. Could China ever be cleaned up? Auden, himself a veteran enemy of compulsory hygiene, was sceptical. We laughed as we pictured Chiang, Madame, and Donald flying frantically about the country by aeroplane, clearing out the drains in one city, buttoning up the coats in another, starting a trachoma-clinic in a third. By the time they had finished the first city would be filthy again and the coat-collars in the second already beginning to come apart.

'As long as you fight for China', Madame had told the Communists, 'we are all friends.' No doubt. But what does she mean by 'China'? Is this struggle to be a mere 'coolies' war', fought to make the country safe for a continuance of the rule of the 'Soong Dynasty', the small and all-powerful clan of bankers to which Madame herself belongs? Can Chiang, with his long record of Communist-suppression, ever form a permanent alliance with men like Mao Tse-tung and Chou En-lai, whose whole lives have been devoted to the workers' struggle? It is certainly hard to believe.

Nevertheless, it is impossible not to feel that the leadership of the Chiangs is vital for China, as long as this war continues. And Madame herself, for all her artificiality, is certainly a great heroic figure. There is one story about her which particularly pleases us. A few months ago the Japanese proposed some extremely impudent peace terms; their offer was made through the medium of a neutral foreign ambassador. The ambassador came to tea and delivered his prepared speech. There was an awkward silence. Somewhat embarrassed, the ambassador added: 'Of course, I give you this message without any comment.' Madame looked at him: 'I should hope so,' she said quietly. Then, switching on all her charm: 'Tell me, how are your children?' This was the only answer the Japanese ever received.

March 15

This evening, as we were walking home to dinner, the air-raid sirens began to scream. One of them, the loudest, bellowed from far away across the river, like a sick cow. The bare trees in the snowy consulate garden had seemed heavy with black leaves; but the leaves were rooks, and now, startled up into the orange evening sky, they circled hither and thither, weaving gigantic intricate patterns. The police began to clear the streets, hustling rickshaw-boys into the cover of archways and doors. The abandoned rickshaws were lined, like kneeling camels, along the gutters of the already deserted road. It was a solemn, apprehensive moment, as if before an eclipse of the sun.

With the Consul and several others we climbed to the roof of one of Hankow's highest buildings, the American bank which stands on the Bund, near to the British Consulate. The electric current had already been switched off, so the lift wasn't working, and we had to grope our way up flight after flight of stairs in the pitch darkness. On the roof there was plenty of light, for the brief dusk was over and the moon was full.

The brilliant moon lit up the Yangtze and the whole of the darkened city. The streets lay empty and dead, except when a lorry, carrying soldiers or ambulance-workers, tore down them, shrieking its brakes at the corners. Already the sirens had sounded for the second time—announcing that the raiders had crossed the inner danger-zone and were within twenty minutes' flying-distance of Hankow. Now at any moment they would be here.

A pause. Then, far off, the hollow, approaching roar of

the bombers, boring their way invisibly through the dark. The dull, punching thud of bombs falling, near the airfield, out in the suburbs. The searchlights criss-crossed, plotting points, like dividers; and suddenly there they were, six of them, flying close together and high up. It was as if a microscope had brought dramatically into focus the bacilli of a fatal disease. They passed, bright, tiny, and deadly, infecting the night. The searchlights followed them right across the sky; guns smashed out; tracer-bullets bounced up towards them, falling hopelessly short, like slow-motion rockets. The concussions made you catch your breath; the watchers around us on the roof exclaimed softly, breathlessly: 'Look! look! there!' It was as tremendous as Beethoven, but *wrong*—a cosmic offence, an insult to the whole of Nature and the entire earth. I don't know if I was frightened. Something inside me was flapping about like a fish. If you looked closely you could see dull red shrapnel-bursts and vicious swarms of red sparks, as the Japanese planes spat back. Over by the aerodrome a great crimson blossom of fire burst from the burning hangars. In ten minutes it was all over, and they had gone.

'Afraid we didn't put up a very good show tonight,' said a British naval officer, as we stumbled downstairs. 'Looks as if they caught the home team on the ground.'

He was right. We heard later that six Chinese planes had been destroyed before they had had time to take the air.

3

Two days later, at seven o'clock in the morning, we left Hankow by train for Cheng-chow.

Our servant Chiang accompanied us to the station. Already before dawn he had arrived at the Consulate to report for his first day of duty—a demure and dignified figure, in his patent leather shoes, black silk robe, spotless linen and European felt hat. His grandeur tacitly reproved our shabbiness—Auden's out-at-elbow sports-coat, my dirty, baggy flannels. We were unworthy of our employee. He was altogether a gentleman's gentleman.

At the ticket-barrier, Chiang began to exhibit his powers. Herding the coolies with our baggage ahead of him he flourished our Government passes (stamped with the Generalissimo's own chop) beneath the awed nose of the sentry. We should have lost face, no doubt, had we deigned to present them ourselves. Then, when everything was arranged, Chiang stepped aside, with a smiling bow, to let us pass. This, his unctuous gesture seemed to say, is how Big Shots board a train.

No sooner had we settled into our compartment, than Chiang bustled off, to carry on the process of face-making among the car-boys. 'My masters', he undoubtedly told them, 'are very important personages. They are the friends of the Generalissimo and the King of England. We are

travelling to the front on a special mission. You had better look after us well, or there might be trouble.' The car-
boys, no doubt, knew just how much of this to believe;
but their curiosity was aroused, nevertheless, and they
all came to peep and smile at us through the corridor
window. We may have undone Chiang's work a little by
winking and waving back. But perhaps we were not un-
imposing figures, with our superbly developed chests—
padded out several inches by thick wads of Hankow dol-
lar-bills stuffed into every available inner pocket. This
seemed a dangerous way to carry money, but traveller's
cheques would have been useless in many of the places to
which we were going.

This train was in every way superior to those running
on the Canton–Hankow line. In peace-time it would have
taken you through to Peking. Nowadays it went no further than Cheng-chow: the railway bridge over the Yellow River had been blown up to check the Japanese advance. There was a handsome dining-car, with potted
plants on the tables, in which we spent most of the day.
This dining-car had only one serious disadvantage: there
were not enough spittoons. Two of the available five were
placed just behind our respective chairs, and the passengers made use of them unceasingly, clearing their throats
before doing so with most unappetizing relish. In China,
it seems, children learn to spit when they are two years
old, and the habit is never lost. True, the New Life Movement discourages it, but without any visible effect. Even
high government officials of our acquaintance hawked
and spat without the least restraint.

Our journey was quite uneventful, despite the usual
prophecies of air-attack. The train ran steadily on through
the golden-yellow landscape. The snow had all disap-

peared, and the sun was hot; but it was still winter here, the trees were leafless and the earth bare and dry. All around us spread the undulating, densely inhabited plain. At a single glance from the carriage-window, one could seldom see less than two hundred people dotted over the paddy-fields, fishing with nets in village ponds, or squatting, on bare haunches, to manure the earth. Their gestures and attitudes had a timeless anonymity; each single figure would have made an admirable 'condition humaine' shot for a Russian peasant-film. What an anonymous country this is! Everywhere the labouring men and women, in their clothes of deep, brilliant blue; everywhere the little grave-mounds, usurping valuable square feet of the arable soil—a class-struggle between the living and the dead. The naked, lemon-coloured torsos, bent over their unending tasks, have no individuality; they seem folded and reticent as plants. The children are all alike—gaping, bleary-nosed, in their padded jackets, like stuffed, mass-produced dolls. Today, for the first time, we saw women rolling along, balanced insecurely as stilt-walkers on their tiny bound feet.

We arrived in Cheng-chow after midnight, two hours behind time. The moon shone brilliantly down on the ruined station, smashed in a big air-raid several weeks before. Outside, in the station-square, moonlight heightened the drama of the shattered buildings; this might have been Ypres in 1915. An aerial torpedo had hit the Hotel of Flowery Peace; nothing remained standing but some broken splinters of the outer walls, within which people were searching the débris by the light of lanterns. All along the roadway street-vendors were selling food, under the flicker of acetylene flares. Chiang told us that Cheng-chow now did most of its business by night. In the daytime the population withdrew into the suburbs, for fear of the planes.

A few yards down the main street from the square we found an hotel with an intact roof and an available bed-room. The proprietor warned us that we should be ex-pected to leave it at 8 a.m.; during the daytime all the hotels were closed. Chiang bustled about, giving orders to everybody, admirably officious to secure our comfort. The beds were unpacked and erected, tea was brought; with his own hands he steadied the table by placing a piece of folded toilet-paper under one of the legs. Where would he sleep himself, we asked. 'Oh, it doesn't matter,' Chiang replied, modestly smiling. 'I shall find a place.' He seemed positively to be enjoying this adventure. We both agreed that we had got a treasure.

I slept very badly that night, dozing only in five-minute snatches until dawn. From the station-sidings came the mournful wail of locomotives, mingling with cries of the nocturnal street-hawkers and the constant shuffling and chatter of people moving about downstairs. Through a window beside my bed I could see the ragged bomb-hole in the roof of the next-door house, and the snapped beam-ends poking up forlornly into the clear moonlight. Why should the people of this town assume that the Japs would only attack during the daytime? Tonight, for example, would be ideal. . . . And I remembered how Stephen Spender had told me of a very similar experience he had had during a visit to wartime Spain. Meanwhile, in the oppo-site bed, Auden slept deeply, with the long, calm snores of the truly strong.

Immediately after breakfast we set out for the Ameri-can Mission Hospital. The Consul-General in Hankow had given us an introduction to Dr. Ayres, its chief. Cheng-chow, viewed by daylight, seemed less dramatic, but infinitely more depressing. It stands at the junction of China's two main railway lines: the Pin-Han, running north and south; the Lung-Hai, running east and west. In peace time, Cheng-chow exploited its key-position to the full. It was a city of gangsters, gamblers, prostitutes, and thieves. All trains, we had been told, stopped there for twenty-two hours—simply in order to give the passengers time to visit the drug-dens and the brothels. When, at intervals, an agitation arose to speed up the train service, the principal hotel-keepers and opium-joint-proprietors would send a delegation to the capital with a suitable bribe, to plead for the maintenance of the original schedule.

The houses of the main streets were pretentious, sinister, and shabby, coated all over with a peculiarly evil-smelling, sticky dust which blew in clouds about the town. We pushed our way down the long, straggling market-lane which led to the hospital gates. At intervals, amidst the booths and shops, were shallow dug-outs, barely a yard deep and no larger than a dog-kennel, roofed over roughly with planks, earth, and straw. In my jaundiced, sleepy mood, everything I noticed seemed miserable and corrupt. Every third person in the crowd appeared to be suffering from trachoma, or goitre, or hereditary syphilis. And the foodstuffs they were buying and selling looked hateful beyond belief—the filthiest parts of the oldest and most diseased animals; stodgy excrement-puddings; vile, stagnant soups and poisonous roots.

It was a relief to find ourselves in Dr. Ayres's sitting-room, with all its wild, grass-widower's untidiness—odd shoes, old coats, sweaters, and surgical instruments scattered everywhere; used razor-blades and tea-cups on the

mantelpiece; medical books sandwiched between last
year's copies of the *Saturday Evening Post*. The place certainly needed a feminine hand. It was dirty, but with the
kind of dirt to which we were accustomed. We felt at
home at once.

Dr. Ayres himself, a charming, drawling southerner
from the State of Georgia, welcomed us like old friends
expected for months. He was just having breakfast, and
presently in burst his colleagues—Dr. Hankey and Dr.
McClure.

'Boy,' cried McClure, rubbing his hands, 'I've got a kid-
ney today! Gee, what luck!'

'Oh, Bob,' said Hankey protestingly. 'You might let
me do it!'

'No, *Sir*! I want to have a stab at it myself.'

Hankey, we discovered during the course of the meal,
was a newcomer to China. He was an Englishman, and
had volunteered for war-work direct from Guy's. Tall,
lanky, and young, beaming behind his thick spectacles,
he amused and delighted the others by his enthusiasm for
every novelty. Everything thrilled him—bomb-craters,
pagodas, stomach-wounds, the faces of old beggars: he
was perpetually whipping out his camera for a photograph.

McClure was a stalwart, sandy, bullet-headed Canadian
Scot, with the energy of a whirlwind and the high spirits
of a sixteen-year-old boy. He wore a leather blouse, riding
breeches and knee-boots with straps. Born in China, educated in Canada, he had earned his college fees by working as a stevedore and a barber. Before the war he had
had his own hospital at Wei-hwei, north of the Yellow
River. It was now in Japanese hands. At present he was
acting as a co-ordinator of Red Cross services; and visit-

ing, in this capacity, all the hospitals and mission-stations up and down the Lung-Hai line.

After our second breakfast we were taken round the premises. In the compound Dr. Ayres had built a big thatched emergency-hut to accommodate the overflow of wounded. Most of the in-patients were suffering from bomb-injuries: fractured legs and arms. Trunk-wounds, the doctors told us, were mostly fatal; the victims were usually brought in too late, and died of sepsis. The Japanese had been very active in the Cheng-chow region lately, attacking not only the town itself, but many of the surrounding villages. McClure himself had had an extremely narrow escape, only a week or two before: the ferry-boat in which he was crossing a river had been destroyed a few moments after he had jumped into the water. Two bombs had been dropped here in the mission compound, just beside the enormous outspread American flag.

The operating-theatre was a scene of lively, rough-and-ready activity. The work of six surgeons had to be done by three—and quickly; there was no time for professional niceties. People strolled in with telegrams or parcels, and remained to help, to the best of their ability; there was something for everybody to hold: a leg, a towel, or a bucket. In the general confusion, while Ayres's back was turned for an instant, one of the operating-tables upset. The patient's head hit the floor with a resounding crack. He looked slightly dazed, but didn't complain.

At lunch McClure told us that he was leaving that evening to visit some hospitals in the direction of Kai-feng. Kwei-teh would be his first destination. Why shouldn't we go with him? We agreed that we should like to, and went upstairs to Dr. Ayres's bedroom to lay in some reserves of sleep.

After a late supper we started out. Chiang was silent this evening, and inclined to be unhelpful; perhaps he was intimidated by McClure's dynamic presence. We were semi-apologetic about the extent of our baggage, uneasily suspecting that McClure considered our possession of beds and a private servant as slightly sissy. He himself carried only a small suitcase. When we reached the station half a dozen coolies sprang out of the darkness, each struggling for a bag. McClure punched one of them hard on the jaw. The man wasn't a bona-fide porter, he explained later, but a railroad thief.

The train, we were told, would leave at ten minutes to two. We had several hours to wait. The platform, unlighted, crowded with troops, was bitterly cold. But McClure's energy warmed us like a brazier.

Himself a Presbyterian, he had no use for dogma in mission-work; it was silly to bother the Chinese with theological language which they couldn't understand. Phrases like 'washed in the Blood' merely disgust them; 'the King of Heaven' suggests to their minds only a sort of super-tax-collector. 'If you stand up on a soap-box you only get hold of the loafer who's on the look-out for an easy job. The people we want are the farmers. And they're too busy to come and listen to a lot of talk. This crusader-stuff is the bunk.'

'In this century mankind's got to choose between alcohol and the combustion-engine. You can't run both. The hospitals are full of saps who try to. If you want to go fast you've got to live clean. . . . Reminds me of a funny thing. I used to work in Formosa, you know. One day an old man came into my clinic. Said he couldn't remember his age; thought he must be close on eighty. "Why, boy," I said, "you've got a physique like a man of twenty-five!"

79

And he had, too. Magnificent! Well, I thought to myself, here's a chance to teach the students something. So I had them all come in. "See here," I said to them, "this is what you get from living clean. Look at him—and now take a look at yourselves!" Then I asked the old man: "You don't smoke, I suppose?" "No, never." "And I guess you don't drink, either?" "I do not." "Don't play around with women?" No, he didn't care to do that, any more. "Well," I said, "to what do you attribute your wonderful health? Tell these gentlemen, please." So he thought for a minute, and then he said: "Twice every day I take a little opium. There's nothing like it." That certainly was one on me, eh—with my Y.M.C.A. stuff?'

Two o'clock came, and half-past, and there was still no train. But McClure didn't despair. The station-master had assured him that a troop-train would be passing through Cheng-chow at three. 'That suits me all right. They're apt to be a bit overcrowded. We'll have to sit on the roof, I guess. . . . Only thing—if the Japs come over you've got to jump. Quick. Those trains are loaded full of ammunition. You wouldn't have a chance. Not a chance.'

The troop-train, not altogether to my disappointment, never arrived. Propped against each other, like sacks, on a hard wooden bench, we dozed and froze patiently until seven o'clock. Then we returned to the mission-hospital for breakfast. At nine McClure was back in the operating-theatre, tinkering away at the casualties with unimpaired vigour.

At tea-time we came in to find McClure and two bearded Italian missionaries listening with grave faces to the wireless. The Italians had brought news that Kwei-teh had already fallen; even the Chinese newspaper admitted that

80

the Japanese had captured a town only twenty-five miles further north. But the wireless-bulletin told us nothing new; and we agreed that we had better attempt the journey, at any rate as far as Kai-feng. 'Whatever happens,' said McClure joyfully, 'we'll be in the thick of it!'

Tonight a train was promised for eleven o'clock. At twelve-thirty we were told that it had actually reached the North Station, only a mile away. McClure decided that he and I should walk there, along the track, leaving Auden and Chiang to look after the luggage. In this way we should be more likely to get seats. As we set out it began to rain. Several hundred yards down the line there was a most unpleasant bridge, open to the water beneath. You had to cross it by stepping delicately from girder to girder, hoping that the gaps, invisible in the darkness, would be roughly equidistant. 'What shall we do', I asked timidly, 'if the train comes now?' 'Jump it,' replied McClure promptly, and proceeded to explain the proper technique of jumping trains, if you didn't want a broken neck.

But, to my surprise and relief, the train actually was waiting. McClure efficiently identified it from among a dozen others. We even found a sleeping-compartment with four vacant berths. At first he was inclined to turn up his nose at so much unnecessary comfort; but I cunningly pleaded with him to accept it for the sake of Auden, who, I hinted, was far from well.

Auden, meanwhile, had had an alarming experience. After a visit to the station lavatory at the far end of the sidings, he had returned to find that Chiang and our luggage had utterly disappeared—swallowed up in a vast, amorphous mass of sleeping soldiers and refugees which grew perpetually larger, like a nightmare fungus, and threatened gradually to cover the entire platform. It had

81

taken him an hour's search to find them again. 'I really began to be afraid', he told us, 'that I'd lost you all for ever.'

At nine o'clock next morning we reached Min-Chuan— a name which, translated, means 'Democracy'. It was no more than a loop-line, a signal, and a hut, set down, without apparent object, beside a bedraggled grove of willows, in the midst of an immense mud plain. Auden called it 'The Bad Earth'.

We had plenty of time to dislike the view, for we stayed at Democracy six and a half hours. Why, nobody could tell. McClure predicted that the Japanese must be advancing up the line, and that presently we should all have to retreat to Cheng-chow on foot. His morale, we couldn't help noticing, was slightly impaired. Indeed, he admitted this himself. 'It's because', he explained, 'my system's running short of sugar. If I can only get something sweet, I'll be all right. What I need, right now, is a box of candy.'

Out of the rainy mist, as if in answer to his request, a crowd began to gather. They were neighbouring peasants who had come to sell their wares, scenting from afar the presence of our train. Standing in the drizzle, in their fur hats and straw capes, they offered boiled chicken varnished red with soya beans, sausage-shaped waffles made from bean-flour, grey vermicelli, sugar-cane and hard-boiled eggs. We bought eggs, waffles, and a stick of cane, which McClure sucked contentedly. Its tonic effect upon him was almost immediately apparent. Soon the Bad Earth was forgotten, and we were listening to a further instalment of his lavishly-illustrated autobiography. Our only hope was that it would continue until this journey was over.

In Cheng-chow he had bought a lorry and run it into a

quicksand, while disembarking from the Yellow River ferry. Within half an hour the sand had been up to the instrument-board, but they had got it out, nevertheless. 'I had to take it apart and clean it, nut by nut. And, boy, when I'd got it apart, I couldn't put the darned thing together again! So I went to Peking, and worked in a Chevrolet garage for a month—learning how.'

'One time I was medical adviser to a General. A real old bandit. Boy, was he tough? Wouldn't pay his fees. After a while, when he owed me five hundred dollars, they told me he was going to give me a testimonial tablet. Of course, I knew what that meant. In this country, if you give a man a tablet, it cancels all your debts. So I went around to the tablet-carver, and I said: "That tablet's not going to be ready till I say the word." Sure enough, every day that old bandit would send word to ask how the tablet was getting along. And every day the carver would tell him: "One of the characters isn't just how I want it. I guess I'll do it again." Was he mad? But I got my money all right, in the end.'

At half-past three, without the least warning, the train moved forward. We had almost forgotten that it possessed an engine and wheels. McClure told us that eastern Ho-Nan is the great wheat-growing district of China. The Chinese is essentially a market-gardener. He cultivates wheat as the English grow roses. He makes a hole for each single plant, and fills it with night soil. In consequence the yield per acre is very high. The British-American Tobacco Company, said McClure, once sent out a party of experts to show the Chinese how to grow tobacco. But, at the end of two years, their experimental farm, equipped with all the latest scientific methods, couldn't produce as big a crop as the Chinese did, on their own.

Where the Chinese failed, he thought, was in their utter lack of co-operative spirit. When the crops are ripe each peasant has to guard his little plot with a gun. If he falls asleep for a moment his neighbours will steal some of it— and the whole village will think this right and proper. When McClure himself had started a co-operative irrigation scheme with electric pumps, the project had had to be dropped, because it would have necessitated closing some wells and deepening others; and no one was prepared to have his own well closed. Similarly, a superior kind of peach has recently been brought to China, but it cannot be grown unless an entire community is ready to agree to its introduction. Otherwise, local jealousy would be such that the fruit would all be stolen before it was ripe.

Fights over property are not uncommon. For example, a woman has a hen. When she is feeding it a neighbour's hen runs up to share the grain. The two women have words and exchange blows. The owner of the hen then tells her son, who immediately attacks the son of the neighbour. Finally, every member of both families joins in, and there follows what McClure calls 'a knock-down and drag-out', in the course of which several people will probably be wounded or killed.

Cheating in business, he added, was nearly universal. Clay beans were manufactured, at considerable trouble and expense, to adulterate bean flour. Wheat was made heavier by the addition of tacks and scrap-metal. The magnetic separator of a flour-mill in this district removes at least one hundred and fifty pounds of metal a day.

Towards five o'clock we arrived at Shang-kui, Kwei-teh's nearest railway station. The distance between Kwei-teh and Shang-kui is about five miles; we covered it in rickshaws, along a flat, rough road, lined with trees. The buildings of the Church of Canada Mission Hospital stand in their own large compound-garden, beyond the air-field, just outside the city. It seems strangely touching, in the midst of the alien plain, to come upon these prim, manselike walls of grey brick, so isolated, so stubbornly Anglo-Saxon, despite the pointed, upcurving eaves of their corrugated iron roofs. After the drill-ground bareness of Cheng-chow, the garden itself seemed wonderfully fruitful and pleasant. The trees were full of birds—crows and beautiful blue-jays, with white throat-collars and long sky-blue tails.

McClure entered like Father Christmas, with a double postman's knock, and soon, amidst back-slappings and kidney-punchings, we were being introduced to his two Canadian colleagues, Dr. Gilbert and Dr. Brown.

Our first questions were, naturally, about the Japanese. Where were they? But nobody in Kwei-teh exactly knew. They might arrive at any moment to attack the city—or they might be still a long way off. The railway line to Süchow appeared to be unbroken, as yet. Trains were going daily east. Here they had had very few air-raids. Shang-kui station was occasionally bombed, but without much damage, so far.

Next afternoon, after a much-needed night of unbroken sleep, we all walked into the city, to call on the Roman Catholic bishop and on the local American Baptist missionary, Mr. White. Seen from outside, Kwei-teh is a town of great beauty; its four massive walls, flanked by corner watch-towers, are surrounded by a wide, reedy moat. The gateways are plastered with advertisements. But these

85

huge, boldly-daubed characters decorate rather than dis-
figure Chinese architecture—at any rate, to our Western
eyes. Within the walls is a maze of muddy, stinking
streets. This place would be a death-trap in an air-raid.
Life seemed unbearably cramped and confined; we were
both conscious of a mild claustrophobia. 'It gives you an
idea', said Auden, 'of what Europe must have been like
in the Middle Ages.'

The bishop, a rotund and cheerful pro-Franco Span-
iard, welcomed us with a bottle of cherry-brandy. 'This
is the one good thing', he told us, 'that comes out of Russia.' He was not displeased at the prospect of a Japanese
conquest. The Japanese, he said, would bring law and
order to China.

Mr. White was an altogether more sympathetic figure
—pleasant-looking, quite young, with tooth-paste-advert
teeth. Unlike the other Protestant missionaries, he had
kept his family with him—a wife and two small children.
They invited us to lunch next day. The American flag in
his garden had stuck half-way up the pole. McClure volunteered, of course, to shin up and get it down. McClure was
in his element here. When the centrifugal pump at the
hospital went wrong, he knew why; when the gas-plant
failed, he could put it right; when the engine was making
the wrong kind of noise, McClure detected it at once. Dr.
Brown, his friend since college days, provided a mock-
admiring audience for all these feats of energy and skill.

On the way home Dr. Gilbert told us that this countryside was once overrun with bandits. Since the war, however, there had been fewer. In China the bandit is usually
a soldier out of work. But the road to the station was still
unsafe after nightfall. Local men of property, coming up
to Kwei-teh in rickshaws, had been attacked and robbed;

the rickshaw-coolies simply ran away. And Dr. Brown himself, driving the ambulance-truck down to Shang-kui late one evening, had been shouted at to stop, and fired on when he refused. McClure, needless to say, pooh-poohed the danger. Bandits were easy enough to deal with, he told us. You merely had to strike first. He had been cycling near Cheng-chow one evening when he spotted some suspicious characters lurking on the road ahead. 'I didn't hesitate. I drew my gun right away, and fired a couple of shots into the air. Those bandits did the vanishing trick, all right! Man, I'll bet they're running yet!' The moral of this story was that both Auden and myself should carry automatic pistols. It wasn't the first time we'd heard this piece of advice, but we had no intention of following it.

Dr. Gilbert then went on to tell us of a local missionary and his wife who happened, a few years ago, to be on a train which was just drawing into Shang-kui station. By the merest chance they decided to leave the coach in which they were travelling and move forward to another, where they could find more comfortable seats. As the train arrived, the two back coaches, which they had just quitted, were uncoupled, and promptly raked with machine-gun fire. The station authorities had got word that they contained some notorious bandits. The bandits were killed, all right; but so were many innocent passengers. The Mayor of Kwei-teh later expressed his regret that this should have been so. 'It was', he agreed, 'very unfortunate for the Pooblic.'

Auden offered his cigarettes, which Dr. Gilbert accepted, somewhat coyly. The standards of Kwei-teh hospital were liberal enough, in comparison with many others; but, even here, nicotine had the daring attraction of a minor vice. Elsewhere in the mission-field, so we had heard, the sternest taboos prevailed. Mission-doctors were obliged to smoke in secret, like schoolboys. If they were discovered there would be a public prayer-meeting for the salvation of their souls. In some places a doctor caught drinking a glass of wine by his minister would be liable to lose his job altogether. (It must be added that, in the course of our Yellow River journey, we witnessed few serious signs of this stupid and contemptible tyranny—no doubt because the tyrants themselves had been the first to abandon their posts and run away from the danger-zone. In general, only the best type of missionary had remained.)

We were just finishing breakfast next morning when Dr. Brown invited us to attend service in the hospital chapel. The hymn they were singing had, as its refrain, the words, 'Arise! Arise!' In Chinese it sounded like: '*Chee*-ee-ee-ee *lai!*' This tune, set to different words, is a favourite song of the Eighth Route Army. The Chinese minister, seeing that there were foreign visitors in the congregation, made the service last as long as he possibly could.

Afterwards, in the operating-theatre, we watched Mc-Clure and Brown at work. The patient had a vaginal-urethral fistula, sustained in childbirth. We took the opportunity of examining her feet. A girl's feet are generally bound at the age of four or five. All toes except the big toe are turned under the foot, and fastened in this position. Subsequent growth will then only have the effect of raising the arch, forming a deep groove across the centre of the sole, which is very liable to sores. The custom of foot-binding is gradually dying out in China. Most of the

bound feet we saw in Kwei-teh were those of middle-aged
or elderly women.

While he operated McClure kept up a running commentary for the benefit of the amused and slightly scan-
dalized Canadian Sister. 'Let's have something to kneel
on. . . . You see, Sister, I'm more devotional than you
think. . . . Now the torch. . . . Let your light so shine. . . .
Oh boy, that's good! Sponge, Brother. . . . More light in
the north-east. . . . Phew, I'm sweating. This is worse than
two sets of tennis. . . . Now then, Bunty pulls the strings.
Which string shall you pull, Brother? If you were in a
sailing-ship, you'd be sunk. . . . Well, that's fixed the ex-
haust. We'll do the differential tomorrow. . . .'

Opposite the hospital buildings, there was a small enclosed plot of land, half kitchen-garden, half municipal
park, which contained an obelisk commemorating the
foundation of the Chinese Republic. Brown had heard
that some bandits had been executed there the day before, so we went over to look. In the park were an old lady
and some soldiers, eating their midday meal under a fruit-
tree. 'Their heads are over in that ditch,' they told us.
We hunted about for some time but could find nothing.
'Oh well,' remarked the old lady, casually, 'then the dogs
must have got them.'

Brown thought it more likely that the bandits' relatives had carried off the heads, during the night. The
Chinese, like the Japanese, have a horror of leaving a
headless corpse behind them, for, without a head, they
cannot hope to enter the next world. Even after a surgical amputation, the doctors have to offer the severed limb
to the patient. He will probably wish to keep it until his
death, when it will be buried with him. This is why, after

a penal decapitation, the heads are usually stuck on poles above the city gates, out of reach of the victims' families.

In Kwei-teh, as elsewhere, the authorities' scale of punishments is fatally simple. In order to scare his cook, who had stolen and re-sold a large quantity of the hospital's sugar, Brown once reported him to the Mayor. Happening to glance out of the window next morning, he was just in time to prevent the cook being led out to be shot. When, later, he expostulated, the Mayor seemed surprised: 'But I thought you wanted me to punish him?'

We lunched, as arranged, with the Whites. There was another guest, a Baptist minister from further down the line. We had fruit-juice, meat-loaf, salad, and cake. It was a resolutely cheerful little American household; Mrs. White was educating her daughter with the aid of correspondence-school books. One couldn't help wondering what would have happened to them six months from now. If the Japanese came, the Whites had arranged to take refuge in the hospital-compound. Neither of them seemed in the least nervous at the prospect.

The meal opened with a slight misunderstanding. 'I have a lot of bandits in my field,' the Baptist minister told us.

'How very unpleasant for you,' said Auden sympathetically. 'Do they steal your vegetables?'

The minister looked somewhat puzzled until Mr. White explained: 'It's the mission-field he means.'

The conversation then became professional: 'In Loyang he heard the Gospel, and it took root.' 'He was quite a skilled silversmith, but when he became a Christian he refused to make dragons and other works of the Devil. So he lost his job.' 'The Japanese remind me of that text in

90

Ezekiel xxix: "But I will put hooks in thy jaws, and I will cause the fish of thy rivers to stick unto thy scales."'

The Whites had a young fox-terrier. Mr. White put a small piece of cake on the table, and asked: 'Do you want it?' The dog cocked its ears but didn't move. 'Are you a Catholic?' Mr. White asked it. There was no response. 'Are you an Anglican?' 'Are you a Presbyterian?' 'Are you a Seventh Day Adventist?' 'Are you a Mormon?' Mr. White turned to us proudly: 'Now watch. . . . Are you an American Baptist?' The terrier jumped for the cake at once.

'But did you notice', said Mr. White, 'how he nearly made a move when I mentioned the Adventists? I'm kind of worried about him.'

Next day was a brilliant warm spring morning. This is the time of year when the coolies begin to discard some of their heavy winter clothes and the lice, emerging from the padding, seek other hosts. 'In the spring', the Chinese say, 'the louse can fly.'

From the road outside came the continual pig-squeal of wheelbarrows going past. To quote McClure, all Chinese wheelbarrows squeak, because the squeak is cheaper than the grease. Also, the boss can tell at once if one of his coolies quits work.

At crack of dawn McClure had set off to visit a mission-station somewhere to the south, riding Dr. Brown's push-bike. McClure is one of the great apostles of the bicycle. He trusts it over any kind of country, as other men trust the horse. Dr. Brown maintains, however, that, owing to the state of the roads, most of McClure's cycling is done on foot. We were more than sorry to see him go.

Really, the proceedings of the Chinese are so mysterious

91

as to fill one, ultimately, with a kind of despair. During
the morning Auden heard an explosion and ran out into
the road to see what had happened. All he could see was
an officer haranguing his men, and a group of peasants
who were burning an old book. Then a woman rushed up
and prostrated herself before the officer, wailing and sob-
bing. The officer raised her to her feet and, immediately,
the two of them began talking quite naturally, as though
nothing whatever had occurred.

Numbers of wounded soldiers arrived in rickshaws from
the northern front. They had been several days *en route*,
and a few of the rickshaws contained corpses. The wounded
were all bandaged in the roughest possible way. Often a
bit of dirty wadding from somebody's coat had been
simply stuffed into the wound. Dr. Brown told us that the
warm intestines of a freshly-killed chicken are a favourite
Chinese antiseptic.

Today we had decided to start trying to leave for Sü-
chow. The being-about-to-start appeared to be an important phase of any journey through this part of China.
Brown drove us that afternoon to Shang-kui, to interview his friend Mr. Lin, the Sectional Engineer. Mr. Lin
was a charming, shock-headed gentleman, fervently patriotic: he had taken a vow, he told us, not to cut his hair
until the Japanese had been driven right out of China.
'When Shan-Tung is retaken, I cut a little. When Hopeh
is retaken, I cut more. When Manchukuo is retaken, I cut
all.' He spoke vehemently of the Japanese atrocities
against women: 'Everywhere they are going, the Japanese
committing adultery.' 'Manchukuo was the beginning,'
he said. 'Then came Abyssinia. Then Spain. And now,
you see, the Germans have take Australia without firing
a single shop.'

We inquired about our journey. Mr. Lin assured us that there would be a train—there were always two trains to Sü-chow every day. True, it might be late, very late—it might even arrive tomorrow morning; nevertheless, it would be today's afternoon train. Meanwhile, if we wished, we could sleep at his house, so as to be nearer the railway station.

Dr. Brown then took us for a walk round Shang-kui. It was a wretched little place, muddy, overcrowded, and infested with hens. We inspected the bath-house, where you were scrubbed in a big communal pool of steaming water, by little boys; and then conducted to a curtained-off apartment, where you could have your toes massaged, drink tea, and get a woman. One of the customers was covered with a syphilitic rash. Nobody minded being looked at; we merely felt embarrassed by our own clothed presence. The whole building was filthy and smelt heartily of urine. A third-class bath, we were informed, cost six cents, including tip.

We then went into a Chinese military hospital—actually a square of miserable, windowless huts, grouped round the sides of a compound. The wounded lay in their uniforms, on straw—three men often beneath a single blanket. The orderly told us that they had hardly any dressings or antiseptics, and no proper surgical instruments at all. We found eleven men lying in a room barely fifteen feet long and eight broad. In one hut the sweet stench of gas-gangrene from a rotting leg was so violent that I had to step outside to avoid vomiting. There was no X-ray apparatus here, of course, so very few of the bullets could be extracted. Those who were badly wounded could only be left to die. Indeed, it argued a strong constitution if they could get to the hospital at all. Some were

93

stranded near the battlefield because they hadn't a dollar to pay for carriage.

Almost all the patients were apparently cheerful—despite the darkness, the stink of urine-sodden straw, the agonizing jolts which their wounds must continually have received from their bedfellows. Indeed, they thanked us for our kindness in coming to see them. Our visit upset all of us—and particularly Brown, who was much worried over his half-formed decision to leave Kwei-teh and join the Eighth Route Army, where he would have to work under similar conditions. I think the sight of these men finally made up his mind for him. He told us that when we returned from Sü-chow he would probably be ready to start.

We returned to the mission hospital for supper, and set off again at ten o'clock, loaded with presents of food from Dr. Gilbert and the Sisters. Brown drove very fast, skidding wildly all over the muddy road; but nobody tried to stop us.

Mr. Lin made us very comfortable. We erected our beds in his outer office. A boy brewed unending cups of tea, and we sat talking far into the night—chiefly about Confucius, of whom Mr. Lin was an ardent disciple. 'Confucius say: "One must live without hurting others." Very bright.' On the wall of the office was a framed Chinese character, executed in sweeping brush-strokes, with a thick, bushy tail—somewhat resembling an impressionist drawing of a cat. Mr. Lin told us that it signified 'Going forward smoothly, step by step.' Certainly, we agreed, this was an admirable motto for a railway engineer.

4

March 24

We slept soundly, woke, breakfasted. Still no train. It arrived at last, about 10.30 a.m. Just as we had got all our luggage on board, a large bell on the roof of a neighbouring building began to toll—the local warning of an air-raid. So, with several dozen others, we retired to the station dug-out, a fine structure of concrete and wooden piles, with three rooms and two exits, built by Mr. Lin himself, in 1936, when the Chinese, seeing that war was sooner or later inevitable, had begun to make their preparations. The dug-out was fitted with telephones; and a long, dramatically candle-lit conversation followed with various stations further down the line. At the end of half an hour we were told that the Japanese weren't coming after all.

So we started. Mr. Lin's influence had procured us a free pass to Sü-chow, and the station master came in person to see us off. We left Shang-kui with faces much enlarged.

The carriage roofs, as usual, were black with passengers. On every journey, we are told, two or three of them fall off and are killed. At the last moment, dozens of people tried to clamber on to the train, and were beaten off with sticks. The train-guards even chased particularly agile boys right along the platform, thrashing them unmercifully. But this, it seemed, was only a kind of game, for the victims' padded coats were so thick that the blows only raised a cloud of dust and lice; and pursuer and pursued roared with laughter.

Our journey took up the whole of the day. There were the usual cups of tea, the usual damp towels (we no longer wipe our faces with them, however, for McClure has warned us of the danger of trachoma-infection), the usual hour-long halts. The stations were mostly small, and much alike, with their rookeries, their basket-ball pitches, their food-vendors, their lurid or cryptic anti-Japanese cartoons. At one place a young officer got so bored that he began firing at the rooks with his revolver, and was severely reprimanded by a hastily improvised court-martial in the waiting-room. Chiang enjoyed himself hugely as face-maker and gossip-bearer. This time, he told the car-boys, quite pointlessly, that we were doctors—much to our alarm; for we expected at every station to be summoned to perform major operations upon the wounded. 'But at least', said Auden, 'we'd be better than nothing.' So we agreed, if called upon, to have a try.

Not far from Sü-chow we passed an armoured train, its metal sides plastered with a camouflage of mud. Behind it was the Generalissimo's special coach. He and Madame, we learnt later, had been in Sü-chow, attending a military conference.

Presently Chiang came running excitedly to tell us that a Japanese prisoner had been taken on board our train. He had been captured somewhere near the Grand Canal. The Generalissimo had personally ordered that he should be kindly treated, and sent down to Hankow for cross-examination. He would go there on the return journey. Prisoners in this war are a kind of zoological rarity; we gaped at this one with furtive and somewhat shame-faced curiosity. A stout, round-faced youth, tied up with rope like a parcel, he seemed as isolated in his captivity as a baby panda. His half-dozen guards grinned at him cheerfully, but he looked sheepish and scared, as well he might —for one of them was negligently twirling a pistol on his index finger. It threatened at any moment to go off and shoot somebody in the foot. The Japanese, said Chiang, had been a tailor in civil life, but this was probably invented, for the prisoner spoke only his native language, and no one present could understand it. There was nothing we could do for him except to put a cigarette between his lips and go away as soon as was decently possible.

We arrived at Sü-chow at about half-past nine in the evening. Here, too, the station buildings have been damaged by air-raids, but not very seriously. No sooner had we emerged into the darkened street outside than we were set upon by a mob of rickshaw-coolies, yelling and snatching for our baggage. Chiang dealt with them most efficiently, though his methods are the very opposite of McClure's. In three or four minutes the bargaining and scuffling were over, and we were bumping over the cobbles, into the city.

We had arranged to stay the night at the Garden Hotel, chiefly because Chiang had been told, on the train, that it was the headquarters of General Li Tsung-jen. Li Tsung-jen and Pai Ch'ung-hsi are jointly in command of the Chinese armies in this zone: the soldiers refer to them as 'The Two'. Before the war these generals were the virtual dictators of Kwang-si Province, and the avowed enemies of the Generalissimo. That they and their troops are fighting up here in the north, hundreds of miles from their home,

97

is one of the most striking instances of China's solidarity against the Japanese. We are anxious to meet Li Tsung-jen, because we want him to give us passes to visit the front. We have a letter of introduction to him from the all-providing Mr. Hollington Tong.

General Li wasn't at the Garden Hotel, after all; but we decided to stop there, nevertheless. The hotel itself was full; we were given a room in a sort of garden pavilion. The place was draughty and cold; we unwisely tried to light the stove, which nearly smoked us out into the street. But, as Auden remarked, it was better to die like Zola than like Captain Scott. And soon, despite the intimate noises which reached us, through the matchboard walls, from the rooms of our fellow-guests, we had both sunk into the heavy dreamless sleep of semi-asphyxia.

March 25

This morning there was an air-raid, of which we saw and heard very little. The bombs seemed to be dropping at a considerable distance. When it was over we started off to call on Dr. MacFadyen, of the Presbyterian Mission Hospital. We had a letter to him from Dr. Brown.

Sü-chow is an attractive city of one-story houses with narrow, cobbled streets. It stands along the old bed of the Yellow River, which is several feet higher than the town itself. The police here are armed with flat swords; they carry them slung on their backs in short red sheaths.

When we arrived at the hospital Dr. MacFadyen was out, so we went on to the house of his colleague, Dr. Greer. This hospital has a very large compound. Besides the main building, the annexe, and the doctors' houses, there is a clinic for women, which is Dr. Greer's special charge.

Dr. Greer herself, a white-haired, apple-cheeked lady of seventy from the Southern States, is, even on casual acquaintance, plainly one of the great figures of the China Missions. She wears a Chinese robe, with flat-heeled leather shoes and several pairs of thick woollen stockings. She welcomed us like long-lost grandsons, clapping her hands as she chatted, to hurry on the servants in their preparation of an emergency lunch.

Married to a missionary, but now a widow, she has spent the whole of her adult life here in Sü-chow, and today her sons and daughters are also missionaries, working in different parts of the country.

'You saw my clinic as you came by? My husband and I wanted that bit of ground for twenty years. And here's how we got it. . . .'

There had been trouble in the city at that time. Sü-chow was in the hands of a bandit army. The plot of land in question had been occupied by bandit-soldiers. Dr. Greer's husband was in bed, very sick. One night, dozing beside him, Dr. Greer awoke to see one of the bandits standing in the corner of the bedroom, holding her husband's revolver. Her first thought was, 'He's going to kill my husband!' So she rushed at him. They struggled. The bandit threw her off and dashed out of the room. Dr. Greer's husband woke up, exclaiming that they'd all be murdered. Dr. Greer hastily gave him his medicine and an injection; then seized the poker and charged downstairs to continue the battle. But now she heard screams coming from her children's room. The bandit had run through it, dropping the revolver on the bed. 'So back I ran—like an old hen after her chickens.' Meanwhile, the bandit had jumped from a window into the garden and escaped. When Dr. Greer's husband got well he complained to the ban-

dit's general, who not only apologized, but immediately
withdrew his soldiers from the neighbouring plot, and so
the Greers were able to buy it, cheap. Dr. Greer's only
comment on this story is: 'I guess the Lord must have
given me strength.'

On Dr. Greer's advice we installed ourselves, uninvited,
in Dr. MacFadyen's house. He would, she assured us, be
only too glad of a bit of company, for his wife was away.
Any qualms we may have felt were dispelled when, presently, the Doctor himself returned. He also is American,
and also elderly—a burly, bullet-headed man, in shabby,
greenish-black clothes, with twinkling eyes and a rich
Southern accent. He seemed to take our presence as a
matter of course. 'Well, well,' he greeted us, 'I kind of
thought it wouldn't be long before some more of you
newspaper-boys got around here.' (The last 'newspaper-
boy' to visit Sü-chow was an American journalist. He
stayed here a week, as the guest of Dr. MacFadyen, trying
to get permission to go up to the front. The authorities
made so many difficulties and excuses that he finally returned to Hankow in despair.)

Sü-chow, it appears, is in no immediate danger of falling. But the enemy are not more than thirty miles to the
north, and they are advancing from the south-east as well.
If and when the Japanese occupy the city Dr. Greer and
Dr. MacFadyen will remain. They plan to give shelter, in
their compound, to a large body of female refugees.

The technique of receiving the Japanese is now well
established in missionary circles. Letters of advice on this
subject have even found their way from one side of the
line to the other. It is very important, everybody agrees,
that a foreigner shall be present when the invaders enter
a town. When the attack is expected you must brick up

all your compound-gates but one. (They are doing this at Sü-chow already.) This gate must always be left open or it may be broken down. During the critical period one or other of the white missionaries must remain in the gate-house all day and sleep there at night. When the first soldiers arrive they must be given tea. You must argue with them patiently, you must be firm but very polite, and on no account must you show that you are frightened. It is important to get hold of an officer at the earliest possible opportunity. With luck he may even post a notice forbidding soldiers to enter your compound. Mission reports agree that the officers—especially if they are Christians—will be courteous and amenable, but they cannot always control their own troops. The common soldiers are all right if they aren't drunk. The Japanese, in general, are very easily intoxicated, however, and then the trouble begins. The lives of the male inhabitants will probably be spared, but most of the women will almost certainly be raped, so it is the women who must be got into the mission-buildings. What drunken and really undisciplined troops will do when they find themselves deprived of girls is uncertain. In one well-authenticated instance the missionaries themselves were murdered.

Dr. Greer and Dr. MacFadyen know all this and accept it as a matter of course. Their unsensational heroism would seem even more extraordinary if it weren't paralleled by many similar cases. At this very moment, for example, a missionary named Hoskyns, who is well over seventy, remains at his post in Y-Hsien, with two elderly ladies. The town is being besieged, and a big artillery battle is said to be in progress.

This afternoon we went to headquarters to see Li Tsung-jen. Li's secretary, Major Pan, received us, a handsome, gentle young man with a puzzled scowl, who spoke adequate English. On the basis of demanding twice as much as one expects to get, we asked for a private car to take us to the front, and an interpreter to accompany us. Major Pan scowled and looked worried. It was he, we learnt, who had had to deal with the American journalist. Perhaps he foresees that we shall be an even greater nuisance. Finally he took us in to meet General Li himself.

Li speaks no English. He is a very polite, nut-brown man, with an enormous mouth and deeply intelligent eyes. Through our translator we asked for passes to the front. Li replied that the front was extremely dangerous. We answered that we didn't mind. Li bowed. We bowed back. Tea was drunk. The interview closed on a note of polite obstructionism.

A few hours later, to our surprise, a soldier came round to the hospital with a couple of signed permits.

March 26

We have changed our plans. It is no good badgering the unfortunate Major Pan, whose final suggestion was that we should go up to the front by train and return the same day—this would mean spending only a few hours in the trenches. Also, the movements of the troop-trains are worse than uncertain. So we have arranged, through Chiang, to hire rickshaws and travel quite independently, by road. Major Pan, whom we have seen again today, to get road permits, is more discouraging than ever. The road, he says, is liable to attack by Japanese mobile units operating behind the Chinese lines. However, after much bowing and tea, the permits were signed.

This morning there was a big air-raid on the station and the centre of the town. The planes were overhead for nearly half an hour. But we could hardly tear ourselves away to look at them, so deeply were we engrossed in the treasures of Dr. MacFadyen's library. Auden is reading *Bleak House*. I have a novel by Oppenheim, called *Michael's Misdeeds*.

Dr. Greer came in later. A bomb, she told us, had dropped just beside the mission church during the service. The glass in the windows had all been shattered, but the congregation was on its knees, and no one was hurt. She had been at the station distributing tracts to a regiment of soldiers who were leaving on a troop-train. They had all clamoured: 'We want a little book!' And she'd said: 'If you snatch you won't get one!' So they hadn't snatched.

Dr. Greer thinks that the Japanese came over this morning because they are trying to destroy the new guns which are passing through Sü-chow on their way up to the line. So far, apparently, they haven't succeeded.

Dr. MacFadyen tells us that there is an earlier city of Sü-chow, buried about twenty-five feet underground by a flood six hundred years ago. At the bottom of the well in his garden there are ruins of a house from which he has excavated all kinds of utensils and implements. Floods have always been a great danger in this region. The dyke along the former Yellow River bank is very old. It is strengthened with a mixture of lime, sand, glutinous rice, and pig's blood—the ancient Chinese form of cement. At the north gate of the city there is a curious bronze ox—placed there as a charm against floods. When the water begins to rise the ox is supposed to bellow.

China, says Dr. MacFadyen, is a terrible place for growths and tumours. In the hospital he has a whole museum of bladder-stones. One of his patients had a polypus growing out of his nose, so long that you could wind the pedicle round his neck. He once removed a three-pointed stone which was sticking simultaneously into the navel, the rectum, and the urethra. Another patient had a tumour on his back weighing sixty pounds. It resembled a meal-sack. Whenever the man sat down the weight of it pulled his feet up into the air. All these phenomena are due, largely, to neglect; few people will come into the hospital until things have progressed so far that they are already freaks. In some cases the relatives are opposed to medical treatment, because they imagine that the sick man brings them luck. In others, the patient himself grows positively to like his own affliction.

March 27

At half-past seven this morning we left Sü-chow in our four hired rickshaws—two for ourselves, one for Chiang, and one for the baggage. The rickshaw-coolies had agreed that they could make the journey to the front easily in one day.

At the north gate we stopped for several minutes, while Auden photographed the bronze ox from every conceivable angle. A big crowd gathered to watch us, laughing and chatting, as well they might: we certainly make an extraordinary trio. Auden, in his immense, shapeless overcoat and woollen Jaeger cap, seems dressed for the Arctic regions. Chiang, neat as ever, might be about to wait at a Hankow consular dinner-party. My own beret, sweater, and martial boots would not be out of place in Valencia or Madrid. Collectively, perhaps, we most resemble a group of characters in one of Jules Verne's stories about lunatic English explorers. Even our oddly-shaped canvas sack, riding ahead of us in its rickshaw like a fat, sullen emperor, might be supposed to contain one of

Verne's fantastic contraptions for investigating the bottom of the sea or flying from the earth to the moon.

The weather was grey and cloudy. As we left the city behind us the sirens began to wail, and we congratulated ourselves on having avoided the delay of the morning air-raid.

Alternately walking and riding, we reached Mao Tsun, the first village marked on the sketch-map which Mac-Fadyen had prepared for our journey. The road was flat and easy, winding across the cultivated plain, with low hills on our left and, on our right, the high embankment of the railway. A few miles out of Sü-chow we had crossed an elaborate trench-system, as yet empty and unguarded, evidently designed to defend the city from the north. We passed a boy leading a donkey with a small red cloth on its back. Chiang, even more officious than usual, stopped to warn the boy that he must remove the cloth at once, or its bright colour would be likely to attract the attention of Japanese airmen!

Beyond Mao Tsun the road got very rough and the country wilder and less inhabited. We had to walk most of the way to Liu Chuan. The sun came out, bright and hot; I shed my sweater, Auden his overcoat and cap. All the while I was keeping a faintly uneasy eye alert for the Japs, but there was no sign of them, either in the air or among the barren folds of the hills.

At Liu Chuan we ate our midday meal at a table in the middle of the street, for the hovel which was the village's only restaurant swarmed with flies. The crowd round our stools was so dense that you couldn't move an elbow without touching a human body. The children were the most inquisitive; the chins of the smallest were ranged along the table-edge, a row of decapitated heads, smeared with

105

mucus and dirt. They scuffled silently for the scraps we threw them, nearly overbalanced by the huge drum-bellies which are due to enlarged spleen. The grown men looked on, smiling and commenting, from behind. Our occasional accidents with the chop-sticks—we are now getting comparatively skilful—amused them greatly.

Chiang questioned everybody but could get very little definite news. The fighting, most people seemed to think, was going on just north of Han Chwang, where the railway line crosses the Grand Canal. We could certainly push on as far as Li Kwo Yi, and spend the night there. Then we should be able to visit the trenches next day, on foot. Here, in Liu Chuan, they had heard the guns very plainly during the night. But now there wasn't a sound.

Liu Chuan was full of soldiers but we met no troops on the road beyond—only an occasional army lorry and groups of refugee peasants going south, laden with sacks. The low empty hills crowded in; we climbed slowly to the top of a shallow, stony pass. Here and there, in the middle distance, we saw a sentry posted at some vantage-point which commanded the windings of the track. The railway was no longer visible; it had curved away to the east. Once, very faintly, I fancied I heard the boom of a gun.

From the top of the pass the view opened. We were looking down the slopes to Li Kwo Yi, with the Grand Canal beyond, and the valley where Han Chwang must lie: not a shot to be heard, not a puff of smoke to be seen —the meadows still and peaceful in the afternoon sun, the blossom beginning on the hill-sides and, in the distance, a blue range of mountains. Auden made me laugh by saying thoughtfully: 'I suppose if we were over there we'd be dead.'

From here we looked down on War as a bird might—

seeing only a kind of sinister agriculture or anti-agriculture. Immediately below us peasants were digging in the fertile, productive plain. Further on there would be more peasants, in uniform, also digging—the unproductive, sterile trench. Beyond them, to the north, still more peasants; and, once again, the fertile fields. This is how war must seem to the neutral, unjudging bird—merely the Bad Earth, the tiny, dead patch in the immense flowering field of luxuriant China.

'Surely', I exclaimed, 'that horse is *green?*' And so it was. We overtook the soldier who was riding it. He explained that all army horses, if they are white, are camouflaged in this way against aircraft. He told us, also, that we shouldn't be able to get to Han Chwang: the northern part of the village is actually in the hands of the Japanese. The southern half, on this side of the canal, is in the Chinese front lines.

On the bridge, just outside Li Kwo Yi, sentries stopped us and examined our passes and cards. We were told that we must first see General Chang Tschen, whose headquarters are at Ma Yuan, a village about two miles to the east. So we set off along a field path running roughly parallel to the canal, towards the village, or group of villages, lying on the edge of the plain under the hills. The sun was just beginning to sink, and Ma Yuan, in the distance, with its walls and rookeries and square, church-like towers, looked so lovely that we could almost cheat ourselves into believing that this wouldn't, on closer inspection, prove to be just another huddle of mud and bamboo huts. From a mile away it couldn't have appeared more beautiful and august if it had housed the combined culture of Oxford, Cambridge, and the Sorbonne.

And indeed, despite the soldiers, the horses, the hens, and their symphony of smells, there was something very academic, dignified, and gentle about the bespectacled officers who received us. General Chang Tschen himself is mild and stout, in carpet slippers. His first words were an apology for the quality of the supper we were about to eat. It was taken as a matter of course that we should spend the night in Ma Yuan as his guests.

'So you wish to visit the front? Ah. . . .' The officers looked puzzled and mildly discouraged. 'The front is very dangerous.' 'Yes, we have heard that.' 'Ah. . . .' There was a pause of polite deadlock. We felt very apologetic for our own obstinacy. Then the telephone rang and the General answered it, in accents which, to our western ears, have always the ring of resigned, dignified despair: 'Wa? Wa? Ah. . . . Ah. . . . Ah. . . .' Then a sigh, as though of extreme pain: 'Aah. . . .' 'We are told', he informed us, 'that the Japanese will soon begin to shoot with their gun. Please do not be alarmed. It is only a very small gun. . . .'

By the time we had finished supper it was already after six o'clock. The General's A.D.C. came to tell us that we might pay a visit to the front immediately before dark. Auden, Chiang, three or four officers, and myself made up the party. Mounted on small Chinese ponies we trotted away over the fields. Auden, during his visit to Iceland, had become a daring, if somewhat unorthodox, horseman. Chiang and I were beginners; indeed, Chiang had never ridden before in his life. But there was no difficulty in keeping your seat on these docile little animals; no sooner had we started than they fell into line, nose to tail, like a circus-troupe.

We dismounted at a ruinous and practically deserted village much nearer the canal. Dusk was gathering, and I narrowly escaped decapitation by a slack field-telephone wire which hung across the street. Here were more officers: there was a five-minute pause for introductions, the exchange of visiting-cards, handshakes, and salutes. 'You are now', the A.D.C. told us impressively, 'in the third Chinese line.'

We admired it duly, and asked if we might be taken on to the second. The A.D.C. hesitated, and sighed. We were certainly difficult to please. In the second line, he warned us, we should be within range of the Japanese gun. We persisted, however, emboldened by the sight of a soldier on the top of the distant earthworks, standing casually, black against the sky. If the Japs couldn't hit him they must be very bad shots indeed.

So, in single file, we advanced across the fields on foot towards another village. Here and there, in a small shallow pit, a soldier would be crouching, with his rifle beside him: why he was posted there neither of us could imagine. Our guides insisted that we should keep well apart; but this precaution seemed unnecessary because, as we later discovered, we were entirely invisible to the enemy. Perhaps the A.D.C., in his kindly way, wished to give us the maximum thrill for our money.

The second line is well constructed—amazingly so, considering that it has all been dug within the last week. It runs right across the plain at an average distance of about half a mile from the canal itself. The front line is the actual canal bank, which ends, to the west, on the shores of the big, shallow Y-Shan lake. The Japanese have, in fact, occupied nearly the whole of Han Chwang—for the southern suburb is extremely small; their main stronghold is the railway station. But this Grand Canal front is only in the nature of a barrage or dam, for beyond it, to the north, Chinese mobile units are besieging the enemy (and Mr. Hoskyns) in Y-Hsien, and attacking them at several other points. Provided, in fact, that the canal-line holds, the Japs are cut off, and will be destroyed piece-meal. General Chang Tschen's idea is, it seems, to clear up these centres of their resistance before ordering a general advance northwards. The Japanese are estimated to have between three and four hundred men in Han Chwang itself: the Chinese rather more. And reinforce-ments are expected tomorrow.

We inspected the whole of the second line, and asked to be taken on to the first; but it was already getting very dark, so we didn't press the point. From the canal an occa-sional shot rang out, and once or twice, like the slamming of a great door, came the boom of the unalarming 'small gun'. In the twilight the earthworks looked mournful and deserted. They might have been the remains of some vast engineering scheme, abandoned long ago. As we picked our way along them a soldier would now and then emerge from his straw-lined hole, to salute. Most of these boys looked pitifully young. We asked what they were doing so near the front line. Did they ever have to take part in an attack? Our guides assured us that they were only orderlies, and seldom exposed to any real danger.

We plodded back across the fields, dog-tired by this time, to the village where we had left our ponies. The ride back to Ma Yuan was much more exhilarating, for the horses, smelling supper, broke their circus-formation, and cantered through the darkness over the uneven plough-land. We passed an apparently deserted farmhouse, inside which a dog was furiously barking. I wondered if its refu-gee owners had left it locked in there by mistake. As we approached Ma Yuan a party of horsemen rode out to challenge us. It was lucky that the A.D.C. was well in front, and could give the password before any misunderstandings arose.

General Chang Tschen has assigned us a room in one of the commandeered houses of the village. It is still furnished with tables and stools; in the corner stands an immense lacquered Chinese bed. It feels very hard, and we prefer our own. Chiang has just put them up. He himself is going to sleep on the table. This evening he seems depressed. He got terribly bumped during his ride and is now feeling very stiff. Also he was scared, we think, at the prospect of visiting the front line tomorrow: we have reassured him by saying that he needn't come with us. This may also ease our way in negotiating with the officers, for Chiang does all our interpreting here, and he isn't above editing our requests and the Chinese replies.

A soldier has just been in to warn us not to go outside our own yard during the night. A sentry, as he put it, might make a stupid mistake.

I am beginning to feel an extraordinary affection for my bed. It gives a kind of continuity to this whole journey which is very reassuring. No matter whether we are sleeping at the Consulate or at Dr. MacFadyen's, or in this hut, it is always the same bed—and so I am always at home.

March 28

Woke soon after dawn to the crowing of a rooster, the braying of a donkey, and the chirping of a tame cricket which hangs in a little cage outside the door. During breakfast we continued our argument with two of the officers about the proposed front-line visit. 'If you go', said one of them, as though this were a startling and final ulti-

111

matum, 'we are afraid we cannot guarantee to protect
you.' 'But we do not ask for protection.' Another difficult
pause. 'Please tell them', said Auden to Chiang, 'that a
journalist has his duty, like a soldier. It is sometimes
necessary for him to go into danger.' This heroic sentiment, or Chiang's rendering of it, had a surprising effect.
Quite suddenly they gave us up: we were altogether too
tiresome for any further comment. Very well, we might
start in an hour.

Meanwhile there was time for a stroll round the village.
It was a glorious, cool spring morning. On a waste plot of
land beyond the houses a dog was gnawing what was, only
too obviously, a human arm. A spy, they told us, had
been buried there after execution a day or two ago; the
dog had dug the corpse half out of the earth. It was rather
a pretty dog with a fine, bushy tail. I remembered how
we had patted it when it came begging for scraps of our
supper the evening before.

We asked whether there were many spies about. Yes,
quite a number. The peasants round here are very poor
and the Japanese offer them handsome rewards for trea-
son. How had this particular man been caught? He was a
peasant who had crossed the Grand Canal by night and
come to Ma Yuan to get news. He had been so indiscreet
as to ask the General's cook where the General lived. The
cook, who suspected him already, had exclaimed: 'Oh,
you spy!' And the peasant had hung his head and blushed.
He was arrested immediately. This is Chiang's version of
the story—obviously garbled. But no doubt, from time
to time, there really is a miscarriage of justice. The Chinese take no chances.

We started at half-past eight. When the horses were
brought round Chiang insisted on mounting one of them

—the largest—and posing for his photograph. He was anxious to have a souvenir of his equestrian exploits. We then arranged that he and the rickshaw-coolies should proceed direct to Li Kwo Yi and wait there until we rejoined them later.

Our own route was the same as yesterday evening. There were the same semi-farcical precautions: the advance in single file across the fields and some dramatic dodging along communication trenches, only to emerge from them right on the crest of the sky-line as brilliantly illuminated targets. Finally we reached the canal bank itself. But this part of the front—as one of the officers, who spoke a little English, had to admit—was only occupied by the Japanese at night, when almost all the real fighting and raiding takes place. During the daytime the Japs retire into Han Chwang village.

Gradually we made our way westwards towards the shattered railway bridge, the village, and the lake. All the soldiers rose at our approach and saluted. We asked how they recognized an officer, for there is no apparent difference in uniform. 'An officer', said our guide, 'is recognized by his face.'

By this time the sunshine was very hot. Our walk was long and rough; I envied Auden his rubber shoes and bitterly repented of the vanity which had prompted me to wear my own uncomfortable, slightly oversize boots. Reaching the bridge we scrambled down into the dug-out which the Chinese have constructed right under the railway embankment. The men here talked in whispers, for the Japanese have machine-guns posted in the row of ruined cottages beyond. You could easily throw a stone across the canal into their positions.

Among the huts of the southern suburb we stopped to

113

drink hot water and take group-photographs of the commander and his staff. The commander insisted that we
should pose with them: 'Your families', he said, 'will be
very pleased to know that you have been so brave.'
Visiting-cards were liberally exchanged. Our pockets
bulged with them. As the hot-water party progressed
our hosts began an excited conversation in Chinese. Auden
and I, left to our own devices, found ourselves discussing
the poetry of Robert Bridges. *The Testament of Beauty*
can seldom have been quoted in less appropriate sur-
roundings.

At length it was time to go on. Our guides led us to the
extreme end of the village, a spit of land projecting into
the lake. Twice, crouching and running, we crossed streets
which were protected only by curtains of matting from
the enemy's eyes. There was a little shrine with two holes
made by shell-fire in its roof. The last house on the opposite bank of the canal was said to be full of troops, but
Auden popped his head above the parapet and took two
pictures without getting shot at. 'I don't believe', he
whispered to me, 'that there are any Japs here at all.'

His words were interrupted by three tremendous deto-
nations. The newly-arrived Chinese guns, somewhere near
Li Kwo Yi, had opened fire. The officers said that we must
start back immediately; at any moment now the Japanese
would reply. We were bustled out of the village in company with a soldier who was ordered to escort us back
into safety. We said good-bye to our hosts, thanking them
hastily but sincerely for all their hospitality and patience.

As we trudged over the fields, lying bare and empty in
the sunshine, the bombardment continued. More Chinese
guns opened fire from the east. The Japanese fired back,
shelling the trenches we had left. The Chinese guns were

far out of their reach—they seemed to have a range of at least seven miles. We could hear the great slam of the explosion, then the express-train scream of the shell right over our heads, then the dull crash of the burst, and a black, escaped genie of smoke would tower, for a moment, above the roofs of Han Chwang, or the open countryside beyond. Whenever this happened the soldier grinned at us delightedly.

Presently the firing slackened and stopped. From the north came the drone of approaching planes. The Japanese were out looking for the Chinese guns. They circled the sky several times, passing quite low above us. Whenever they came over, the soldier signalled to us to lie down. It was an unpleasant feeling lying there exposed in the naked field: one couldn't help remembering the many anecdotes of aviators' caprice—how a pilot will take a sudden dislike to some solitary figure moving beneath him, and waste round after round of ammunition until he has annihilated it, like an irritating fly. Auden seized the opportunity of catching the two of us unawares with his camera. 'You looked wonderful', he told me, 'with your great nose cleaving the summer air.'

In Li Kwo Yi we found Chiang and the coolies waiting. The village authorities gave us lunch on a lavish scale— twenty-seven boiled eggs were provided for three people. Just as we had finished eating the bombardment recommenced; its concussions shook the window frames. The prospect of another visit from the Japanese planes speeded up the rickshaw-boys considerably; they pulled us to the top of the pass in record time. They were pleased to have got out of the danger zone, but also, it seemed, proud to have been in it. All the way down to Liu Chuan they chattered gaily to each other and sang. Through Chiang

115

we questioned them about their wages. The general exodus from Sü-chow during the first threat of Japanese invasion had created a rickshaw boom. Coolies had charged eight dollars to take passengers to the railway station. Some of them made as much as twenty-four dollars a day.

We reached Mao Tsun without incident about six o'clock. A troop-train was just leaving and we were lucky enough to get a lift in it, through Chiang's diplomacy with the station-master, back to Sü-chow in time for supper. We paid off the coolies, who would return to the city on foot next day.

We both agree that it is nearly impossible for casual foreigners like ourselves to assess Chinese military morale. Judged by western standards the impressions brought back from a visit like this are bound to be superficially depressing. In Europe one is so accustomed to cocksureness and boasting that the reticence of a Chinese officer seems positively defeatist. While we were at the front this morning our guide said: 'Over there are the lines to which we shall retreat.' 'But you *mustn't* retreat,' Auden interjected, in spite of himself, rather severely. The Chinese merely smiled. And later, when we had seen everything, we were asked for our opinion of the trench system. The officers seemed genuinely disappointed when we praised it, and I don't think this was only politeness. They would really have welcomed even an ignorant English civilian's suggestions and advice.

The average Chinese soldier speaks of China's chances with an air of gentle depreciation, yet he is ultimately confident or, at least, hopeful. 'The Japanese', said one of them, 'fight with their tanks and planes. We Chinese fight with our spirit.' The 'spirit' is certainly important when one considers the Chinese inferiority in armaments (to-

116

day's new guns were a remarkable exception) and their hopeless deficiency in medical services. European troops may appear more self-confident, more combative, more efficient and energetic, but if they had to wage this war under similar conditions they would probably all mutiny within a fortnight.

5

Next afternoon as I was writing up our travel notes Auden (who had been out to call on Major Pan) rushed in to say that a train for the west was leaving in half an hour. We packed in a scramble, said good-bye to Dr. MacFadyen, and got to the station with only a couple of minutes to spare.

This train, we discovered, was the very same in which we had come from Kwei-teh to Sü-chow five days before. Chiang and the car-boys greeted each other delightedly like old friends, and he set to work at once intriguing that we should all be given free passes for the journey. The ticket-collector proved very amenable. After a glance at the Generalissimo's chop he bowed himself out of our compartment. Our one ungrateful regret was that we had ever been so silly as to buy tickets on this railway at all.

We now intended to travel straight through to Sian, covering almost the entire stretch of the Lung-Hai Railway. The minimum length of this trip, under present conditions, would be one whole day and two nights. But at Tung-kwan, where the line runs close beside the Yellow River, the Japanese had mounted guns on the northern bank, so this part of the journey had always to be made during the darkness and might cause twenty-four hours' delay. McClure, with all the relish of a Job's comforter, had told us about Tung-kwan already: 'Why, boy, it's nothing but a shooting-gallery. The Japs have their guns sighted on the track. And they've got searchlights, too. If once they spot you you haven't a chance—not a chance.'

In the middle of the night we stopped at Shang-kui. Dr. Brown was rather on our consciences; we had half-promised to pay him and Dr. Gilbert a visit when we returned from Sü-chow. But we couldn't face the prospect of abandoning our train and at length compromised by telling Chiang to get on the telephone to Kwei-teh Hospital and ask Dr. Brown if he was ready to join us at once. After a long time Chiang returned to say that only the night-watchman seemed to be awake, and that he could get no satisfactory reply.

All next morning we ran steadily westwards. The train had become a model of punctuality; nowhere did we stop longer than a quarter of an hour. Even the ill-omened 'Democracy' was left behind without undue delay. The car-boys, Chiang told us, were optimistic. If we could reach Loyang by six o'clock, they said, we should pass Tung-kwan during the night and be in Sian next day before noon.

Beyond 'Democracy' the sandy plain is desert to the horizon, patched here and there with scanty green, where peasants scratch miserably for their living, like fowls. Two-wheel carts, drawn by donkeys, toil over the waste, creaking as if their frames were loaded with the whole immense weight of the sky. We passed Kai-feng. By midday we were in Cheng-chow. We noticed that the sidings behind the station were full of derelict railway trucks, splintered and smashed by bombs.

Now the loess region begins. We skirted the gaping

119

sand-canyons, guarded by fantastic sandy spires and pin-
nacles—an entire landscape of Lot's wives. The cliff-faces
are dotted up and down with the dark entrances of cave-
dwellings. Here and there the slope has been architec-
tured into terraces, upon which wheat is growing. The
walls of the terraces are strengthened with a kind of mud-
stucco, so that, from a distance, the hillside resembles an
old Babylonish city.

Presently the canyon-country flattens down into a broad
rich river valley of orchards and green parks. Sails move
slowly above the waters of the hidden stream. There are
wells everywhere; donkeys plod round them in circles,
working the wooden irrigation-wheels. The poorer farmers, who cannot afford them, are raising the water by
windlass. Here and there, breaking the monotony of the
countless blue-clad figures, you catch sight of a pair of
scarlet trousers or a coat. 'Surely you must admit', the
bland evening seems to say, 'that these people are happy
and good?'

We reached Loyang punctual almost to the minute.
The platform was crowded with troops. A soldier leant
out of the opposite train-window laying his forefingers together and shouting something which made the others
laugh and applaud. 'England and China', Chiang translated, 'together! Italy and Japan together, too!'

I slept uneasily that night—in my trousers and shirt:
not wishing to have to leave the train and bolt for cover
in my pyjamas. Auden, with his monumental calm, had
completely undressed. There were frequent shuntings and
stops, excited conversations in the corridor, darkened
stations where men gesticulated mysteriously with lanterns and electric pocket-lamps. At last I tired of waiting

for Tung-kwan—if, indeed, we hadn't passed it already—
and relapsed into a long, boring, travel-nightmare which
did not leave me until dawn.

We both woke with a start in full sunny daylight.
Where were we? Certainly not in Sian. Certainly not past
Tung-kwan, even; for, away to our right, spread the broad
beach of the Yellow River. On our left was a little station:
we read its name-board, Ling Pao. The station buildings
were pitted with shrapnel-holes and all the windows were
smashed. A piece of loose iron on top of the water-tank,
camouflaged with branches, clattered in the hot violent
wind. Behind the station in a sandy hollow lay the mean,
dusty village. Chiang came in with bad news. There had
been a railway accident farther down the line. We
shouldn't be able to move on till eight o'clock that night.

We did move, nevertheless, into a deep cutting between two tunnels, where the train could take shelter
from a possible attack by enemy planes. The other passengers seemed to take the delay much more philosophically than we did. They scrambled up the steep slopes of
the cutting or went to sleep on the shady side of the line.
The engine driver got out a bundle of straw—perhaps kept
specially for this very purpose—and lay down comfort-
ably under his locomotive to read a book. The sun blazed
down, the bottom of our ravine was heated like a brick-
oven. Presently a string of peasants came trooping through
the tunnel from Ling Pao, and, within half an hour, the
cutting was a market resounding with the screams of
women and boys crying their wares.

Peevishly anxious for news, we asked Chiang to fetch
the conductor. He arrived, apologetically smiling. Yes, it
was quite true, there had been an accident. An engine had
run off the rails. They were laying a loop of new track

121

around the wreck. We should probably be able to start tomorrow at noon. '*Tomorrow*, at *noon!*' we echoed in dismay. 'What's the good of that? You can't pass Tungkwan by daylight.' The conductor smiled vaguely, bowed, and left us.

Meanwhile the car-boys had ceased hovering at the door of our compartment; they now came boldly inside and sat down. They seemed to have nothing whatever to do. The liveliest of them was called Chin-dung; his long floppy hair framed a charming, flat-nosed, impudent face. Chin-dung was exceedingly vain: he was eternally combing his hair or admiring his figure in the glass. He wore a thick rubber belt, like a bandage, which squeezed his pliant body into an absurdly exaggerated Victorian waspwaist. None of the car-boys spoke English, but they made themselves perfectly at home, prying into our luggage, examining and trying on our clothes, eating nuts, splitting seeds with their teeth, and helping themselves liberally to our cigarettes.

After lunch—without the least warning, and leaving a good quarter of its passengers behind on the cutting slope—the train moved off. But it was only backing through the tunnel into Ling Pao to water the engine. It stayed there several hours. Chin-dung presented us with a signed photograph of himself looking loutish and rather touchingly ridiculous in his best holiday suit of clothes. The other car-boys soon joined him, bringing with them a portable gramophone which played wailing opera-airs. We both began to feel that we had lived in this compartment for the whole of our lives.

Towards evening the train raised our wildest hopes by starting again—this time in the right direction. It carried us as far as the next station, a bleak upland village, standing back from the river, whose name-board, in the gathering darkness, we couldn't read. We christened it 'Wuthering Heights', and fell asleep early, to the whining of the wind between the motionless carriage-wheels.

'Wuthering Heights' was certainly preferable to Ling Pao. The morning air when we woke was cool and fresh. But poor Auden was in a terrible state: his legs and arms were covered with bug-bites. The bugs must be nesting in the upholstery of the shabby old Belgian sleeping-berths. We decided to have a radical spring-cleaning. First we called for basin after basin of hot water and washed ourselves all over. Then we set Chin-dung and the other car-boys to scrubbing the windows, while we ourselves took all our bedding out on to the platform, beat it with our walking-sticks, and hung it on the station fence to air in the sun. At first the Chinese passengers looked on, giggling with amazement. Then they began to follow our example. In a short time windows were being washed and bedding hung out down the whole length of the train. We felt sure that Madame Chiang Kai-shek would have approved.

After lunch we moved on a few more miles to the next station, Wen Chung Shan. It lay in the cup of a vast sand-plateau, high above the river. There was nothing here but the station buildings, and a few bamboo huts. Walking along the platform to stretch my legs I was accosted by one of the passengers, a sly, spotty boy with hair like a Japanese doll. He glanced quickly to left and right, nipped me suddenly and painfully in a sensitive place and murmured: 'Nice girl?' I smiled and followed him to the station exit, curious to see how the nice girl would be produced. From one of the huts beside the line an old woman

123

emerged on minute bird-like feet, leading by the hand a child of ten. She beckoned invitingly. I laughed, shook my head, and turned back towards the train.

Meanwhile Auden was teaching Chin-dung English. They were learning the parts of the body, naming them alternately in English and Chinese. A big crowd of passengers and beggars looked on, roaring with laughter whenever the anatomical lesson reached an intimate area. Chin-dung was rather stupid, but some of the younger spectators were very quick. They capered about the platform, slapping themselves all over and shouting the new, rude, foreign words.

But the lesson soon ceased to be a joke and became a hearty nuisance. Thrown back upon each other's well-worn company, we got through the long hours as we could best contrive—emptying out our heads like waste-paper baskets for the least scrap of amusement or interest. We told the old anecdotes, each secretly hoping that the other would remember or invent some new detail, however palpably untrue. We improvised parodies and limericks. We lost ourselves in interminable arguments and speculations: 'What would happen if the world ran out of oil?' 'What would you describe as the unhappiest day of your life?' 'Does a man become a different person in a different place?' 'If I know that I have no soul does that prove that nobody else has one, either?'

Meals were our greatest solace. Constipated though we were we could still eat, and the food provided by the kitchen-truck was, considering the circumstances, excellent. Our chief luxury was the American coffee which we had brought with us from Hankow in tins; Chiang always prepared this himself. Tonight there was no electric current on the train: we had to eat by candle-light. Chin-dung came in with a Chinese flute which neither he nor any one else present could play. His efforts to do so were so painful that at length we had to turn him out of the compartment altogether.

'Is there anything else you would like?' Chiang asked. And Auden answered jokingly: 'Yes. Bring us some whisky.' To our astonishment Chiang returned with a bottle of Red Label three-quarters full. He had found it in a corner of the kitchen-truck, where it must have been lying unnoticed for months.

During the night we reached Pan Tao, about fifteen miles distant from Tung-kwan itself. Another day of boredom and inaction seemed inevitable. But after breakfast we discovered that a breakdown train was leaving Pan Tao immediately for the scene of the accident. Mr. Wong, the Inspector of Railways from Sian, was on board. He kindly agreed to take us with him. Mr. Wong spoke fluent French; he had worked with the Belgian engineers when this part of the line was built, between 1931 and 1936.

We asked Mr. Wong about the Japanese at Tung-kwan. He was very reassuring. Oh yes, they shelled the line but they didn't do much damage. As for searchlights, they had them certainly, but didn't use them often. Mr. Wong pointed out some shrapnel-holes in the iron wall of the truck in which we were travelling. This train had been fired on early yesterday morning, but nobody was hurt. 'Had the Chinese any guns?' we asked. 'Certainly. Now we have some big guns.' 'I suppose', said Auden, 'you shell the Japanese?' 'No, we don't do that. You see, we don't want the Japanese to know that we've got them.'

Three miles beyond Pan Tao the line emerged from its

deep cutting on to an exposed, curving ledge, built out
from the sandy slope of the hills. Far beneath, at the foot
of the precipice, lay a big village surrounded by trees and
cultivated fields, spreading down to the beaches of the
Yellow River, whose golden-red bluffs showed through a
faint haze behind the northern shore. Right ahead, towering into the western sky, was a jagged chain of gigantic
blue mountains. This might have been the valley of Rus-
kin's fairy story. No one could possibly have chosen a
more beautiful spot for a disaster.

The derailed locomotive lay on its side right on the very
edge of the embankment amidst wreckage and twisted
track. One coach had slithered half-way down the steep
sand-slope beneath. We asked Mr. Wong exactly how the
accident had happened. Two trains, he said, had been
travelling west, one very close behind the other. As they
rounded this curve a wheel had come off a truck on the
rear train. Its driver, hearing the noise, had imagined that
the Japanese were firing at him from across the river and
had accelerated so violently that he collided with the
train in front and crashed off the rails. Nine people had
been killed and fifteen seriously injured. We asked if
there were many accidents on the Lung-Hai line. 'Oh
no,' said Mr. Wong, 'we've only had two in the last three
weeks.'

The new loop-track was laid already. Throughout the
long, hot morning, we watched the travelling crane as it
laboriously shifted the position of the damaged engine.
Mr. Wong took us down to lunch in the village: the hut in
which we ate was papered entirely with old copies of
American 'tabloids' and magazines, shipped out here by
the ton and sold for such architectural purposes. Wher-
ever you looked, the crimes of gangsters and the love-

secrets of divorcées were proclaimed from the ̇bamboo walls.

During the afternoon, without any warning, a Japanese aeroplane appeared, flying straight towards us out of the north-western sky. The breakdown gang stopped work and watched it without attempting to take cover. But many of the onlookers scattered, and three or four of the most panic-stricken actually glissaded right down the embankment slope to the village in a cloud of sand. The Japanese pilot was only scouting, it seemed. He changed his course and headed along the railway, flying east.

We returned to Pan Tao on foot, walking down the track. By the time we arrived it was already getting dark. Supper was a somewhat cheerless meal that evening; the car-boys had run out of firewood, so all the food was cold. There was no more sugar, either. Chiang brought us some sticks of candy to dip in our coffee. They looked like blackboard-chalk and tasted of Edinburgh rock.

About half-past nine everything was ready to start. The guards hurried from compartment to compartment, extinguishing all the candles. We took up our positions in the corridor at a window which I had insisted on opening, for fear of shattered glass. Auden, of course, was certain that nothing would happen. 'I *know* they won't shoot,' he kept repeating, until I began to be superstitiously afraid that the demons of the air would hear him and take offence.

We stopped twice at blacked-out stations where officials shouted excitedly to the engine driver, as though giving him last-minute warnings and instructions. 'They won't shoot,' Auden repeated. The train gathered speed, lurching so violently from side to side that I began to agree with him—we should probably be derailed long be-

fore we reached Tung-kwan at all. Putting out our lights
had been an altogether superfluous precaution, for the
glare from our stokehole lit up the entire cutting, and
swept the huge, flickering shadow of the engine along its
flying banks. The scream of the whistle, announcing our
approach, must have been audible for miles. The corridor
was a fog of sulphur and smuts.

There was a curious sense of relief, even of pleasure,
in those final moments. There was nothing we could do
either to hinder or to assist. Everyday life, so complex and
anxious, was soothingly simplified to the narrowness of a
single railway track. Our little egotisms, our ambitions,
our vanities, were absorbed, identified utterly with the
rush of the speeding train. The cutting deepened, and a
tunnel swallowed us in roaring darkness. Now. . . .

We burst out of it into clear starlight; the high embankment rose sheer from the river's edge. And there, right
opposite, blazing from the blackness of the opposite shore
like the illuminations of a pretentious road-house, were
the Japanese searchlights. We yelled at them and waved
our arms, suddenly hysterical as a drunken charabanc
party: 'Come on! Shoot! Shoot!' Then another tunnel
choked our shouting with its fumes. A couple of minutes
later we were clattering crazily over the points past the
deserted sidings of Tung-kwan station. And soon after the
guard came to tell us that we might relight our candles.
We were safe. The train slackened speed a little. The passengers began to get ready for bed. 'You see,' said Auden.
'I told you so. . . . I knew they wouldn't. . . . Nothing of
that sort ever happens to *me*.' 'But it does to *me*,' I ob-
jected; 'and if it had this time you'd have been there,
too.' 'Ah, but it didn't, you see.' 'No. But it might.' 'But
it didn't.'

There is no arguing with the complacency of a mystic.
I turned over and went to sleep.

We arrived in Sian without further incident at half-
past seven next morning.

Our first impressions of the city were formidable. As we
left the railway station its gigantic town-wall towered
ahead, extending to left and right as far as the eye could
see till it was lost in the thick, clammy, morning mist. We
might have been about to enter a gaol. And here, at the
gate, were the gaolers, surly and unsmiling—typical soldiers of the sullen north-west. Despite Chiang's well-
proven technique, they were not to be appeased with a
mere flourish of visiting-cards. They demanded our military passes and examined them suspiciously for a long
time before they let us through.

The Guest-House at Sian must be one of the strangest
hotels in the world. A caprice of Chang Hsueh-liang created
it—a Germanic, severely modern building, complete with
private bathrooms, running water, central heating, and
barber's shop; the white dining-room has a dance-floor in
the middle, and an indirectly rose-lit dome. Sitting in the
entrance-lounge, on comfortable settees, you watch the
guests going in and out, with the self-assured briskness of
people accustomed to luxury and prompt service, inhabitants of a great metropolis. Those swing-doors might open
on to Fifth Avenue, Piccadilly, Unter den Linden. The
illusion is nearly complete.

Nearly, but not quite. For, now and then a tattered
rickshaw-coolie, popping his head in to joke with the
page-boys, reminds you of what is really outside.

Sian has shrunk too small for its own immense peniten-
tiary-walls. Most of the houses are mere shacks, dwarfed

129

by the crazy old medieval gate-towers. Like shabby, dis-
pirited spectators of a procession, they line the edges of
the wide, rough, cart-track streets. Everywhere there are
plots of waste ground littered with ruins. When the sun
shines the city is swept by great clouds of dust blowing
down from the Gobi; when it rains the whole place is a
miserable bog. Beyond the walls, all along the southern
horizon, you can see the broken line of the big, savage,
bandit-infested mountains.

If Cheng-chow smells of disease, Sian smells of murder.
Too many people have died there throughout history, in
agony and terror. In 1911 the Chinese population fell
upon the Manchus and massacred twenty-five thousand
of them in the course of a single night. In 1926 the city
endured a terrible seven-months' siege. The Guest-House
itself has been the scene of more than one execution.

At the time of our arrival the guests of the hotel were,
almost exclusively, military or official—little band-box
officers, slim and smart and chattering; older, more responsible men, whose hair was cropped close to the skull,
who wore felt slippers and whose uniform hung loosely on
them like crumpled pyjamas. There were only four Europeans—Mr. Smith, the British postmaster, and Dr. Mooser, with his two Swiss colleagues of the League of Nations
commission, which was to advise the Chinese Government
on the prevention of infectious diseases.

Mr. Smith was something of a local character. Without
his tragic grimaces and dramatic, story-telling gestures,
no foreign party was quite complete. He had worked for
several years in Harbin and his description of the postal
services there and in Shen-si Province was fascinating.
The posts in Shen-si are conveyed by runners, who cover
amazing distances in record times. The runners make

their own non-aggression pacts with the local bandits
and are very seldom molested. Transport other than by
foot presents enormous difficulties. Even Mr. Smith was
often quite unable to get trucks when he wanted them
from the Provincial Government, owing to the petrol
shortage.

Trucks interested us, too. We hoped, somehow, to get
a lift in one when we left Sian, as far as Cheng-tu. From
Cheng-tu we planned to reach Chung-king and so return,
by river-boat down the Yangtze, to Hankow. The only
alternative was to go by bus from the rail-head at Pao-ki.
But Dr. Stockley and Dr. Clow, the two Scotch surgeons
at the Mission Hospital, told us that this would be nearly
impossible. Pao-ki was crammed with refugees already,
all waiting to get away. There were only two buses, each
holding fifty people, and the company had issued three
thousand tickets up to date.

We went for advice to Mr. Russell, the missionary, one
of the oldest and most experienced foreign residents in
Sian. Tall, thin, grave, blue-eyed, looking much younger
than his years, Mr. Russell was guilty of one mild eccen-
tricity: there were three clocks in his house, each set to a
different time. Time, anyhow, is a tiresome factor in Sian
life. There is post-office time, which regulates the activities of the town, and Shanghai time (three-quarters of an
hour later), which the railway authorities observe. To
these Mr. Russell had added London time. When last he
returned to China from leave he found himself unable for
sentimental reasons to alter his own watch.

Mr. Russell promised to take us to see the secretary of
the Military Governor, who would, perhaps, be ready to
help us. But we should have to wait a little; for next day,
April 5th, was Ching Ming, the festival of The Sweeping

of the Graves. All the officials would be leaving town to hold a service at the tombs of the Jo emperors, and the Government offices would be closed.

Instead he showed us the Pe-lin museum, known as the Forest of Tablets. Among them is the famous Nestorian Tablet, which proves the existence of Christianity in classical China. Some of the engraved stones are wonderfully beautiful—the lines could hardly be more flowing and delicate if they were painted with a hair-brush on silk. Outside the museum was a little shop where rubbings of the tablets were for sale. While we were admiring them and drinking tea with the shopkeeper, a raid began on the air-field outside the city. The Japanese dropped about twenty-five bombs. There was no anti-aircraft fire or any attempt at resistance by the Chinese planes.

Mr. Russell was a very interesting companion. He had worked in the China Mission for the last thirty years, partly here, partly at Yen-an-fu, which, since 1936, has been the capital of the Chinese Soviet Republic in the north-west. During this period he had acquired an intimate knowledge of bandits, their code of morals, their peculiarities and their tactics.

On one occasion the bandits raided Yen-an itself and were only persuaded, through Mr. Russell's intervention, to withdraw on condition that they should be sent a certain number of rifles and a certain quantity of ammunition from the arsenal of the city militia. After a great deal of argument the militia were talked into agreement, against the vote of a minority, who exclaimed: 'Rather than give up our arms we'll become bandits ourselves!' and immediately deserted into the hills. The city authorities then deputed Mr. Russell and a Catholic missionary to ride out to the bandits' mountain stronghold, taking the arms with them, loaded on a donkey. They arrived towards nightfall, after the donkey had collapsed, and they had been obliged to pile the rifles across their own saddles. In the twilight they narrowly escaped being shot at by the bandits' outposts. But they were recognized in time and escorted to a cave, where they were hospitably received. During the night three fully armed men entered the cave. Mr. Russell and the priest woke up expecting to be murdered immediately. But the three bandits had not come to kill them. They were tired of their life with the gang and wanted to escape to another province. Would the missionaries give them letters of safe conduct to show to the Government authorities? They also had another request: they wished to become Christians. But here a delicate problem arose: how many were to be Baptists, how many Roman Catholics? This the priest solved very simply by baptizing all three of them into the Roman Church. Mr. Russell politely made no objection.

Next day both missionaries rode back to Yen-an. They found the city authorities in high spirits. The mayor explained gleefully that they had played an excellent trick on the bandits. The cartridges which they had sent them had all been emptied of powder and the rifles damaged so that they couldn't be used. Wasn't it clever? 'No,' said Mr. Russell. 'Not clever at all. It was very stupid, and I'm afraid you'll regret it.' The mayor laughed at his fears. Even if the bandits did attempt reprisals, he said, they would never be able to enter the town. A strong force of Government troops were already on their way to protect it.

But the Government troops never arrived and soon the bandits returned. Coming home late one evening, Mr. Russell found several of their leaders sitting waiting for him in his own study. This time he really expected instant death. But the bandit chiefs were quite friendly. 'We know you are our friend,' they told him. 'You played fair with us. It wasn't your fault about the rifles—you didn't know. . . . But now you must not interfere. Stay here indoors and you will be safe.' Mr. Russell pleaded with them but it was of no use. The bandits were determined on revenge. So he stayed indoors and survived the big massacre of the population which followed.

From this day onwards his friendship with the bandits was secure. When he wanted to visit his mission-stations in the south of the province it wasn't even necessary for him to warn the bandits in advance: they knew of all his comings and goings through their spies. He would ride into a village and find it apparently quite deserted: not a shop open, nothing for sale. But a man would sign to him from a doorway, and there, inside the house, a meal would be waiting. 'We have been ordered to get it ready for you,' he was told. Indeed, such was Mr. Russell's prestige that a Chinese general who had a journey to make through dangerous country came and appealed for his protection. The general wanted to bring an armed bodyguard, but this Mr. Russell refused. 'Either you take your soldiers,' he told the general, 'or you take me alone.' The general chose Mr. Russell. When they had gone some distance they met a party of men on the road and stopped to talk to them. The general never knew until after they had arrived at their destination that these were the bandits themselves.

Mr. Russell supplemented the account Dr. Stockley had already given us of the siege of Sian in 1926. A Chinese war-lord attacked the city in April and held it block-aded until November, when the defenders were relieved

by the 'Christian General', Feng Yü-hsiang. The length
of the siege surprised and dismayed the missionaries, who
had expected it to be an affair of days. Many peasants
from the outlying villages were trapped inside the town,
but these Mr. Russell managed to evacuate, in parties of
two hundred, through the lines of an enemy commander
who was less intransigent than his allies. Here again Mr.
Russell's good intentions were the cause of trouble, for
his Chinese secretary took advantage of the truce to
smuggle into Sian a message from the besiegers hidden in
a melon. The message was addressed to some disloyal officers among the garrison. It invited immediate surrender
on favourable terms. But the melon was opened by the
city guards and its secret discovered. Mr. Russell himself
was viewed with suspicion, and he had the greatest difficulty in saving his secretary from execution.

In October the foreign women and children were allowed to leave Sian. The men could have left too, but they
decided to remain in order to protect and feed the refugees who were living in their compounds. Food was now
very scarce. The missionaries had bought supplies of
wheat earlier in the siege. They had to keep them buried
in their gardens in stone jars, for every day the soldiers
came to search. 'If you can find it', Mr. Russell told them,
'you can have it!' But the soldiers couldn't find anything.
The missionaries dared only eat at night, grinding the
flour with their own millstones. During September and
October thousands of people died of hunger, collapsing
suddenly as they went about their business. Corpses lay
where they had fallen in the streets.

When the city was at last relieved there was a great
rush to the south gate. Mr. Russell said that never, as long
as he lived, would he forget the sight of the first village

carts, stacked high with fruit and vegetables, being mobbed by the starving townspeople.

Throughout the siege the missionaries in Sian got no word or sign of help from the British authorities, and this, Mr. Russell felt, was a good thing in the long run, for it did much to convince the Chinese that the missionaries had no connection with the British Government, and were not, in any sense, its agents or spies.

Sian is remarkable for its rickshaws. They have blue or white hood-covers, embroidered with big flowers, of an oddly Victorian design. We used the rickshaws a good deal, out of laziness, despite Dr. Mooser's warning that their upholstery often contained typhus-lice. Typhus is one of the great scourges of Shen-si Province. One of Mooser's two colleagues, an engineer, went down with it soon after his arrival, but, thanks to an inoculation, the attack was comparatively slight.

Dr. Mooser himself was a stocky figure, eagle-eyed, with a bitter mouth and a smashed, rugged face. He wore a leather jerkin, riding-breeches, and big strapped boots. He rushed at life, at China, at this job, with his head down, stamping and roaring like a bull. The dishonesty and laziness of the average Chinese official was driving him nearly frantic. 'While I'm here', he bellowed at his assistants, 'you are all Swiss. When I go away you can be Chinese again, if you like—or anything else you Goddam well please.'

Not that Mooser had much use for his countrymen either, or, indeed, for any Europeans at all. 'The Swiss are crooks, the Germans are crooks, the English are the damn lousiest crooks of the lot. . . . It was you lousy bastards who wouldn't let ambulances be sent to China. I have all the facts. I shall not rest until they are published in the newspaper.' With his colleagues he spoke Swiss dialect, or English—boycotting High German, the language of the Nazis.

Dr. Mooser had established several refugee camps in Sian, as well as a delousing station. The refugees were housed in empty buildings. As soon as could be arranged they were sent off into the country and distributed amongst the neighbouring villages. There were about eight thousand of them in the city, including one thousand Mohammedans, who had a special camp to themselves. These people belonged mostly to the middle class of China— nearly all of them had a little money. The really poor had no choice but to stay where they were, and await the coming of the Japanese. The really rich were already safe in Hongkong.

There was no doubt of Mooser's efficiency. The camps were well run, the floors and bedding clean, the children's faces washed, and there was hardly any spitting. Mooser was a great favourite with the children. Whenever he visited them his pockets were full of sweets. 'I had to sack three camp commandants in the first week,' he told us. 'They call me The Chaser.'

Mooser didn't quite know what to make of us—especially after he had heard from me that Auden was a poet. He had no use for poetry because 'it changes the order of the words'. While he was working in Mexico he was summoned to the bedside of an Englishman named David H. Lawrence, 'a queer-looking fellow with a red beard. I told him: "I thought you were Jesus Christ." And he laughed. There was a big German woman sitting beside him. She was his wife. I asked him what his profession was. He said he was a writer. "Are you a famous writer?" I asked him.

"Oh no," he said. "Not so famous." His wife didn't like that. "Didn't you really know my husband was a writer?" she said to me. "No," I said. "Never heard of him." And Lawrence said: "Don't be silly, Frieda. How should he know I was a writer? I didn't know he was a doctor, either, till he told me."'

Dr. Mooser then examined Lawrence and told him that he was suffering from tuberculosis—not from malaria, as the Mexican doctor had assured him. Lawrence took it very quietly. He only asked how long Mooser thought he would live. 'Two years,' said Mooser. 'If you're careful.' This was in 1928.

6

April 6

Today there are some interesting new arrivals at the hotel. They are the four members of the German medical mission, which has come to inspect the war areas. The mission is headed by Dr. Trautmann, the son of the German Ambassador to China. They all came clumping in, dressed, with truly national tactlessness, in a kind of German Army Medical uniform. They keep very much to themselves, sitting at a table in the corner and calling loudly for beer.

The uniforms have already created the worst possible impression. People here are convinced—no doubt most unjustly—that the Mission has political motives. But Dr. Trautmann and his colleagues seem quite unaware of the difficulties they are about to encounter. They have announced their intention of going north to visit the Eighth Route Army. It seems most unlikely that they will get permission to do so. And Dr. Mooser certainly won't help them. Whenever they appear he glares across the room at them like a tiger about to jump.

This morning, with Mr. Russell, we went to call on Mr. Liu Yin-shih, of the Ministry of Pacification. Mr. Liu presented us to General Chiang Ting-wen, the military governor. General Chiang speaks no English: Mr. Liu translated. We asked the usual questions: what did he think of the situation? when would the Chinese attack? what would be the outcome of the war? And received the usual answers—polite, optimistic, vague. The General told us one interesting detail, however. It seems that the Japanese forces opposite Tung-kwan are very small and therefore obliged to do a good deal of bluffing. They move trucks up and down the bank, creating an appearance of great activity—but the trucks are full of stones. There are also wooden figures set up to represent soldiers. The General laughed as this was translated to us, with the chuckling, indulgent air of placid superiority which the Chinese so often assume when the Japanese are spoken of.

We asked Mr. Liu to transmit to the General our request for seats in a lorry to Cheng-tu. The General merely smiled and passed this off with a compliment: Mr. Liu was to tell us how greatly he admired our spirit in undertaking this adventurous journey. But Mr. Liu himself, when we talked to him alone later, seemed more helpful. He promised to let us have definite news in a day or two.

Our dealings with the military on the Sü-chow front have accustomed us to being saluted: it is a form of vanity which grows on you very quickly. Indeed, I am now quite piqued when soldiers don't salute. Today, for instance, I found myself glaring at a young sentry who was lolling against the barrack-gates, so ferociously that, after two or three seconds, he sprang guiltily to attention and presented arms.

We both hope that the transport problem will soon be settled. Life in this hotel is alarmingly expensive, and its comforts are making us daily less inclined to return to the tiresome little hardships of our journey. The food here is pretentious, dull, and bad. Every day there is chicken, and every day there is pork. There are also eggs and ham.

Sometimes the ham gets into the soup, which is made of chicken, and always thick white. The fish is high. There is one bottle of whisky in the bar, which we are steadily drinking: it should last our time. *Après nous*, the unspeakable Shanghai sherry—for the duration, presumably, of the war.

The menu is full of weird items: 'Ham egg.' 'Hat cake.' 'Lemen Pie.' 'FF Potatoes.' After the meal cocoa is served, in small coffee-cups.

April 7

This morning Mr. Liu kindly sent a staff officer to escort us round the various sights of Sian. The staff officer's presence was necessary in case we should wish to take photographs—for here, in Shen-si, the regulations are very strict.

We had intended to begin with the Drum Tower, which stands in the middle of the town, but just as we were climbing its steps the air-raid alarm sounded. The Drum Tower is used as an observation post, so the officer said that it would be better to return there later. We would drive out first to see the Big Goose Pagoda, about a mile outside the city walls. The people of Sian take air-raids very seriously. The police drive them helter-skelter off the streets with sticks, and the general atmosphere of alarm is consequently much greater than in Sü-chow or Hankow.

Ahead of us, bumping along the road which led from the city gate, was a motor-bus. Just outside the city Auden stopped our car to photograph some Mohammedan tombs. To our surprise the bus stopped too, and out of it jumped twenty figures in blue overalls, nearly all of them Europeans, blonde-haired, snub-nosed, chattering

141

in Russian. They scattered over the fields, shouting to each other, laughing, turning somersaults, like schoolboys arriving at the scene of a Sunday-school picnic. Our guide told us that they were Russian mechanics from the air-field, and that they are always evacuated like this when a raid is threatened.

Here was a partial answer to one of the questions we have been asking everybody about the extent of Russian aid to China. Many Chinese deny categorically that there are any Russians in Sian at all. Others have told us that it is the Russian mechanics who won't allow civil planes of the Eurasia Company to land on the aerodrome, because the Eurasia pilots are Germans. We have also heard that trains are going through the station every night loaded with Russian munitions and trucks which have come into China across Sinkiang. It seems nearly imposs-ible to get any definite information.

The Big Goose Pagoda, like nearly everything else we saw this morning, is a thousand years old—so our guide told us. It is less ornate, more massive, simpler in outline, than the kind of pagoda you see in travel magazines. From the top, looking out over the fields, you can see the traces of a much larger city, the Sian of the T'angs. The Pagoda used to stand on its outskirts. On the highest story there is a little shrine, and on the wall behind it—as in so many other appropriate and inappropriate places—somebody has scribbled one of the conventional anti-Japanese draw-ings: China as a giant martyr, stuck full of swords and pestered by a tiny Jap aeroplane which buzzes round his head like a wasp. On reaching the bottom of the Pagoda stairs I had a violent attack of cramp, and for the rest of the morning could only hobble. Auden suggests that it is probably the prelude to some rare Oriental disease.

After this we saw the Little Goose Pagoda, which is a semi-ruin, split down the middle by an earthquake, and the Mohammedan mosque in the city, and the Drum Tower. This afternoon we drove out to Lintung, a famous hot springs resort lying right under the mountain, in the direction of Tung-kwan. We bathed at the bath-house in its willow-pattern garden of pools and bridges. The water has no very remarkable properties: it neither stinks nor fizzes, nor is it in the least discoloured. But it is nice and warm.

It was here that the Generalissimo was arrested by the commander of the Young Marshal's bodyguard on the 12th of December, 1936. You can still see the dent of a bullet in one of the scarlet wooden pillars outside his sleeping-pavilion, and high above, on the mountain path, the rocks bear an inscription in red characters telling how, at this spot, Chiang Kai-shek, who had escaped from the bath-house in his nightshirt, was caught by the pursuing soldiers.

Beyond Lintung is the largest tomb in China, that of the Emperor Ch'in Shih Huang Ti (200 B.C.), who burnt the scholars' books at a spot where grass has never grown since. According to legend, he had a marvellous palace, illuminated by candles which would burn for a thousand years, and protected by mechanical archers who shot unwelcome guests. On the mountain-top, we were told, is a beacon with a 'Wolf! Wolf!' story attached to it. The beacon summoned the Emperor's generals in time of danger, and the Empress lit it for a joke. The generals, arriving and finding that they had been tricked, were cross, naturally. So that, later, when the Empress was really in the hands of bandits, they saw the fire and didn't come. So she died.

143

When we got back to the hotel I decided to have a massage. We arranged with the manager that one of the coolies from the neighbouring bath-house should be sent up to our room. A speciality of this country is toe-massage, which is simply toe-pinching—and how they can pinch! The coolie also played a syncopated drum-rhythm on my legs, producing a series of quite loud hollow pops, interspersed with arpeggios of astonishingly painful thumb-stabs. Then with finger and thumb he carefully felt for, grasped, and tweaked my ulnar nerves. I yelled. It was like a violent electric shock. But the coolie didn't even smile. His terrifying, impersonal ferocity reminded me of the demons you see in temple-paintings, devouring the bodies of the damned. Perhaps he did my cramp good. At any rate, I feel very stiff.

April 8

Today it is raining heavily. The city is a wilderness of mud through which the rickshaws toil with their hoods up—long hoods which protect the coolie as well as his passenger, who sits, invisible and blind, behind a high waterproof bib.

This afternoon we have been to see Mr. Liu again, and our last hopes of getting down to Cheng-tu are destroyed. We should be obliged to charter an entire truck, and it would cost at least three hundred dollars. So we have decided to go back to Hankow the day after tomorrow by rail.

Mr. Liu was very friendly. He begged us to stay and talk. He used to be a professor of modern history at Nanking University. He speaks good English, and is extremely intelligent and widely read.

Without our even asking—for the subject is so taboo as

144

to seem almost indecent—he talked quite openly about the Russian military supplies. The Russian trucks, says Mr. Liu, bring them as far as Tiwha, where the Chinese trucks meet them. The journey from Tiwha to Sian sometimes takes three weeks. Aeroplanes are often flown across from Russian territory direct to Lanchow. But Russia only supplies thirty per cent of China's petrol: the rest comes from the Americans and the English via Hongkong.

We asked Mr. Liu's opinion of the possible duration of the war. He predicted another fifteen months. Then, if China still held out, Japan's finances would collapse. 'But what about China's finances?' we asked. Mr. Liu smiled: 'China has no finances. That is our strength. . . . China doesn't pay silver. She imports arms entirely on credit.' After the war China would need the Western Powers for many years to come. They would get their money back on reconstruction and economic development. Extra-territorial rights would have to be abolished, of course. He assured us that China would never make peace until Manchuria had been restored to her.

Asked what kind of government he would like after the war, he became a little vague. Oh yes, there would be a Parliament with three parties: Kuomintang, Social Democrat, Communist. But it was plain that he expected friction between the Communists and Chiang Kai-shek before long. And, of course, the country would, in practice, be governed by a military dictatorship. Outer Mongolia and Thibet would remain outside the direct influence of the Government. They were valuable as buffer-states. No, there could be no real democracy, at present. The electorate wasn't sufficiently educated. Elementary primary education has begun in certain provinces, but it is con-

145

cerned for the moment chiefly with inculcating patriotic principles. Reading and writing will come later.

We asked whether there is any form of conscription in China. Oh, no, Mr. Liu replied, it wasn't necessary. China has far more able-bodied soldiers than she can possibly use. The coolies volunteer everywhere, and they are brave as a matter of course—they set no value on their lives. 'If you asked *me*', Mr. Liu added jokingly, 'to take a rifle and fight, I wouldn't do it, of course!' He believed that education tended to make the Chinese unsuitable for military purposes. The officers who have been trained at West Point or in England expect their men to wash themselves and brush their teeth—and the men don't like it. Returning to the subject of conscription, Mr. Liu also told us that the carrying-on of the family is such an important article of Chinese religious feeling that the eldest son never becomes a soldier.

(Mr. Liu's remarks may be true of Shen-si Province, but we have heard elsewhere that compulsory military service is very strictly enforced. You can only avoid it by paying for somebody else to go in your place. Thus the richer members of a village will club together and subscribe enough to buy its necessary quota of recruits from the poorer families which badly need the money.)

This evening we went up to Mooser's room to drink with a party of Chinese doctors and the Swiss. Somebody told the story of how another foreign medical expert arrived in Sian, alone: he spoke no Chinese, so on leaving the station he got into a rickshaw and waited to see what would happen. The rickshaw-coolie took him straight to General Staff Headquarters, where he was immediately arrested and locked in a room for several hours, until an

English-speaking officer arrived, and the matter was explained.

While we were talking, fire-crackers began to explode all over the city. And presently we got the news of the big Chinese victory on the Grand Canal front, at Tai-erh-chwang. We were all excited, except for one of the Chinese doctors, who became sad and thoughtful. He had a Japanese wife.

April 9

Today, as we were sitting in the hotel entrance-lounge, in walked Dr. Brown. He is on his way north to join the Eighth Route Army and will leave for Yen-an tomorrow, with one of the Swiss doctors.

Dr. Brown was in the highest of spirits. He seemed to have grown ten years younger. He told us how, shortly after we left Kwei-teh, Dr. Gilbert, who was cycling home one evening, was stopped by bandits within a few hundred yards of the hospital gates. They took away his money and his watch but didn't hurt him. The bandits hadn't been caught.

April 10

This afternoon at five o'clock we left Sian by train for Hankow. Dr. Mooser and the Swiss engineer are travelling in the next compartment. They are going down to a medical conference at Changsha. Trautmann and his Germans are also on board. Having failed to reach Yen-an they are making for Sü-chow. This is the same old train, and Chin-dung and his friends have lost no time in re-establishing their claims on our cigarettes. They are, luckily, a little awed, however, by our fellow-passenger—an important military official who reclines in the oppo-

site bunk, reading poetry with an air of extreme fastidi-
ousness. When the car-boys look in, he eyes them dis-
tastefully and touches his temples with a handkerchief
moistened in eau-de-Cologne. From Chiang we learn that
he has been up in the north-west, supervising the transport of Russian munitions. Unfortunately he speaks hardly any English, and is obviously much too grand to be
cross-examined through an interpreter.

We are rather annoyed with Chiang just now. The long,
lazy stay at Sian has corrupted him. He has become bossy,
impudent, and careless. When he packed this morning he
left a number of our things behind in the hotel. Now, as
the losses are discovered, he takes refuge in his bad English until we could gladly box his ears.

'So you didn't pack the soap, Chiang?'
Chiang looks at us and smiles: 'Yes.'
'Well, where is it, then?'
'I don't know.'
'But you *must* know. Look for it.'
Chiang looks, not very carefully. His manner suggests
that the search is quite hopeless.
'Did you pack it, or didn't you?'
'Yes.'
'You mean you *did* pack it?'
'No.'

April 11

During the night we arrived at Hwayin Hsien, one of
the last stations before Tung-kwan. We shall stay here
until this evening. A train has just come through from
the east with one of its windows smashed by shell-fire—
otherwise no damage. In the distance you can hear the
booming of artillery. The Chinese batteries have revealed

themselves at last. They are said to have put one of the Japanese guns out of action already.

Hwayin Hsien is a pretty little town with clean cobbled streets and several ancient shrines. Behind it towers a sacred mountain, a magnificent blue crag like a shattered molar tooth thrust up from the pine-forests beneath. Cavalry units are quartered here and the plain is dotted with cantering riders. From every pool and ditch frogs sound their tiny klaxons in the brilliant sunshine. All this morning we have been lying in the grass smoking and talking a few hundred yards from the train, under the shadow of the town wall. There was an air-raid warning, but no Japanese appeared. Now and then a group of passing soldiers and peasants would stop and speak to us. When we showed that we didn't understand they would make the signs of Chinese characters with their forefingers on the palms of their hands. Though there are so many dialects in China, the written language is almost universally understood—and so the country people believe that English is merely yet another dialect. This sign-language has been tried on us over and over again.

April 12

Here we are back at 'Wuthering Heights'. We passed Tung-kwan safely during the night. More sitting about, more English lessons with the car-boys, more short strolls with one eye on the train. Quite literally, we don't trust it any further than we can see it. It is liable to start without the least warning at any moment. At a station where we stopped earlier this morning it very nearly succeeded in leaving Dr. Mooser and his colleagues behind.

Auden did a lot of photography among the platform crowd. Shortly after his return from one of these camera-expeditions we looked out of the window to see a beggar rolling on the ground and roaring as though in fearful pain. The Englishman, he yelled, had stolen his spirit and put it into his little box. He wanted five dollars compensation. We were both rather alarmed by this new form of blackmail, but the onlookers seemed to be on our side. They merely laughed.

April 13

We reached Loyang at noon. Chiang came to tell us that we should stay here six hours in order to reach Cheng-chow at the correct time. The train would leave at exactly twenty-five minutes past six. 'Rubbish!' said Auden. 'I bet you a dollar it doesn't!' Chiang smiled blandly.

Chiang and I went into the town during the afternoon. I wanted to buy a tea-pot as a present to an English friend. We examined hundreds. The heat was stifling. Later we drank tea, and Chiang told me about his wife and children. They are still in Nanking, and apparently quite safe, though he hasn't had news of them for some time. Chiang himself fled from Nanking before the Japanese occupation; he was afraid of being conscripted for forced labour. It must be said for him that he really is eager to improve his English. Nearly every day he brings us a list of words which he has heard us use and wishes to have explained. This afternoon he was particularly anxious to know how to describe his job. After we had exhaustively discussed the meanings of 'interpreter', 'valet', 'servant', 'butler', 'major-domo', 'steward', 'guide', and 'travelling-companion', Chiang decided that 'valet' was the most suitable and the nicest of all.

The train started at 6.25, to the minute. Auden handed

150

over his dollar. We wondered if the engine-driver was going to get a commission.

We were in Cheng-chow by half-past ten. The Hankow express was already waiting, but the doors of the first-class coach were locked. However, the attendant recognized us and, perhaps remembering our enormous tipping-powers, let us into a sleeping-compartment in defiance of the regulations. Chiang, stingy as ever, had underpaid the luggage-coolies. While they were arguing two station-guards ran up, smacked the coolies' faces and drove them away with their rifle-butts before we had had time to interfere.

April 14

At breakfast in the dining-car we met Mr. Jao, a live-wire, hard-headed Chinese war-correspondent who had been with us in Hankow when we visited the opera. Mr. Jao has just returned from the front. He was one of the first to enter Tai-erh-chwang after its recapture by the Chinese troops. When they got into the town they found everything dead—men and women, ducks, dogs and cats. One house only was left intact. Its owner, instead of being thankful, had come round to headquarters crying and scolding because one of her chairs had been smashed.

Some troops, passing a shell-hole near the road to Tai-erh-chwang, thought they saw something move. It was a wounded Japanese soldier, who had covered himself in blankets and was attempting to hide. They shouted to him to give himself up, but he refused and opened fire on them. After a battle lasting nearly an hour the Japanese was killed.

Despite the reward of 160 dollars offered for every prisoner taken alive, very few Japanese are ever captured.

They are told by their officers that the Chinese behead their prisoners, so they prefer to commit suicide before the enemy arrives. Some Japanese corpses are even found with notes attached to their clothing, begging the Chinese not to cut their heads off after death.

April 20

We have been back in Hankow now for nearly a week.

Spring has transformed the entire city. It is Siberian no longer; it is sub-tropical. The weather is as warm as an English July. In six weeks the period of real clammy heat, which makes a Hankow summer nearly intolerable for Europeans, will have begun.

The trees are all in leaf, the gardens are full of blossom. The rickshaws have folded back their hoods and the rickshaw-coolies run sweating, stripped to the waist. The troops have removed the padding from their uniforms or exchanged them for light cotton clothes. The civilians begin to appear in white drill jackets and shorts.

In the early evening there is usually a little knot of spectators round the gates of the British Consulate, peering into the garden, where the neat, athletic figure of the Consul-General is to be seen, practising with his golf-clubs. The exquisite accuracy of the Consul's putting seems somehow very reassuring, amidst all the chaos and inefficiency of wartime China. Perhaps the Chinese onlookers feel this, too.

The fine weather favours the air-raids by day and by night. The Japs are now not only a danger but a positive nuisance. If Auden and I go out shopping in different parts of the town we have always to arrange an emergency rendezvous—for there is usually no time to return to the Consulate, and the alternative may be an hour of

152

solitary boredom standing in a doorway or sitting in a café, waiting for the 'all clear' to sound. The night-raids are worse, with their false alarms and endless delays. Twice we have hardly slept at all. I have moved my bed out on to the balcony so as to be able, at any rate, to watch the planes without getting up. When the raid is over, a Chinese plane, with a red and a green light on its wing-tips, circles over the city, to guide the defenders back to the air-field. Looking for this plane we stare so hard into the sky that soon the stars themselves appear to move. I see them dancing in front of me long after I have shut my eyes in an angry and hopeless attempt to fall asleep again.

April 21

Today, having written up our Yellow River material and finished a series of newspaper articles, we reopened our social life by attending a tea-party at the Terminus Hotel. Mr. Han Li-wu had arranged it in order that we should meet the leading Chinese intellectuals at present in Hankow. The intellectuals were grouped at small tables, in parties of five or six, and our hosts moved us gently but firmly from one to another, whenever an interesting conversation was beginning to develop. The gathering was certainly most distinguished. We were honoured by the monumental presence of Feng Yü-hsiang, the 'Christian General' (who is said once to have baptized a whole regiment of his troops with a fire-hose). Feng speaks no English—nor does he need to. He is one of those huge, benevolent human whales whose mere silence is all-sufficient. Our compliments were translated to him and he beamed. Then everybody else talked English, disregarding him completely, and he continued to beam. Strangely

153

enough he had a perfect right to be there, for he is also a poet. He writes verses in peasant dialect about country life, and war. Once the declared enemy of Chiang Kai-shek, he now forms part of the military united front—but so far, it seems, the Government has given him very little to do.

Other notable guests were Messrs. Tien Shou-chang, the dramatist, Hoong, the translator, and Mou Mou-tien, the best modern poet, we are told, in China. A lady named Miss Chen Ye-yun, M.A., talked super-enthusiastically about women's war-work. She was lively, dry, and neat—very little different from her counterpart type in Europe. Towards the end of the meal we were interviewed by a young journalist on the *Ta Kung Pao*, one of China's leading newspapers. He had the exotic name of Macdonald (anglicized from Ma Tong-na). This westernization of names is quite usual, it appears, among the intellectuals. What did we think of Chinese morale, customs, morality? What of the military situation? What of the new type of Chinese woman? We answered most inadequately, but it didn't matter—Mr. Macdonald was already writing before we had opened our mouths.

Meanwhile, at another table, Mr. Tien was having the poem he had written in our honour translated by Mr. Hoong.

> Really, the ends of the world are neighbours:
> Blood-tide, flower-petals, Hankow spring,
> Shoulder to shoulder for civilization fight.
> Across the sea, long journey, how many Byrons?

Not to be outdone, Auden replied with a sonnet, which he finished writing yesterday, on a dead Chinese soldier. We both find functions of this sort extremely tiring.

154

There is no lack of goodwill on either side—indeed, the
air positively vibrates with Anglo-Chinese *rapprochement*
—but are we really communicating with each other at
all? Beaming at our hosts we exchange words: 'England',
'China', 'Poetry', 'Culture', 'Shakespeare', 'International
Understanding', 'Bernard Shaw'—but the words merely
mean, 'We are pleased to see you.' They are just symbols
of mutual confidence, like swapping blank cheques. Never
mind. It is all in a good cause. So we move from table to
table, trying to say something to everybody, and our faces
ache with smiling. One smiles so little, it seems, in the
West. For a newcomer to China the muscular effort is
enormous.

We had just time to change our clothes for the party
which was being given by the Admiral and the Consul-
General in a luxury flat over the Bank. The Admiral is in
command of all the gunboats on this part of the Yangtze
River. His hobbies are photography and collecting Chinese vases. ('I don't know if it's Ming, Sing, Ting, or
Wing—but I like its shape.') Hankow is full of British
naval officers, most of whom are parted from their ships
by the Wuhu boom: they lead an unnatural, widowed life
of office-work, polo-playing, gossip, and drinks, ruled by
a meaningless but unexacting discipline which demands
only that they shall wear the correct uniform at certain
hours of the day. We like nearly all of them very much
indeed. 'You're idealists,' they tell us, 'but you can't alter
human nature.' A few of them come into the Consulate
regularly for their meals. Auden plays to them on the
piano. They teach us new songs and the ritual of 'Cardi-
nal Puff'.

The Admiral, with his great thrusting, naked chin (he
detests beards) and the Consul-General, looking like a

white-haired schoolboy, received their guests. There was Sir Archibald Clark Kerr, the British Ambassador, Scottish but funny, with the deprecatory, amateur air which marks the born diplomatist. There was Lady Kerr, his wife, a tiny Chilean blonde, whose beauty lent a brilliant, almost theatrical lustre to the whole proceedings. There was Mr. Jarvis, the American Consul—owner of an anthology of seventeenth-century lyrics, which Auden has borrowed, and which a puppy at the Consulate began to eat during the night, getting as far as Milton (Mr. Jarvis was very nice about this). There was Peter Fleming and his wife the actress, Celia Johnson, charming in her thick horn-rimmed spectacles. Fleming with his drawl, his tan, his sleek, perfectly brushed hair, and lean good looks, is a subtly comic figure—the conscious, living parody of the pukka sahib. He is altogether too good to be true—and he knows it. This time Fleming is in China as a correspondent of *The Times*; he has just returned from Chung-king, where the Ambassador was paying his first official visit to the President of the Chinese Republic.

The party was a great success.

April 22

An extract from today's News Bulletin:

'With the tide of war surging on many fronts the "permanent wave" is now at its very ebb in China. This is one of the numerous harbingers of China's final victory in her war of self-defence, for from the ebbing of the "permanent wave" have already arisen hundreds of thousands of Chinese girls bravely and conscientiously taking their share of their country's all-front resistance. . . .

'War has introduced a new concept of beauty in China.

Girls with pencilled brows like moths, powdered face, manicured finger-nails and toe-nails and above all with the "permanent wave" in their hair, no longer command admiration. They are often considered unpatriotic. In present-day China the true wartime beauty in a woman must carry a martial air. She uses no cosmetics on her face and her hair is pressed backward under a smart cap that matches her army uniform. . . .

'Chinese girls, crazy for modernity, borrowed the curliness in their hair from the barber shops. With the change of affairs prevailing in wartime, many of the barber shops in China have shelved their paraphernalia for hair waving.

'In Hankow, for instance, such paraphernalia is in operation only in a small number of barber shops located in the French Concession, where are concentrated most of Hankow's singsong girls. These fair ones have to continue to keep their hair waved for the simple reason that they have to live.

'But even the singsong girls have changed their style. They want the "permanent wave" that would turn their hair into the likeness of an airplane—the airplane that is fighting in the air against the Japanese.

'True to the patriotism into which their hair is shaped, the singsong girls in Hankow have done laudably for their country's cause by helping in raising funds in the interest of China's wounded soldiers and refugees.'

You can see the singsong girls any evening, dancing with their friends and customers at the 'Wee Golf Restaurant'. (The 'Wee Golf' is so-called because it has, or had, a midget golf-course on the premises. There is also a 'Majestic Golf Restaurant' further down the street.) The singsong girls are not, as we had at first imagined, professional prostitutes. Indeed, it is very difficult to start an affair with one of them. Introductions, and a period of courtship, are necessary; and, if the girl doesn't like you, she won't have you. In general, the Chinese aren't very highly sexed—so people tell us. The average young man will be quite content to spend the evening dancing, flirting, and drinking tea with his girl friend. Sex is an affair of jokes and compliments and gaiety; a graceful minor art, harmless, pretty and gentle as flower-painting on a fan. Most of the girls are attractive, but few are really beautiful: as a rule their faces are too broad and flat. Nearly all of them have superb figures. They wear sleeveless Chinese gowns of patterned silk, tight under the armpits, with a high collar clasped close round the throat. The gown falls to the ankles, but its sides are slashed, so that the wearer's legs when she moves are visible right up to the knee.

This morning we were visited by Mr. C. C. Yeh, a shy young man whom we met yesterday at the literary tea. He is the author of a book of short stories in Esperanto, *Forgesitaj Homoj*, written under the pseudonym of 'Cicio Mar'. Yeh was once a pupil of Julian Bell, when Bell was a professor at the Wuhan University. Like Macdonald he belongs to a propaganda group in the political department of the Military Council. This group includes a number of writers who, until recently, have been in prison for their liberal or left-wing opinions. Yeh himself was in Japan when the war started. The Japanese police arrested him on the suspicion that he was an anarchist. 'You must not mind', he told us, 'if I seem a little stupid sometimes. You see, they struck me very often upon the head.' Like all these amazingly tough Chinese revolutionaries, he gives one the impression of being gentle, nervous, and soft.

While we were talking, in burst a spring vision—Agnes Smedley, in a light, girlish dress. She was triumphant and gay. Her manuscript has turned up after all, most mysteriously, in New York; and the new Red Army book will soon be published in England, Russia, and the States. She seemed delighted to see us back and invited us to come and see her at her new room. (She has moved from the 'Moscow-Heaven Axis', for Bishop Roots has already left Hankow.) She is now living in the Chang Gai—the same street as the Eighth Route Army Headquarters. 'But the coolies around there call it Pa Lu Gai—"Eighth Route Street". When you take a rickshaw don't ask for Chang Gai. Just say "Pa Lu Gai", and see if they understand. I want to find out if it's known all over the town.' We promised that we would.

In the afternoon we drove out with the Ambassador, Lady Kerr, and a professor named Kuo, to visit the Wuhan University. It is on the south side of the river, near Wuchang. The university buildings are quite new: they were started in 1931. Their neo-Chinese style of architecture brilliantly combines the old horned roofs with the massive brutality of blank concrete. From the distance the huge central block, with its rows of little windows, standing magnificently in a wild hilly park beside a big lake, reminds you of pictures of Lhasa. Actually this effect of size is achieved by a clever architectural fake—what appear to be the tops of great square towers are, in reality, comparatively small buildings set upon the crest of the hill, so that they rise above the lower façade. The interior is disappointing, chiefly, no doubt, because the war has cut short the work of decoration.

There are only a few students, most of them post-graduates, at Wuhan nowadays. A part of the buildings is even being used as a barracks. Education is cheap. A student needs no more than two hundred Chinese dollars a year for his fees, board and lodging included. Even very poor boys, we are told, are often able to get into the university. For family sentiment in this country is so strong that the most distant relatives feel themselves bound in honour to subscribe something towards the education of a really promising scholar.

About a dozen professors and their wives received us: they seemed particularly delighted that Lady Kerr had come. After we had seen everything we were given tea at a small guest-house in the grounds. Beneath their politely assumed gaiety the professors all seemed apprehensive and sad. They are wondering, no doubt, what will become of the university if Hankow falls. Wuhan has been their life-work, and the ambition has only so recently been realized. Must all they have struggled for be lost again, so soon? Nevertheless, today is not tomorrow; and they have no wish to sadden their honoured guests. So they giggled and chattered, pressing us to immense helpings of the rich cream-cakes. (We had an uneasy feeling that this extravagant banquet must have cost them a good part of their month's wages.)

Before we said good-bye each member of our party was presented with an inscribed silk scroll, on which was painted a panorama of the Wuhan buildings. And Ling Su-hua, wife of Professor Chen, gave Auden and myself two fans, which she had painted that afternoon. They re-

160

present landscapes near the lake. On my fan Madame Chen has written two lines from an old poet:

The mountain and the river in the mist not broken in
  pieces.
We should only drink and forget this immense sorrow.

Beneath which she herself has added:

During this country struggle
I paint in wonder to forget my sorrow.

Madame Chen is a great admirer of the works of Virginia Woolf. She has given us a little box to take back to Mrs. Woolf as a present. Inside it is a beautifully carved ivory skull.

April 23

Macdonald came in to see us this morning. His interview with us at the tea-party was printed in the *Ta Kung Pao* yesterday, together with a manuscript facsimile and Chinese rendering of Auden's sonnet. Macdonald had been specially praised by his editor for getting this interview, and was feeling very pleased with himself. He translated it all to us, word by word: 'Mr. Tien then read his poem to Mr. Au and Mr. Y, who were very much influenced. Then Mr. Au read his poem, and everybody was very much influenced.'

We got Macdonald to retranslate the Chinese version of the sonnet. The translators had evidently felt that one line:

Abandoned by his general and his lice,

was too brutal, and maybe, even, a dangerous thought (for generals never abandon their troops under any circumstances). So, instead, they had written:

The rich and the poor are combining to fight.

Today is St. George's Day, and we devoted the rest of it to the Navy. There was a lunch-party at the Consulate, a cocktail-party at the Race Club, and a supper in one of the Russian dance-restaurants (known collectively to the British officers as 'The Dumps').

Lunch was argumentative and political. Somebody present believed that Franco was a gentleman and a sportsman, because he played a good game of golf, and had attended a British Consul's funeral in the Canary Islands on his way to start the rebellion in Morocco. Somebody else gave an interesting analysis of Chiang Kai-shek's Easter Speech. He believed that the Government's removal of the ban on religious teaching in mission schools suggests that the New Life Movement will now become more specifically Christian. Perhaps, also, the Chiangs' Christianity will prove an increasingly effective political weapon to counter the propaganda of the Anti-Comintern Pact. The old accusations against the Communists and their allies of 'godlessness' are getting more and more difficult to sustain. Mao Tse-tung himself is said to have attended Mass as a gesture of goodwill towards the missionaries. Perhaps the historian of the future will have to thank Bishop Roots.

Not only the Race Club buildings but even the grounds surrounding them might well be in the heart of Surrey. Here, as Auden remarked, all trace of China has been lovingly obliterated. We drank to 'St. George's Day—England's Day', and looked forward to 'the match tomorrow with our brother Scots, and an excellent tiffin with the St. Andrew's Society'. We were chiefly impressed by the surprising number of English civilian residents still remaining in Hankow.

Today is also the eve of the Russian Orthodox Easter.

162

Just before midnight we joined the group of onlookers at the doors of the Russian church, which stands a little way down the road from the British Consulate. The church itself was crammed. From the interior came whiffs of incense and hot leather—the nostalgic perfume of exile. Nearly the whole of the White Russian colony must have been assembled, including the taxi-girls from 'The Dumps'. Their high-boned faces, illuminated by the candles which each member of the congregation held in his or her hand, looked beautiful and cold and pure. Many of the taxi-girls were accompanied by their men friends, heavy, blue-chinned figures in dinner-jackets, waiting, somewhat impatiently, for midnight, when custom would permit them to exchange the ambiguous Easter kiss.

7

We now began to make plans for our visit to the south-eastern front—if, indeed, it could be described as a 'front' at all. The Japanese forces were working their way inland from Shanghai, thrusting forward like the spokes of an irregularly-shaped fan. To the north-west the fan covered Nanking; to the west it approached Wuhu, where the Chinese had barred the Yangtze with their boom; to the south-west it touched Hang-chow. About the country which lay in between these points information was contradictory and vague. The Japs would advance along a valley and retreat again. They would occupy a village or a railway station, and hold it like a fort in the midst of an area overrun with hostile guerrilla units. It was even said that with a knowledge of the lie of the land you could easily penetrate their lines, unchallenged, to the very outskirts of Shanghai itself.

We, too, hoped eventually to reach Shanghai without having to return to Hankow and make the usual journey via Hongkong. The river-ports of Ningpo and Wenchow were still open. From either of them we ought to be able to get a boat direct to the Bund of the International Settlement.

Next morning we went to see Agnes Smedley in her

164

new home. She was living in an otherwise deserted building, a former military headquarters. After wandering down empty and semi-ruinous passages it was strange to come upon her gay, prettily-furnished room, with its vases and screens. When we arrived, Capa and Po Ku were both with her. Miss Smedley's first question was: Had we remembered to ask the rickshaw-coolies for the Pa Lu Gai? Yes, we had; and they had brought us here without hesitation. Miss Smedley was delighted. She seemed to regard this as a definite victory for the workers' cause.

Capa had just returned with the others from Tai-erh-chwang. He had got a lot of pictures, and Ivens had shot a whole section of his film. But Capa was dissatisfied. He had found the Chinese face unsatisfactory for the camera, in comparison with the Spanish. He was plainly longing to return to Spain. 'I'd like to get back to Paris for the Fourteenth of July', he said wistfully, 'and dance in the streets. Then off to Madrid. . . .' But, meanwhile, he was accompanying Ivens and Fernhout to Yen-an and the north-west. He wanted us to help him send off his photographs uncensored to America, where they would be published as a book.

'You make much money!' said Po Ku with an explosive, giggling laugh. Po Ku laughs at everything—the Japanese, the war, victory, defeat. We asked for the latest news of the Eighth Route Army. What were conditions like nowadays? 'Terrible!' Po Ku giggled. 'They have no shoes!' 'No shoes!' echoed Miss Smedley, with a moan of the wildest despair. She began to pace the room with her hand to her mouth. 'Tell me, Po Ku, what shall we do? No shoes! I must cable to America at once!'

They began to discuss the shoe problem. In Hankow

there is a type of rubber-soled sandal which can be bought wholesale, very cheap. They argued expertly about its merits and defects. It was fascinating to watch them—both, in their different ways, so practical, so deadly earnest: the smiling East, the melodramatic West. The Red Army, one sees, is Agnes Smedley's whole life—her husband and her child. "When I was with them', she told us, 'for the first time I felt at one with the universe.' Here in Hankow she was miserably homesick for the north-west. But here she could do more to help by keeping in touch with sympathetic organizations abroad. And so she stayed.

We talked of the south-eastern front, and Po Ku repeated his promise of a letter to the Communist Fourth Army headquarters at Nanchang. He said also that he would try to arrange an interview for us with Chou En-lai.

In the afternoon of the next day we drove out to the suburbs to visit Hankow's film-studio—the largest of its kind in wartime China. There were two buildings: a big shabby villa, once the property of a Chinese general, now used for dark-rooms and the accommodation of the actors; and the more recently built studio itself. In the garden half a dozen young actors and technicians were playing netball beside a dismantled set representing a shell-wrecked village. Dresses were hung out to dry on a clothes-line. The whole place looked very domestic and untidy and cheerful. Our hosts explained that no work was done during the daytime, because of air-raids. After dark the shooting in the studio would begin.

Mr. Lo, the sound-engineer, showed us round. Neither he nor any of his colleagues had studied abroad, nor had they ever imported foreign advisers. He had learnt everything out of books, constructing his own sound-recording apparatus and enlarging-camera. This home-made equipment was excellent. Technical problems had been solved with astonishing economy and ingenuity. We particularly admired the interior set itself. It was the living-room of a farm-house, prepared for a wedding, with an eye for detail which would put most western art-directors to shame. The properties had none of that unnatural newness which is such a besetting vice of the English studios. Mr. Lo showed us a whole arsenal of machine-guns, rifles, and uniforms, most of which had been actually captured by the Eighth Route Army from the Japanese.

At present the studio was producing only war-films. Just now they were at work on the story of Shanghai's 'Doomed Battalion'. It would be called *Fight to the Last*. We were shown some of the rushes. The war-scenes were brilliant. The producer had an astonishingly subtle feeling for grouping; his weakness lay in the direction of the actors themselves—he had indulged too often the Chinese talent for making faces. All these grimaces of passion, anger, or sorrow, seemed a mere mimicry of the West. One day a director of genius will evolve a style of acting which is more truly national—a style based upon the beauty and dignity of the Chinese face in repose.

Besides these fragments we were shown several news-reels. There were the ruins of Tai-erh-chwang; the entry of the Chinese troops into the town; a woman's naked body, horribly mutilated; a speech to the soldiers by Feng Yü-hsiang (who must surely, to judge by his tones and gestures, be one of the best orators in China); and an amusing and touching shot of some Manchurian prisoners dancing for joy on finding that they were not to be executed. One of the prisoners was a White Russian. A considerable number of them, we were told, are fighting in the Japanese Army.

In the evening Miss Smedley came round to see us at the Consulate, deeply depressed. The Police have just raided the bookshops in Hankow and Chung-king, and confiscated large quantities of Left-wing and Communist literature. Even General Feng Yü-hsiang's poems have been banned, because he writes about the poor. It is difficult to tell just who gave the order for this police action; probably one of Chiang's more reactionary advisers. It may not mean very much, but it is disheartening. It shows that there are still people in the Government who can't forget the old feuds.

Agnes Smedley took a very serious view of the matter. She feared that these raids might indicate a change of policy towards the Communists on the part of the Kuomintang. She suspected even that the Eighth Route Army was being deliberately kept short of money and equipment, lest it should become too important as a military and political factor when the war was over. She told us also that three prominent Chinese business men in Shanghai had just been caught organizing a kidnapping racket to supply the Japanese brothels with Chinese women.

We paid another visit to General von Falkenhausen's headquarters. Our friend the A.D.C. was in an indignant mood. He had just read the news of an interview given by a prominent American journalist to the Press in Shanghai. The journalist had praised China's solidarity, adding that Germans and Russians were 'fighting side by side'. 'Never in my life', the A.D.C. assured us, 'have I spoken to a Soviet Russian!'

That same morning we had been shown a report issued by the German Chamber of Commerce in Shanghai. It was a tactfully worded but extremely thorough criticism of Berlin's Far Eastern policy. The German Government's support of Japan, it claimed, was responsible for the ruin of German business interests in China. Many firms were failing already. By the end of the year they would have closed down altogether.

We had tea with Mr. Han Li-wu. He was anxious to invite a delegation of British artists and writers to visit China in the near future and wanted us to suggest some suitable names.

From another informant we had heard, unofficially, that Japan was already angling for peace terms on the basis of the pre-war *status quo*. We asked Mr. Han if he thought that China would agree to let Japan keep Manchukuo. Mr. Han replied that this depended largely on the attitude of the British Government. If Britain insisted China might have to agree.

In one of 'The Dumps' that evening we talked to the proprietor, an ex-Cossack officer in the Tsarist army. 'Well, thank goodness', he said, 'I shall be finished with this place next Friday for ever! I've got a job as instructor to a cavalry unit at Loyang. There'll be six of us working together—three of them are Soviet officers from the Red Army.' 'Won't that be rather awkward for you?' we asked. 'Of course not,' said the proprietor, 'why should it be? All those politics are a thing of the past. If Japan attacks Russia I shall join the Red Army myself.' He told us how, a few days before, he had talked to one of the Soviet airmen at present in Hankow. 'Are you a Communist?' he had asked the airman. 'Naturally.' 'Then I suppose you're an internationalist?' The airman had laughed: 'Me an internationalist? No! I'm a Russian.'

For some time we had been anxious to have an interview with Du Yueh-seng. At length next morning, through Macdonald, this was arranged.

Before the war Du Yueh-seng was one of the most influential Chinese politicians in Shanghai. A Big Business chief after the classic American pattern, Du not only employed labour, he controlled it. His political organization, the Green Jade Band, held the Chinese city in a state of undeclared martial law. In the International Settlement also, Du was a great power behind the scenes. After the Communist *coup d'état* in 1927 which put Chiang Kai-shek into power, it was Du and his men who helped Chiang to turn upon his former allies, and kill or drive into exile all the most dangerous radicals among them. When the Japanese entered Shanghai they destroyed much of Du's property, and thereby made for themselves an implacable enemy. Du was now a high Government official, holding an important position on the Red Cross Central Committee. He was said to be completely illiterate.

To visit Du's flat was to enter a strongly-guarded fortress. At least a dozen attendants were posted in the hall, and, when we sat down to talk, there were others who stood in the background behind our chairs. Du himself was tall and thin, with a face that seemed hewn out of stone, a Chinese version of the Sphinx. Peculiarly and inexplicably terrifying were his feet, in their silk socks and smart pointed European boots, emerging from beneath the long silken gown. Perhaps the Sphinx, too, would be even more frightening if it wore a modern top-hat.

Du speaks only Chinese, but several of the doctors present were able to translate our conversation. We talked entirely about the Red Cross. We were told that there were eight thousand qualified doctors in China: eighteen hundred of them were engaged in Red Cross work. Though arrangements were still very imperfect a number of mobile operating units had already been sent out, and were working in or near the front lines. Du asked us for our own experiences and impressions, and nodded his head slowly and heavily as they were translated to him. As we stood up to go he said something to one of the doctors, who told us: 'Mr. Auden and Mr. Isherwood, Mr. Du Yueh-seng wishes to say how much he appreciates your interest in China's Red Cross. He wishes to thank you—in the name of humanity.'

One of the top names on Du Yueh-seng's 1927 black list had been that of Chou En-lai, organizer of the armed insurrection and the general strike. Auden was lucky enough to meet him next morning, quite by chance, when he went round to the Pa Lu Gai to photograph Agnes Smedley. That Miss Smedley had agreed to be photographed at all was a great concession. 'If you weren't a leftist writer', she told Auden, 'I shouldn't let you do this. I hate my face.'

Today she was in a cheerful mood because Chou En-lai had written an article exposing the lies of the Whampoa clique—the extreme Right wing of the Government. Kao Tzse, head of the Second Bureau of the Political Department, had published a pamphlet purporting to be the verbatim account of a speech by Po Ku. According to this pamphlet Po Ku had frankly admitted that the Communists had been guilty in the past of murdering many inno-

171

cent people. It also pretended that he had told his audience that the United Front was only a tactical formation, to be dissolved when it had served the Communist Party's purpose.

Chou En-lai believed that the longer the war continued the more complete would be China's victory, and the closer would be the understanding between the Communist Party and the Kuomintang. What he most feared was a compromise peace between the Kuomintang and Japan at the Communists' expense. He was not at all satisfied with the munitions situation. Many private firms had offered their services and asked for Government support —but nothing had been done.

When Auden left, Miss Smedley gave him an apple and a card to the New Fourth Army headquarters in Nanchang. To our lasting regret the photographs he had taken of her were all blurred or spoilt.

This, April 29th, was our last day in Hankow. It was also the birthday of the Emperor of Japan. The Japanese celebrated it in their usual manner with a big air-raid. When they arrived, the 'home team' was already up to meet them—twenty of the newly-delivered Gloucester Gladiators and thirty Russian machines.

Soon after lunch the sirens began to blare. We put on our smoked glasses and lay down flat on our backs on the Consulate lawn—it is the best way of watching an air-battle if you don't want a stiff neck. Machine-guns and anti-aircraft guns were hammering all around us, but the sky was so brilliant that we seldom caught a glimpse of the planes unless the sun happened to flash on their turning wings. Presently a shell burst close to one of the Japanese bombers; it flared against the blue like a struck match.

Down in the road the rickshaw coolies were delightedly clapping their hands. Then came the whining roar of another machine, hopelessly out of control; and, suddenly, a white parachute mushroomed out over the river while the plane plunged on, down into the lake behind Wuchang. This must have been a Chinese, for the Jap pilots, it is said, are not allowed parachutes. They are even rumoured to be padlocked into their cockpits.

Guided by the gesticulations of the rickshaw-boys we ran to another part of the garden in time to watch two planes manœuvring for position. They emitted long streamers of smoke as if writing advertisements. Then another plane, a Japanese, came tumbling out of the eye of the sun, shot to pieces, and turning over and over like a scrap of glittering silver paper. A spent explosive bullet hit the road in front of the house with a tremendous crack. (For a moment we really thought that the Consul-General must have gone mad and opened fire on the enemy with his shot-gun.) Today the Japs annotated their bombs with propaganda leaflets; one of them fluttered down to rest on the roof of the Consulate. It assured the Chinese that Japan was their truest friend.

As soon as the 'All Clear' had sounded we telephoned for a car and drove at top speed down twisting, crowded lanes to the banks of the Han River. On the opposite shore smoke was still rising in clouds from the buildings of the Hanyang Arsenal, and from the slum-suburbs which surrounded it. The Japanese had dropped many of their bombs here—a striking proof of the inefficiency of the Japanese Intelligence Service, for the Arsenal had been evacuated several months before and was now practically disused.

The current of the muddy little river as it swirls round

173

the bend into the Yangtze is terribly swift. People are frequently drowned here. We wondered how we should get across, and regarded with deep misgivings the crazy old sampan in which a boy of twelve and a one-eyed crone were offering to ferry us over. But there was no time to waste. The old lady worked us upstream like a rock-climber, grappling her way from one moored sampan to the next with her boat-hook; then out we shot, obliquely, into the middle of the river. As we approached the further bank, with the speed of a motor-car, a serious crash seemed almost inevitable, but the little boy broke the shock with a glancing stab of his bamboo pole, and, a moment later, we were scrambling up the steep mud bank below the Arsenal wall. One of the bombs had blown a derelict boiler clean over this wall and dropped it into the water, all but sinking a small cargo-steamer. Naked coolies, up to their waists in the current, were already working to shift it.

There was a crowd outside the Arsenal gates amidst the havoc of plaster, tiles, and splintered bamboo which, an hour before, had been a row of cottages. A flourish of passes and cards got us past the police guards into the grounds of the Arsenal itself. The authorities were certainly doing their job efficiently: the wounded had long since been removed, and the fire brigade had things well under control; only one small building was still actually in flames. Judging from the size of the bomb-craters the Japanese had wasted a big sum of money.

Over by the other gate lay five civilian victims on stretchers, waiting for their coffins to arrive. They were terribly mutilated and very dirty, for the force of the explosion had tattooed their flesh with gravel and sand. Beside one corpse was a brand-new, undamaged straw hat. All the bodies looked very small, very poor, and very dead, but, as we stood beside one old woman, whose brains were soaking obscenely through a little towel, I saw the blood-caked mouth open and shut, and the hand beneath the sack-covering clench and unclench. Such were the Emperor's birthday presents.

We heard later that five hundred civilians had been killed in the raid and thirty planes destroyed—nine Chinese and twenty-one Japs. Several other Japanese planes had been seriously damaged and were not expected to be able to reach their base. That night Hankow celebrated its greatest aerial victory.

The Navy and our friends from the Consulate gave us a tremendous send-off. We staggered on board the river-steamer for Kiukiang just as the gangways were going up. Later I found myself involved in a semi-maudlin, semi-aggressive conversation with two German passengers, who assured me solemnly that never, under any circumstances, could England and Germany be friends. Germany would never forget how she had been treated, in the Far East, at the outbreak of the 1914 war. I retired to bed, having lost the argument. I am never much good at defending the British Empire, even when drunk.

There was time to shave, dress, have breakfast, and be heartily sick before Kiukiang swam smoothly round the curve of the river—a pretty Europeanized waterfront of balconied houses and trees, with H.M.S. *Gnat* lying in the foreground at anchor, flat as a nursery tea-tray laden with clean white crockery.

On the river-stairs we were accosted by a big, bald man with the face of a good-humoured don or judge; he wore

175

horn-rimmed glasses, sports jacket, Chinese stockings and shorts. This was Mr. Charleton, proprietor of Journey's End, an hotel (or, as he preferred to call it, an inn) situated several miles from Kiukiang, in the Kuling hills.

We had heard of Journey's End, of course, already. It was advertised regularly in the Hankow English newspaper:

JOURNEY'S END

850 feet above sea level. Up here, all is fresh, clean, and beautiful. The Mount Lavinia of the Yangtze Valley. Grilled rainbow trout. Crab home-grown salads. Fresh prawn curries.

Sunrise.

Fresh as a maid, all grace and beauty,
Cool as the trout in our Lien Hwa Tong,
Green as the grass of our lakeside pasture,
Gold as the comb in our wild bees' home.

Eventide.

Red as the rays of an Iceland sunset,
Tired as a child at bedtime's hour:
Dark, dark as the mane of a blue-black Arab:
Quiet, all quiet as a leopard's paw.

Such days and nights in China's Switzerland are both fine things, little brother: Come and see for yourself.

'Good morning, sir' (this was to Auden). 'Are you by any chance a relation of the author? Your wife is German, I believe? You wonder how I know? Heard it over the bamboo wireless. News travels fast in this country.' (This, as we discovered later, was a typical example of Mr.

176

Charleton's love of mystification. He had, as a matter of fact, been told all about us by one of our fellow-passengers a few moments before.) 'You're an author too, sir?' (Charleton turned to me.) 'You really must forgive me for not knowing. I live in Sleepy Hollow. I say, I do hope you're not angry with me? I ought to have said: Are you both, by any chance, relations of the authors? Never mind—you two youngsters must bear with an old man who's got one foot in the grave. I hope when you come to my age you'll be able to say: I enjoyed every minute of it! Oh, I've been very lucky. I've had a wonderful life. I'm the luckiest man in the world. My father was the most upright man I ever knew: he was a manager of the Bank of England. I knew Brooke, you know. We were at Cambridge together. I admit I'm a gambler. I could have had anything I wanted from life. Anything. But I played too hard and I lived too hard. They offered to make me a don. Not because I was a great scholar; it was for my rowing. I made a fortune in Shanghai. Lost every penny of it. Who cares? What is success if you're miserable? I'm the happiest man alive!'

I suppose we had already agreed to stay at Journey's End. Or perhaps we hadn't. Anyhow, here we were, bundled into an ancient car with steering-gear like a roulette wheel, bumping through the green countryside, towards the lucid blue of the Kuling mountains. From the village where we stopped Charleton led us uphill, along a path which crossed and recrossed the mountain stream by stepping-stones and tumbledown rustic bridges. The house, with its deep porches, stood on a terrace, looking down the glen. Beneath it the torrent had been dammed to make a swimming-pool ('like swimmers into cleanness leaping', Mr. Charleton had quoted in his latest adver-

tisement). On a board in the garden he had painted
Dorothy Frances Blomfield Gurney's notorious lines:

The kiss of the sun for pardon,
The song of the birds for mirth.
One is nearer God's heart in a garden
Than anywhere else on earth.

Running out to meet us came a drilled troop of house-
boys in khaki shorts and white shirts, prettily embroidered with the scarlet characters of their names. Mr.
Charleton's boys were famous, it appeared, in this part
of China. He trained them for three years—as servants,
gardeners, carpenters, or painters—and then placed them,
often in excellent jobs, with consular officials, or foreign
business men. The boys had all learnt a little English.
They could say: 'Good morning, sir,' when you met them,
and commanded a whole repertoire of sentences about tea,
breakfast, the time you wanted to be called, the laundry,
and the price of drinks. When a new boy arrived one of
the third-year boys was appointed as his guardian. The
first year, the boy was paid nothing; the second year, four
dollars a month, the third year, ten. If a boy was stupid
but willing he was taken on to the kitchen staff, and given
a different uniform—black shirt and shorts. All tips were
divided and the profits of the business shared out at the
end of the year.

The boys also learnt boxing, and were allowed to use
the swimming-pool daily, unless one of them had been
responsible for a dirty spoon or fork. They also were taught
to be quiet. Any boy who shouted lost a good conduct
mark. As Mr. Charleton said: 'God has given you a pair
of beautiful legs, and He meant you to use them. If you've
anything to say come up close and say it.' Boys were sum-

moned by striking with a small hammer one of the numerous shell-cases which were disposed about the house
and grounds. On the subject of dress Charleton exercised
a more than military strictness. On certain days all the
boys were obliged to wear their stockings up to the knee;
on others the stockings were rolled down to the ankles.
'It depends', he explained, 'on my mood.'

Our rooms were large and the beds very comfortable.
Each bedroom was provided with a Bible and a volume
of pornographic French literature. If you stayed at Journey's End long enough you could work through twenty
of them at least. 'You'll have tiffin under the camphor-
tree; it keeps off the insects,' said the headmaster (for
surely this was a preparatory school?) or the abbot (for
perhaps, after all, it was a monastery). 'This is Hu Sur-
chen. He'll look after you. Each guest has a boy attached
to him.' Hu Sur-chen smiled faintly. He was a delicate-
looking youth of nineteen, unusually shy for a Chinese.

So we had tiffin under the camphor-tree, aware, in a
trance of pleasure, of the smell of its leaves; of the splash
of the stream over the stones; of the great gorge folding
back, like a painting by Salvator Rosa, into the wooded
hills behind the house. There were snipe to eat, and rainbow trout. It was all far, far too beautiful to be real. 'If
I make the sign of the Hammer and Sickle', I said, 'everything will disappear.' And Auden agreed: 'It's the Third
Temptation of the Demon.' One could arrive for the week-
end and stay fifteen years—eating, sleeping, swimming;
standing for hours in a daze of stupefied reverence before
the little Ming tomb in the garden; writing, in the porch,
the book that was altogether too wonderful to finish and
too sacred ever to publish; pleasantly flagellating the flesh
by a scramble up the mountain to the Lily Cave and the

179

Dragon Pool; and, in the evening, inventing imaginary sins to repent of, under the expert guidance of the schoolmaster-abbot.

Chiang, it seemed, had also succumbed to the Third Temptation. Never had he been so lazy—though, indeed, there was nothing whatever for him to do. He spent the day lounging in a deck-chair, or gossiping with the servants of Mr. Kung (brother of the great banker), who, excepting Herr Meyer, one of the German military advisers, was Charleton's only other guest. Mr. Kung is said to resemble Confucius, whose lineal descendant he is. He reminded us strongly of Balzac.

Charleton admirably refrained from bothering his visitors. Although the place was so small he respected their privacy. If he saw you didn't want to talk he passed your chair with a simple fascist salute. Sometimes he made suggestions: would you like to walk to Kuling, or take a bath? If you agreed he raised his thumb with the gesture of an emperor at the Roman games. But if you were in the mood for conversation you could have that, too. Too inconsequent to be for a moment boring, he sideslipped from Cambridge into Shanghai, from big business to small pleasures, from the blood-sports to the fine arts, from Love to Death. He was sure that he would die soon, he told us. He had lived, played, gambled, worked too hard. Never mind. He was ready for the call.

Herr Meyer was not ready for the call, however. He wanted most emphatically to get well, to finish his job, to return to his wife and children in Hanover. He was a dumpy, sensible, good-natured, middle-aged man; the most senior of all the German advisers. He had been through every recent campaign and survived their risks until, recently, an attack of typhus had affected his heart.

He was optimistic about the outcome of the present war. His own troops were stationed at Loyang, and he would go there at the end of his convalescence in a few days' time. He had been training the same corps ever since he came to China. Meyer repeated what we had heard already in Hankow—that the German advice had been frequently disregarded, that promises of supplies had sometimes been broken, that there had been far too much red tape, that the Japanese could have been defeated long ago. He did not believe that Manchukuo could be recaptured. He was certain that a Japanese victory would mean the end of foreign influence in the Far East.

The relationship between Meyer and Charleton was the only noisy thing at Journey's End. They made up for their respective lack of English and German by shouts and laughter. The chief cause of their serio-comic friction was one of Charleton's house-boys. Meyer had offered the boy a job but stipulated that he must come away at once. Charleton insisted that the boy should stay at Journey's End till September to help with the summer visitors. Meyer retaliated with typically German banter about the hardness of his bed, the badness of the food, the heat of his room, and the number of insects. Charleton, who didn't understand a word, roared: 'That's a nasty one!' or 'Sorry! I don't speak Welsh!'

Next morning the Demon began to exercise his power. We were to have left for Nanchang, and we didn't. It was chiefly my fault: I had wanted to go up to Kuling, the mountain village which is the missionaries' holiday resort. But today the clouds were down on the hills; the gorge was choked with mist; and the swimming-pool, after a night of heavy rain, was pouring itself out over the rocks like a miniature Niagara.

Were we, perhaps, going to stay on here for ever? The rain was so soothing. . . . After all, why go to Nanchang? Why go anywhere? Why bother about the Fourth Army? It could take care of itself. What was this journey? An illusion. What were America, England, London, the spring publishing season, our families, our friends, ambition, money, love? Only modes of the First Temptation of the Demon—and why should one temptation be better than another? True, our cash would run out, but Charleton wouldn't let us starve. He'd put us into shorts, and we should wash the dishes and clean the thunder-boxes and take out guests for walks. Later we'd learn to fish and hunt mountain leopards and shoot snipe. We should become real hill-men, and perhaps even beat Charleton's record time up to Kuling—one hour and thirty-five minutes. 'No, no!' cried Auden, almost in despair. 'We must leave tomorrow morning!'

In the afternoon Hu Sur-chen took us to see the Iron Pagoda—which wasn't, as we had expected, a building, but a three-foot monument in a temple a few miles away. The priests at the temple gave us tea. On the way back there was a thunderstorm, and the rain fell in torrents. We arrived home happily drenched, feeling like old Journey's End boys already.

In the sitting-room was a stuffed dog—once Mr. Charleton's prize-winning spaniel, 'Lady Lovable'. Being in a surrealistic mood we made it sit with us at supper. There was something very sinister about 'Lady Lovable': one of her glass eyes had fallen out, the other glared at us with the ferocity of a Chinese dragon. Auden said that she would probably visit us during the night, dragging her

182

paralysed hindquarters after her, with a dry slithering sound, along the passage to the bedroom door.

After supper Mr. Charleton drank Chinese wine and was nearly overcome by the extraordinary happiness of his life. 'We've all had that picture, 'Love Locked Out', in our rooms!' he shouted at Herr Meyer, who replied that the lemonade had been adulterated with petroleum. The rain poured down on the roof, and the insects descended upon us in myriads—there were beetles in the tea, midges in the air, and great whiskered creatures trying to crawl out of the beer-glasses. 'Haven't I given you three tins of *pâté de foie gras* at three dollars fifty each?' cried Charleton; and Meyer retorted: 'At Christmas I shall come back with a couple of friends and smash this lousy hole to bits.' 'I'll never have another Fritz inside my door,' said Charleton. 'The last one couldn't pay his bill—and do you know what he left me instead? A German flag!' At this point the house-boys created a diversion by bursting the bathroom boiler. 'The whole place is flooding,' observed Charleton, philosophically. 'I don't care. I hope you two kids will have a grand life. Drink to the poor old man next Christmas Eve. I shall be dead by then. God bless.'

During the night the Demon left us abruptly in a tremendous gust of wind which flung wide the bedroom doors and extinguished the lamps. It was no longer difficult to tear ourselves away from Journey's End. Next morning even the novices of this all-too-charming monastery appeared in a more prosaic aspect—they were merely Chinese servants awaiting their cumshaws. Having received them they giggled shamefacedly—as Europeans giggle over Sex—and asked for a little, a very little, just a trifle more.

183

So Charleton gave us his last Roman salute and away we drove down to the station at Kiukiang, only to find that the train had left an hour before its advertised time, and that there was no other that day. If we had been true poets—the kind of poets Charleton respected—we should, no doubt, have laughed gaily and wandered off, hand in hand, into the fields to make each other crowns of wild flowers. But, alas, in our fussy, materialistic way, we were cross. Kiukiang had nothing to offer us beyond two beds in the China Travel Hotel. It was drizzling. The *Gnat* had sailed away. And Auden felt ill. The after-effects of an attack of dysentery were undermining his iron nerves. He remarked that our room would be a peculiarly suitable place to die in. We spent a sombre afternoon chain-smoking, talking about diseases, and reading a three-volume edition of Motley's *Rise of the Dutch Republic*. Motley depressed us both intensely with his catalogue of tortures, massacres, and battles. 'And it's exactly the same nowadays,' Auden exclaimed. 'Really, civilization hasn't advanced an inch!'

In the evening we went to the cinema. The big picture was about a Chinese weakling who turned traitor to his country and agreed to make signals to Japanese aircraft in exchange for cocaine injections given him by a fiendish Jap doctor. He was shot, of course, and the audience clapped. And then the avenging Chinese troops captured the town—and everybody clapped still louder. We both wondered how long it would be before we were applauding similar trash, only a shade more sophisticated, at all the London cinemas.

8

The sun was shining this morning. The junks in the creek outside our hotel hoisted their great tattered dragon-wing sails. Kiukiang seemed charming again, and curiously Dutch. We caught the train with plenty of time to spare: it left shortly after eight.

The Kiukiang–Nanchang railway has none of the drama of the Lung-Hai. There were no air-raid alarms, no long halts. The carriage roofs are painted with large spots, like a nursery rocking-horse. The countryside is as green as Devonshire, with flowering hedges, and little hills and lanes. We noticed that the faces on the station platforms were less typically Chinese (according to western ideas) than in the other provinces we have visited. The eyes are larger and rounder. The noses are straight, even, sometimes, hooked or beaky.

The Burlington Hotel at Nanchang is more up to date even than the Sian Guest-House, and considerably cheaper. The food is good, too. As befits the birthplace of the New Life Movement, the hotel prohibits gambling, prostitutes, shouting, musical instruments, and opium on its premises. There is a beautifully bound copy of the Bible in Chinese on the writing-table in my bedroom.

May 4

After breakfast we started off to find the headquarters of the New Fourth Army. The outward appearance of Nanchang is most deceptive. From across the river it looks almost as imposing as Hankow. The Burlington Hotel stands on a fine broad ring-boulevard, laid out with grass and planted with trees soon after the proclamation of the New Life Movement. But the inner town remains filthy, tortuous, and picturesque; stinking lanes, full of pot-holes, wind their way round evil-smelling, stagnant lakes. After nearly an hour of inquiries we discovered the house we were looking for—a half-empty mansion with big, weed-grown courtyards, near to the Three-Eyed Well. Anything less military could hardly be imagined. We were received very politely by two men and about a dozen little boys, who told us that all the responsible officers were away somewhere near the front, but that they would be returning to Nanchang soon.

Next we went to the offices of the Salt Gabelle to call on M. Berubé, who is a friend of the Consul-General in Hankow. The Chinese manager most kindly lent us a car to drive out to a little camp of ply-wood huts, standing in a fir-plantation about a mile outside the city. M. Berubé and his staff have moved there to escape the air-raids, which have been very frequent and have caused a great deal of damage. This camp used to belong to an Italian firm of aircraft manufacturers. The Italians were found to be in league with the Japanese, so they had to leave in a hurry. Berubé has nicknamed the place 'Frascati's'.

A confirmed Anglophile, small and dapper and facetious, he speaks excellent idiomatic English. During the war he served with the French Air Force: his father was a spy in Copenhagen. He has an English wife. He prefers P. & O. boats to the Messageries Maritimes because there is more discipline, and the passengers are obliged to dress for dinner. He quoted with relish a dictum of Anatole France: 'A British boat is a floating democracy. A French boat is a drifting demagogy.' His most thrilling adventure in China was his capture by bandits on the Shanghai–Peking express in 1923.

In the afternoon we went round to the American Mission Hospital so that Auden could be examined. This is the largest hospital we have so far seen in China. Among the patients who were waiting to be treated was a round-faced young Chinese, about twenty years old, whose eyes had an expression of the most painful anxiety and bewilderment. He came up with his brother to speak to us: 'Please can you tell me the fact?' 'What fact?' we asked. 'The fact about thinking. Is it done by radio-waves? I am very nervous.' The brother explained to us that their whole family had been killed in an air-raid, and that the young man was suffering from shock. He hoped to get treatment here in the hospital. He had been a clerk in the post office, and spoke good English. 'I'm going to find out', he told Auden, 'whether you are a radio man. Can you, please, introduce me to the President? I want to know if I'm still in the experiment. Then I shall be comforted.'

May 5

We returned to the hospital again this morning. The doctors, here as elsewhere, are admirable and efficient; but there is a very voluble lady missionary, smug and fat, who displays an irritating professional familiarity with the Almighty, whom she evidently regards as the private property of the American Nonconformists. She is not, we are glad to hear, a regular member of the hospital staff, but only in Nanchang on a visit.

After tea we visited the Governor of Kiang-Si Province, General Hsiung Shih-hueh. Slim and erect, in his plain blue uniform and elastic-sided shoes, the Governor looks a mere boy, nearly twenty years younger than his age. His pale oval face and sloe-black eyes have the repose of a great actor or a Buddhist saint. As Auden said, his mere presence would make him a fortune on any stage.

The results of the interview were not very encouraging. The Governor thanked us for our visit, and hoped that we shouldn't be detained very long in Nanchang. He plainly didn't approve of our plan to leave China via Ningpo. The bridges along the Kin-hwa–Ningpo road were broken. If we attempted the journey, he regretted that he could not guarantee us against 'something very unfortunate'. We had much better return to Hongkong. However, he promised to make further inquiries, and to let us know in a few days' time. We asked if we might be allowed to visit the propaganda-school for cadets which, we have heard, exists in Nanchang. After some consultation, the Governor replied that this was unfortunately impossible, 'owing to the political situation'. We bowed ourselves out.

May 6

At the Out-patients' Department of the hospital today we again saw the young man who is worried by 'the fact about thinking'. The fat lady missionary came up to talk to him, and his brother told her of the family tragedy. She simply didn't listen. 'Don't worry,' she told the young man. 'Leave it to Jesus. You go home to your father and mother and eat some of mother's good food. Jesus will look after you all right.'

Never forgetting our admiration for the missionaries of the Yellow River, it is only fair to tell the story we heard recently from an American airman in Hankow. Some years ago the airman and a friend were flying near Loyang. The weather shut down, so they made for the nearest emergency landing-field, on the outskirts of a small, dirty town. The airman suggested that they should try to get a bed at the mission-station, and, sure enough, the missionary received them hospitably, and showed them up to a bedroom, where they shaved, washed, and changed their clothes. They didn't see their host again until the evening. Downstairs, supper was ready: the food looked good, and they were both very hungry. Then the missionary, having said Grace, suddenly asked: 'Does either of you gentlemen smoke?' The airman didn't, but his friend did. 'Do you drink?' Yes, they both took a drink occasionally. 'Then I'm sorry,' said the missionary, 'there's no place for you under this roof.' They could hardly believe their ears; but the missionary wasn't joking. Out they had to go, leaving the supper uneaten, to sleep on chairs in the local Chinese inn. 'And now tell me', our informant concluded, 'what would *you* have said to that missionary?'

May 7

Yesterday afternoon we went out shopping with Berubé. Auden bought his favourite kind of panama hat. This particular example is made, apparently, of cardboard. It certainly won't survive the first shower. Berubé was so much amused that he has written an indecent poem about it, which he brought us today.

This morning Auden went again to the hospital and returned in a state of delighted fury against the lady missionary. Hearing that we were off to the front she had said: 'Are you insured with Jesus? Jesus has positively guaranteed eternal life. . . . This life' (holding up her thumb) 'is just a teeny span.' Auden wishes he had bitten it.

We have now decided to leave at once for Kin-hwa. It is no good waiting for the result of the Governor's inquiries, or the return of the Fourth Army officers to Nanchang. If we can't get through to Ningpo or Wenchow later, well, we can't. There will be plenty of time to bother about that after we have visited the south-eastern front.

Today we at last met Wingeter, the American engineer and civil pilot who is working at the air-field here. Wingeter lives at the Burlington, and it is a great pity we didn't get to know him sooner, for we both like him very much. Wingeter is leading a lonely, worried life—uncertain whether to return to New York and rejoin his wife, or renew his contract here. He and Berubé are the only English-speaking Westerners, apart from the missionaries, in Nanchang. On the air-field there are a number of Russian pilots, but they keep very much to themselves, and are constantly being changed. After a few months' service a pilot returns to Russia and a new man comes out to take his place. When the Japanese attack Hankow the Nanchang planes often fly out to cut off the raiders' retreat. If the Nanchang air-field itself is bombed the Russians take up their heavy bombers and fly them away out of danger until the raid is over. But the Chinese guards remain on the field, ready to run out and plant flags in the bomb-craters, so that the Russians, on their return, may be able to make a safe landing. Wingeter says that the Chinese behave on these occasions with incredible bravery. Many of them get killed. If there is a night-raid Wingeter jumps into his car and drives out to the hills, for the Burlington is too near the air-field to be safe. A bomb has actually destroyed one of the houses on the boulevard just opposite the hotel.

Chiang suggested that we should try to get free passes on to the train to Kin-hwa. So we went along to interview the Director of the railway. By this time it was already a quarter past seven, and the train was due to leave at eight o'clock, so the interview was somewhat unnerving: we had only a quarter of an hour in which to get through the handshaking, the bowing, the card-exchanges, the tea-drinking, and all the other slow-motion phases of Chinese politeness. At last the passes were signed, and we dashed in Wingeter's car to the station. Luckily the train started ten minutes late.

May 8

When we woke early next morning the train was crossing a wide valley of paddy-fields. The rising sun struck its beams across the surfaces of innumerable miniature lakes; in the middle distance farmhouses seemed actually to be floating on the water. Here and there a low mound rose a few feet above the level of the plain, with a weed-grown, ruinous pagoda standing upon it, visible for miles around. Peasants with water-buffaloes were industriously ploughing their arable liquid into a thick brown soup.

We arrived in Kin-hwa at about four o'clock in the afternoon. Hardly had we stepped out of the train when we found ourselves surrounded by a group of soldiers and police. An officer, running up and saluting, requested us to come into the station guardroom. 'We have been expecting you,' he explained. 'We have been down to meet two trains already.' Somewhat bewildered we followed him. More officers were introduced. 'And now', said one of them, who appeared to be the local chief of police, 'I shall escort you to your hotel. A room has been reserved.'

We glanced at each other nervously. 'Do you think', Auden whispered, 'that we're really under arrest? They'd probably be far too tactful to tell us so.' 'Perhaps they think we're spies,' I said. 'Anyhow, we shall never know —until we're actually taken out to be shot.' 'Oh, they'd never shoot us. Far too crude. We shall simply disappear.'

The truth, of course, proved to be far less dramatic. A letter from somebody in Hankow, a wire from Hollington Tong, a mention of our names in the Nanchang paper have combined to convince the Kin-hwa authorities that we are people of importance—and we are going to be treated as such. From now on we must resign ourselves to fulfilling all the obligations of public characters.

It has started already. Hardly had we dumped our bags in the bedroom of the bungalow China Travel Service hotel, when the first official caller was announced—the Kin-hwa Director of the railway. He was followed by the chief of police, who looked in to tell us that a special constable had been put permanently at our disposal. He would sit in the entrance-lounge all day, awaiting our orders. What, exactly, does one do with a special constable, we wondered, as we thanked the chief of police profusely.

Next came Mr. T. Y. Liu, the secretary of the civil government, and correspondent to the *South-Eastern Daily News*. He is a gnome-like little man, with the delicate bones of a very young child, and the weird, upcurving eyes of an immemorially ancient Chinese dragon. In some moods he has the face of a sixteen-year-old boy; in others he sits blinking and yellow as a man of eighty. Mr. Liu, we feel already, is to be our great friend in Kin-hwa. And he will come with us to the front. As he himself says: 'When I am in danger I have no fear.'

After much tea—this evening all records for tea-drinking were easily broken—we drove out with Mr. T. Y. Liu to visit General Huang Shao-yung, Governor of Che-kiang Province. The Governor's headquarters are in a small village at the foot of the mountains. By the time we had arrived there it was already quite dark. Guided by soldiers with flashlights, we crossed an unevenly paved bridge over the mountain-stream, and stumbled through a garden to the door of a cottage. Just inside the cottage hung a linen curtain upon which was projected, as in a post-war German horror-film, the huge, distorted, crouching shadow of the Governor himself.

The Governor wasn't at all horrific, however. He was a ponderous, crop-haired man with a jolly laugh, somewhat resembling a Prussian officer of the least formidable type. He offered at once not only to give us passes to visit the front but to send us there in his own car. We could see everything, we gathered, quite easily and quickly, and be back at Kin-hwa within two or three days. The Governor also explained the military situation. He seems to think that we shall have no difficulty in getting down to Ningpo when this journey is over.

This evening we dined at the hotel with Mr. Liu, his wife, and a charming, boyish major who has been wounded three times in the fighting round Shanghai. 'Major Yang', we were told, by way of introduction, 'does not fear death.' Major Yang speaks no English; he could only smile and repeatedly raise his glass to our health. He and Mr. Liu drink cognac as though it were a light table-wine. We did our best to follow suit. Meanwhile, T. Y. Liu described the very serious operation he had undergone two years ago in Shanghai. By the end of the meal Auden and I were so drunk that we even ventured to criticize the Chinese habit of spitting. Mr. Liu agreed that it was disgusting, unpatriotic, and must be stopped. He and Major Yang continued to spit, with the utmost relish, throughout the rest of the evening.

May 9

This morning we made a ceremonial tour of the town, accompanied by Liu, Yang, Chiang, and suite—including our private constable. Kin-hwa is, perhaps, the most attractive small city we have so far visited in China. The narrow, flagged streets are wonderfully clean, and the shops are so well stocked that they might well be transported bodily into a museum, to exemplify the various crafts and trades. There was nothing you couldn't get, from a fan to a jade sealing-stone. Auden bought two tiny embroidered scarlet jackets for a godchild, but there our purchases ended, because it became quite clear that the municipal government will insist on paying for everything we ask for in this town. The Governor has already sent word that we are his guests as long as we care to stay at the China Travel hotel.

At the municipal government office we were received by the city governor and the chief of police, and shown the dug-out in which many of the employees had sheltered when a big Japanese bomb landed in the garden. At present it was full of water, a fact which the chief of police discovered too late, when he had stepped into it, up to his knees. The Japanese, we are told, never bomb the city nowadays; but they sometimes attack the railway station.

We lunched at a restaurant which has just been opened by refugees from Hang-chow. (Before the war started Hang-chow used to be the provincial capital of Che-kiang. Since the Japanese occupation the Government has moved

194

to Kin-hwa.) The building itself is very pretty. Its pillars are scarlet and turquoise blue, festooned with tiny electric bulbs and coloured paper streamers—like the entrance to a fun-fair. Here the politeness-game, which we had been playing all morning, reached its height. We were a party of twelve, and, for some time, it looked as if we should never get upstairs at all—there was so much playful scuffling to yield the places of honour, so much bowing, so many 'after you's. As a pro-British gesture, our hosts insisted on eating the European menu—a suffocating cavalcade of soup, chicken, Mandarin fish (on a Chinese list of dishes, every fish seems to be described as 'Mandarin'), pork, more chicken, more fish, and sweets. Toasts were drunk and re-drunk in every conceivable combination, till our heads swam. We kept swapping specially dainty morsels with our neighbours. Auden and I developed a private game: it was a point of honour to praise most warmly the dishes you liked least. 'Delicious,' Auden murmured, as he munched what was, apparently, a small sponge soaked in glue. I replied by devouring, with smiles of exquisite pleasure, an orange which tasted of bitter aloes and contained, in its centre, a large weevil. On the whole the food was very nice, but our hosts disparaged it out of courtesy—and of course we had to protest: 'Horrible stuff, this. We must apologize. . . .' 'No, no! Not horrible. Wonderful!' 'Very poor after your English cookery.' 'English cookery disgusting! Chinese cookery marvellous!' 'We are so sorry.' 'The best lunch we ever had in our lives.' 'Miserable.' 'Excellent.' 'Bad.' 'Good.' 'Bad.' 'No!' 'Yes!' And so on. We kept it up throughout the meal.

After lunch, stuffed and intoxicated, we staggered home to rest, but not for long. We had promised to address the three hundred students who are being trained in Kin-hwa as teachers and propagandists. The students will go out into the villages of the surrounding countryside and explain to the peasants the causes and aims of the war. It is strange to have to talk to an audience which does not understand a single word you are saying. One's natural instinct is to shout at them as though they were deaf, or simply to make horrible faces and wave the arms like a windmill. 'After this war', Auden bellowed, 'you will have to fight a more terrible enemy than the Japanese. You will have to fight disease, bad housing, illiteracy, dirt....' 'You must win this war', I boomed, 'to save China, to save Japan, to save Europe.' At the end of every five or six sentences, we had to pause, to let Mr. Liu or the chief of police translate. Goodness knows what they said to the audience. It seemed to us that they were making quite a different speech, much longer, all on their own. When we had finished the Governor thanked us. He wanted, he said, to give us three letters stating China's case—one to show to England, one to Japan, and one to the world. I took this literally, at first, and had an alarming vision of ourselves toiling up and down embassy staircases all over London. But the letters, it later appeared, were only figures of speech.

What did the students make of us? Most of them listened attentively. A few were giggling or drawing pictures. One or two were asleep. While we were having tea after the ceremony a good many of them came in with autograph albums for our signatures.

We went on to inspect the military hospital, which is in a magnificent old temple on the outskirts of the city. Each ward is a shrine, with a gigantic plaster Immortal towering benevolently above the beds. These figures have real horsehair beards. The hospital is fairly well equipped.

The operating-theatre is very clean but there is no X-ray apparatus, and all the water must be brought from a neighbouring well.

May 10

Before nine o'clock this morning the Governor's car, a splendid Nash saloon which was once the property of the mayor of Hang-chow, came round to call for us at the hotel. There were six of us in the party—T. Y. Liu, Major Yang, the chauffeur, a freckled boy with projecting teeth, and ourselves. The boy is a rather mysterious figure. We tried to prevent his coming with us, for the car, when all our luggage had been put into it, was already overcrowded; but we were assured that his presence was absolutely necessary. He had to carry a brandy bottle, he knew the road (this was untrue) and he 'could find gasoline'. Auden suggested that he must be a new type of dowser.

Chiang we were leaving behind. He would be of no use to us, for Liu talks fluent English—and we haven't forgotten his obstructionism at Han Chwang. This arrangement certainly suited Chiang. He will have a wonderful time at Kin-hwa while we are away, running up bills at the Governor's expense and enjoying our reflected glory.

The chauffeur reminds us of a character in a novel by D. H. Lawrence—the groom in *St. Mawr*, or one of those 'dark', sinister Mexicans in *The Plumed Serpent*. Indeed, with his square, heavy figure and brilliant, dangerous smile, he looks more like a Mexican Indian than a Chinese. When the car started his eyes glazed over in a mindless, sub-human stare. His foot sank heavily on the accelerator, and remained there, despite the twistings of the road, until he had deposited us at the brink of a river, about three miles beyond the city.

During this first stage of the journey we had two rivers to cross. The car was ferried over them on a raft propelled by bamboo punt-poles. It is advisable to get out of your car while making such a passage, for the current is strong and the raft very small. Mr. Liu told us that a motor-bus had recently been upset in the middle of the stream, drowning all its passengers.

There was plenty of water traffic: small junks with a single sail, and caravans of long, narrow log-rafts shaped like Canadian toboggans—drawn by gangs of coolies who plodded slowly along the bank, at the end of an immensely long rope.

At Lanchi—a town with several very beautiful pagodas, eighteen miles from Kin-hwa—we came to our third river, and had to wait, because the troops of the Nineteenth Division were crossing in the opposite direction. They were on their way from the south-eastern to the Tsin-pu front. The Nineteenth is a crack division from Fu-kien and Sze-chwan which fought at Shanghai.

We sat on the bank and watched them scrambling ashore from sampans, with their ponies, and machine-guns, and cooking-pots. They had the air of real, hardened soldiers, inveterate and practical as tramps. Experience had taught them exactly what equipment to carry—a thermos flask, a straw sun-hat, chopsticks, an umbrella, a spare pair of rubber shoes. A face-towel hung from each man's belt, like a dish-clout, together with two or three hand-grenades which resembled miniature Chianti bottles. Gaining the shore they formed immediately into a straggling line and marched off, shuffling shabbily and quickly along, with their feet muffled in old rags, laughing and joking—perfectly adapted, it seemed, to their life of hardship, dirt, and pain.

Beyond Lanchi the road leaves the river-valley and turns off into the hills. Soon we were hurtling round the curves of a mountain pass. The scenery was superb, but we were too frightened even to look out of the window. Instead, Auden tried to distract our thoughts from the alarming Present by starting a conversation about eighteenth-century poetry. It was no good: we could remember nothing but verses on sudden death. Meanwhile, the road twisted and struggled, and the car clung to it like a mongoose attacking a cobra. Pedestrians screamed, cyclists overbalanced into paddy-fields, wrecked hens lay twitching spasmodically in the dust-storm behind us. At every corner we shut our eyes, but the chauffeur only laughed darkly as befitted one of the Lords of Death, and swung us round the curve with squealing brakes. Neither Major Yang nor Mr. Liu showed the least symptoms of nervousness. 'The road is very difficult,' Mr. Liu observed peacefully, as we shot across a crazy makeshift bridge over a gorge, rattling its loose planks like the bars of a xylophone. 'It wouldn't be difficult', I retorted, 'if we weren't driving at seventy miles an hour.'

We stopped at a small town for gasoline and a late lunch. In the square was an ambulance-truck full of wounded—the first we had seen that morning. Mr. Liu bought some tablets of Tiger Balm, the cure-all tonic which is advertised all over China. He was feeling in need of them because, as he explained, he had slept badly the night before. 'If I sleep well I am very strong. If I do not sleep I can do nothing.' Today he seemed actually to have shrunk into a little ivory-faced manikin, with a big wet baby's underlip. Nevertheless, he remained the perfect host. 'You are the guests of China,' he kept repeating. 'We must try to satisfy you. You are our friends.'

199

After this short respite the D. H. Lawrence *Todesfahrt* continued. But we were braver now. With food inside us we ventured to admire the view. There were water-mills in the river far below. The hills were cultivated to their summits; the striped, wheat-covered folds of the mountains looked like yellow corduroy. 'Oh, my Gard!' exclaimed Mr. Liu, and was abruptly and violently carsick. A few miles further on Major Yang, who had been looking very thoughtful, followed his example.

Towards the end of the afternoon we descended into the plain. There were more villages here, and a good many buses and lorries. Twice our chauffeur escaped a head-on collision by inches. 'The Chinese', somebody once told us, 'are very lucky drivers.' But not always. Along this part of the roadside we counted five hopelessly shattered wrecks.

A little further on we passed an embankment where a line of track was under construction. 'That', Mr. Liu told us, 'is the secret railway.' We were much intrigued: 'Why is it secret? Who is it secret from? How can you keep a railway secret?' we asked. 'It is secret,' Mr. Liu replied.

Just after six o'clock we reached Tunki—the end of to-day's journey. We are staying at the Yellow Mountain Hotel, whose trellised verandah overhangs the shallow, straggling river, with a background of dark, bumpy mountains stained by the setting sun. All along the bank, women are washing clothes in the pebbled stream; there are willow-groves along the shore; in a distant field some soldiers are playing blind-man's-buff. This might be a small town in the north of Italy. Tomorrow, says Mr. Liu, we shall go up to the front by car, returning to Kin-hwa the day after.

About half an hour after I had finished writing the above, there was a clatter in the passage and the sound of

some one talking English. This was Dr. Robert Lim, head
of the China Red Cross. He was in Dr. Mooser's party when
we travelled back to Hankow from Sian. Dr. Lim was educated abroad and speaks English in preference to Chinese.
He was dressed like a rover scout, in smart grey shorts and
a jaunty forage-cap. 'I heard you were here,' he told us.
'I saw Peter Fleming in Nanchang. Has he arrived yet?'

'Fleming?' The name was echoed by a young Chinese
who, at this moment, strode into the room. 'Which of you
gentlemen is Mr. Fleming?'

'Neither.' We introduced ourselves. The young man,
who was A. W. Kao, a newspaper man, seemed displeased.

'What are you doing here?' he asked

'We want to go to the front.'

'Oh. . . .' Mr. A. W. Kao frowned. 'But they didn't say
that any other journalists were coming. I'm very surprised.'

He had no reason to be surprised, we retorted; we had
nothing to do with him. Our guide was Mr. T. Y. Liu
(whom we now introduced). We were travelling to the
front quite independently.

But our tone failed to impress Mr. A. W. Kao. He was in
charge here and nobody, not even an unwelcome guest,
should escape his jurisdiction. He has a smooth, adoles-
cent face, whose natural charm is spoilt by a perpetual
pout and by his fussy school-prefect's air of authority.
His eyes behind their horn-rimmed glasses are as nearly
priggish as it is possible for Chinese eyes to be.

Negligently tossing his hat and mackintosh to the servant who followed him, he unfolded a large sheet of blank
paper on our bedroom table. 'Tomorrow', he announced,
'a representative of General Ku will come here to answer

any questions. But now I will try to explain the general strategic situation to you with a simple map.' Producing a pencil, postulating our interest as a matter of course, he drew highroads, shaded in towns, arrowed troop movements; lecturing us like the brilliant sixth-form boy who takes the juniors in history while the headmaster is away. Everything was lucid and tidy and false—the flanks like neat little cubes, the pincer-movements working with mathematical precision, the reinforcements never failing to arrive punctual to the minute. But war, as Auden said later, is not like that. War is bombing an already disused arsenal, missing it, and killing a few old women. War is lying in a stable with a gangrenous leg. War is drinking hot water in a barn and worrying about one's wife. War is a handful of lost and terrified men in the mountains, shooting at something moving in the undergrowth. War is waiting for days with nothing to do; shouting down a dead telephone; going without sleep, or sex, or a wash. War is untidy, inefficient, obscure, and largely a matter of chance.

We asked about the New Fourth Army and were told that, two days ago, they had been moved to the Wuhu front. The officers we had tried to see in Nanchang left Tunki yesterday, to return there. 'But why do you wish specially to see the Fourth Army?' said A. W. Kao reprovingly. 'It does not differ from the other units, except that it has a more highly developed propaganda machine. Wuhu is very quiet just now. The most active sector is near the Tai Lake. That would be more interesting for you, I think.'

We got rid of him at last, on the understanding that he would come back in the morning with some one from headquarters. Then we could decide what we wanted to do.

202

We are now wondering if it will be possible to leave for the front before he returns.

May 11

Charming as this hotel is, it isn't ideal to sleep in. It is being used as an unofficial military headquarters, and the coming and going of messengers was continuous throughout the night. Mah-jongg players kept up a perpetual clatter, banging down their pieces on a table somewhere upstairs. In the early hours of the morning old men and women come wandering into the rooms, selling bread and fruit. The electric light in my bedroom won't turn out at all. If you don't want it you must simply unscrew the bulb.

During breakfast we asked Major Yang if he knew any comic soldiers' songs. He said that he did, but added that, in this war, all the army songs were patriotic and serious. After some persuasion he sang the following verses, which Mr. T. Y. Liu translated:

THE RIVER IS FULL OF RED
My angry hair, standing up, pushes my hat.
I stand near the rail of the balcony
And watch the continual rain.
I lift my head to look at the sky, and give a long laugh.
Now I am thirty, my great ambition is anxious and hot.
All the great deeds I did are just like the dust and the soil
    to me.

Eight thousand *li* of distance;
Nothing but the moon and the clouds.
Don't waste your time.
Don't let your hair grow white.
It makes you sorry.

Then Mr. Liu told us the words of a coolies' song:

> We get up at sunrise
> We go to bed at sunset
> We work hard
> We plough the field to grow food
> We dig the well to get drink—
> There is nothing for the King to do.

(I may as well insert here another song which we heard later in Shanghai. It is a song of the Chinese guerrilla units which operate behind the Japanese lines. This is Mr. Zinmay Zau's translation.)

When the season changed, so changed the strategy,
We took off our uniforms and put on the old cotton
  cloth.
Let the enemies fire their guns in vain and be happy for
  nothing;
They will capture an empty city like a new coffin.

Our heroes will put out their wits and tricks
To entertain enemies like fathers:
When they ask for wine we'll give them 'Great Carving
  Flowers';
When they ask for dishes we'll give them 'Shrimps and
  Eggs'.

When they get greedy for happiness they become afraid
  of death,
They won't listen to the orders of their superior
  officials;
They'll insist that the others should go in front when they
  go to the front:
A handful of tears and a handful of snot.

The enemies will be bewitched to their end:
Aeroplanes won't dare to go into the sky;
Tell them to attack, and they'll retreat;
Tell them to fire and they will let out their wind.

A shout of 'KILL!' and we'll fight back,
Rakes and spades will be mobilized:
This time our army will come out from the fields,
They will be like storms and hurricanes.

Tens of years of insults, we now have our revenge;
Tens of years of shame, we now have washed clean:
Those who scolded us, we now will flay their skins;
Those who hit us, we now will pull out their veins.

Those who boasted now will be like dumbs
Eating aloes and galls;
Those who killed and never minded fishy smell,
They will today become mincemeat themselves.

Those who burned our houses
Will now have nowhere to bury their bodies;
Those who raped our girls
Will now have their wives as widows.

Widely opened are the eyes of our God,
What you did to others will now be done to you.
Let's wait for the certain day of the certain month,
When we will have both the principal and interest back
    without discount.

    After breakfast we walked out into the town. In front
of a clothing shop a man and a boy were singing a highly
syncopated sales-duet about a pair of trousers. All the
passers-by grinned at us, and we wondered if there was
anybody in the whole street who didn't already know our

names and our business in Tunki. When we returned Mr. T. Y. Liu informed us: 'I have spent the morning with the dictionary and learnt two new words—Jingoism and Rumour.'

Here, in Tunki, T. Y. appears to have lost some of his self-confidence—perhaps because he is outside his own province. He seems intimidated by A. W. Kao, and shows no willingness to sneak off without him to the front. Possibly he doesn't exactly know where it is.

A. W. arrived after lunch, accompanied by Major-General Shiu, who is General Ku's chief of staff and head of the military Red Cross in this area. We all crowded somehow into Auden's little bedroom and the map-making began again. Once more we asked about the Fourth Army, and were politely snubbed. A. W. had the whip-hand, and he knew it. We couldn't go anywhere without him.

'How long would it take us to get to the nearest fighting?' Auden asked.

'About ten days, there and back. You would have to walk or ride.'

'We were told we could see everything in two or three days.'

A. W. looked scornful. He was deciding, one could see, that we weren't really keen. He said firmly:

'If you want to see anything interesting it will take you ten days as a minimum.'

'But we're with Mr. T. Y. Liu. We don't know if he can keep the car so long. Can you, Mr. T. Y.?'

'Can do.'

'Oh, very well. . . .'

'Good.' A. W. nodded his head triumphantly. 'We shall leave tomorrow morning.'

9

A few minutes later Peter Fleming himself walked into the room. 'Hullo, you two,' he greeted us, with the amused, self-conscious smile of a guest who arrives at a party in fancy dress. Though indeed his dress was anything but fancy—for this occasion it was almost absurdly correct. In his khaki shirt and shorts, complete with golf-stockings, strong suède shoes, waterproof wrist-watch and Leica camera, he might have stepped straight from a London tailor's window, advertising Gent's Tropical Exploration Kit. 'I saw all I wanted to see at Sü-chow,' he explained, 'so I thought I'd get down here before the rush starts.'

Fleming then introduced his companion, Mr. Ching, of the Hankow publicity office. Mr. Ching was short and sleek and plump. He wore a pretty canary yellow shirt. He looked worried, as if he viewed this journey with considerable misgivings. A. W. Kao greeted him rather haughtily, as he had greeted our own T. Y. Fleming alone he recognized as an equal. It was settled between them that Wuhu and the Fourth Army should not be visited; we were to start tomorrow in the direction of the Tai Lake.

In the afternoon we all went to call on General Ku. The car took us several miles out into the country and stopped in the middle of an almost deserted plain. On

207

foot we made our way along the little dikes which divided the paddy-fields, towards a distant copse. Dusk was gathering, and the over-arching trees formed a proscenium beyond which the General and his staff stood grouped with beautifully theatrical effect. At the edge of the glade we stopped and bowed. The General returned our bow. We advanced a few paces. Our hosts did likewise. More bows. Another advance. We met. We shook hands. It was like a scene from a Shakespearian comedy—or, as Fleming said, like the prelude to a duel.

The interview took place in a wooden hut, round a table loaded with delicacies—fruit, brandy, and expensive imported chocolates. Fleming, as our representative, handled the exchange of courtesies with consummate skill; it was unnecessary for either of us to open our mouths. 'Will you please', he asked A. W. Kao, 'thankGeneral Ku for seeing us at such a difficult time—and will you apologize for our clothes?' He knew just what questions to ask: 'Would the General give us his views on the relative merits and defects of the Japanese soldier?' He knew just how to bring the meeting to a close: 'Will you tell the General that, although war correspondents are supposed to be absolutely impartial, we do not think we should be going too far in asking him to drink with us to a Chinese victory?'

Before we left we examined a pile of war material recently captured from the Japanese. It was now quite dark. Holding electric torches we poked about among diaries, photographs, and private letters of dead men. There was a picture of a young cadet, posed in his new uniform; and a letter from a brother which said that they were all praying for his safety, but that it was a noble thing to die for one's country. There were flags, machine-guns, helmets, rifles. Mr. A. W. Kao read out translations of the diaries and letters, construing every sentence into a proof of the decay of Japanese morale. On the whole he wasn't very convincing.

We arrived back late for supper, and all drank a good deal of brandy. The brandy had a depressing effect on Major Yang. Presently he said something to T. Y. Liu, who told us:

'Major Yang wishes to apologize.'

'Oh, really? Why?'

'Major Yang says he wishes to apologize for being alive.'

'But why shouldn't he be alive?'

'He says it is a disgrace for any Chinese officer to have left Shanghai. They should have held it, or died where they stood.'

We protested that Major Yang had no reason to apologize. He was a hero. We were proud to be sitting with him at the same table. Major Yang bowed and clasped his hands in the customary gesture of thanks. But he remained gloomy and morose for the rest of the evening. Auden tried to distract his thoughts by asking him about the future of the Communists, but without much success. 'If they will follow the three principles of Dr. Sun Yat-sen', he told us, 'we shall allow them. Otherwise they will have to be suppressed.' Fleming sat silently smoking and grinning. From time to time he punctuated the conversation in truly Chinese fashion with a resounding belch.

Next morning the noise outside our doors made all further attempts at sleep impossible. The hotel servants were emptying buckets of refuse on to the heads of the washerwomen squatting along the river bank. Yells and curses mingled with the clatter of the servants' feet, which

209

resembled the clumpings of a country dance. I went out on to the balcony, to find, to my amazement, Fleming still fast asleep. His pillow was a hard leather satchel, in which he carried his writing materials. He didn't wake up until we had nearly finished breakfast.

On the river a man was fishing from a boat with tame cormorants. The cormorants perched all round the gunwale of the boat, squawking and flapping their wings. They had short strings tied to their legs, but were quite free. We watched one of them fighting a free-lance kite for possession of a fish. Somebody told us that a well-trained cormorant costs as much as twenty-five dollars.

At half-past nine we started. There were two car-loads of us: A. W. Kao, Ching, Yang, and a young radio expert named Shien; T. Y. Liu, Fleming, and ourselves. There was a good deal of argument as to who should ride with whom—but we clung firmly to our pet and mascot, T. Y., pointing out that the others would then be able to talk Chinese amongst themselves.

Our first destination was the divisional headquarters near Hwei-chow, a charming house in a large garden which had once belonged to a famous historical scholar. Here we were offered biscuits and bowls of sweet warm milk, before beginning our morning strategy-lesson. Fleming was very conscientious about 'lessons'. He took exhaustive notes and made us feel ashamed of our laziness. Also, he knew enough Chinese to understand roughly what was being said. He protested, most impressively, when the translation failed to tally with the original. This, needless to say, put A. W. Kao on his mettle. His phraseology became increasingly schoolmasterish and pedantic.

In a building near by there was a Japanese prisoner, a

transport officer, who had been captured by Chinese irregulars. Driving behind the Japanese lines, he had had a motor accident, and the irregulars had caught him before he could escape. Presently he came in, shuffling between two guards—a tall, crop-haired man, dressed in Chinese uniform and clumsy football boots. He looked ill, and deeply depressed, but he answered our questions with great natural dignity. In civil life he had been a schoolmaster. He had been called up, at the outbreak of the war, to serve in a supply department. Asked who he thought would win, he replied tactfully that it depended on whose morale would last the longest.

T. Y. Liu was chiefly impressed by the prisoner's unusual height. (Even the smallest Chinese sneer at the Japanese as dwarfs.) 'I think', he said, 'that this man must be the Longfellow of Japan.' Today, T. Y. was in the highest possible spirits. When we had lost the way and stopped to wait for the others beside a stream, he lay down under a tree, curled up his legs and kicked—exactly, as Auden said, like the wizened little changeling baby in a fairy story. We roared with exaggerated laughter at his jokes, tickled him, pinched him, and deliberately misunderstood everything he said.

Near Yü-tsien we stopped to have dinner at another divisional headquarters. Swallows flitted round the carved beams of the temple courtyard. We drank Hsaio Shen wine, and a special brand of Tien-mu-shan tea—pale green shoots which barely flavoured the glasses of almost boiling water. A. W. Kao drew one of his sketch-maps and translated the commanding officer's statistics: 'In this village sixty per cent of the women have been adulted.' 'Along this line the Chinese forces will offend the Japanese.' In one engagement, he told us, there had been five hundred Japanese casualties and only eighty Chinese. 'Will you congratulate the Major-General', drawled Fleming, 'on such an excellent proportion?' We repeated our Chinese victory toast, and were brought water to rinse out our mouths with, after the wine. Along the edge of the courtyard ran a stone gutter into which you could spit or empty slops.

It was then decided to drive on a further ten miles to Tien-mu-shan, the road-head at the foot of the mountains. We could sleep at the hotel there—the proprietor was an old friend of Mr. T. Y. Liu—and cross the pass next day to army headquarters at Pao Fu Chun. From Pao Fu Chun it would be another day's journey to Meiki, which was said to be about forty Chinese *li* from the front lines.

At the road-head we were met by a party of soldiers, who led us up a path to the hotel through woods of pine and cedar, silent and strongly scented in the deep blue moonlight. Before the war Tien-mu-shan was a favourite summer resort. It was half-past ten when we arrived, but there was no question of going to bed. Mr. Wang, the proprietor, awaited us, fairly bursting with information. We sat down at once to our evening lessons.

Mr. Wang was the civil governor of six counties, and he had prepared an exhaustive report on the atrocities of the Japanese against the civilian population. In Mr. Wang's area eighty per cent of the houses had been burnt. Out of 1,100 houses in Siaofeng only 200 remained. Out of 2,800 in Tsinan only 3. Three thousand civilians had been killed during the past four months. Children were being kidnapped by the Japanese and sent to Shanghai— for forced labour or the brothels. Out of 110,000 refugees only ten per cent had been able to leave the district. The rest were returning, where possible, to their ruined homes, with money from the Government to buy seeds for the spring sowing. If they belonged to areas occupied by the Japanese they would be given work—either in repairing the roads or in their own handicrafts.

The guerrilla units—known as the Red Spears—were very active in this province. The Japanese had tried to counteract their influence and confuse the political sympathies of the peasants by organizing a rival force, called the Fish Spears. The Fish Spears were not being a success, however. So far, they had enrolled only a hundred members.

On this front the Japanese advance-guard was living, literally, in a state of siege. The troops could only venture out from their strongholds in large bodies, or they ran the risk of ambush. A seventeen-year-old Red Spear had caught ten enemy soldiers drinking in a cottage and killed them all with a sword. A peasant named Da Man had been ordered by a Japanese officer to guide him back to his unit. To reach the unit it was necessary to ford a river; the officer told Da Man to carry him across on his back. In mid stream Da Man threw the officer into the water and bashed his head in with a stone. 'Oh, jolly good!' exclaimed Fleming, politely assuming the tone of one who applauds a record high jump or a pretty drive to leg.

We got up at five o'clock next morning and went down to an ample but unappetising breakfast of chicken and warm lager beer. As a rule the Chinese do not carve a chicken, they chop it transversely into slices, so that even the tiniest morsel contains a fragment of bone.

After breakfast the coolies came round with carrying-chairs mounted on long bamboo poles. A. W. Kao an-

213

nounced, in advance, that he would never make use of the chairs: 'My psychology does not allow me to do so.' For the moment, in any case, everybody was prepared to walk. Fleming supervised our departure with his customary efficiency. One saw his life, at that moment, as a succession of such startings-out in the dawn. He stood pulling at his pipe, giving orders to the coolies, tying up loose ends, adjusting the weight of bags, encouraging each member of the party with a joke or a word. At the bottom of the path the horses were waiting. We said good-bye to Major Yang, who had decided not to accompany us. He was afraid of straining his newly-healed wounds.

The way up the pass was no more than a winding mule-track, very steep in places, and slippery with mud from mountain streams. Far below us the torrent rushed over the boulders. Lizards with blue tails flickered across the path and there were dragon-flies and tiger-beetles, turquoise and viridian. Fleming eyed the copses for signs of game and delighted us by exclaiming: 'How I wish I had a rook-rifle!' Our preliminary defensive attitude towards him—a blend of anti-Etonianism and professional jealousy—had now been altogether abandoned. He, on his side, confessed to a relief that we weren't hundred per cent ideologists: 'I'd expected you two to be much more passionate.' Laughing and perspiring we scrambled uphill; the Fleming Legend accompanying us like a distorted shadow. Auden and I recited passages from an imaginary travel-book called 'With Fleming to the Front'.

Near the top of the pass we stopped to rest at a farmhouse. Auden went inside and came bounding out again with loud cries of dismay, nearly knocking over an old woman. 'My God!' he exclaimed. 'It's full of bees!' The old woman was astonished and angry at his behaviour—

neither she nor the rest of the family seemed to mind the bees at all. She hobbled off, muttering to herself. 'If we'd been Japanese', I told Auden, 'this could be turned into a first-class atrocity story.'

Because of the bees we had to sit outside in the hot sun drinking bowls of icy spring-water, and eating bean-cakes. The water tasted delicious. It was the first we had drunk, unboiled, since we entered China.

At the summit of the pass, which is 4,000 feet high, we stopped again and waited for the others to catch up with us. The long climb, like Life, had strung them out. Already it was possible to predict how they would behave during the rest of the journey. A. W. Kao and Shien, the radio-expert, were wiry and tough; T. Y. Liu and Ching were going to be the lame ducks. T. Y., who had told us yesterday that he could walk a hundred *li* a day, was now complaining that he hadn't slept well, and that a horse had trodden on his foot. He sat sulkily huddled in one of the chairs, his yellow goblin face shrunken to a pair of cheek-bones and a pout of misery. A. W. Kao was unsympathetic. 'A horse trod on *my* foot, too,' he said scornfully, 'but *I* don't mind!' Poor Ching was too exhausted to be able to utter a word. He had plodded all the way on foot and looked as if he had lost pounds of weight already. Fleming, seeing his distress, suggested that he should give up the march and return to Tien-mu-shan on one of the horses. This he indignantly refused.

On our way down the other side of the pass Auden and I tried riding in the chairs. But this was nearly as tiring as walking, for our bearers were obliged to tilt us at such acute angles, as they stepped expertly down from rock to rock, that we had to strain every muscle to prevent ourselves from falling out. So we took to our feet again. At about half-past three that afternoon we limped into Pao Fu Chun, the beautiful little village at the foot of the gorge, standing among trees beside the stream.

Army headquarters were in the old temple with its cool white courtyards and elaborately-carved wooden pillars. Fleming, who had outwalked us all, sat chatting and drinking tea with the General and his Chief of Staff. He was the only one of us who had covered every yard of the distance on foot, and he looked as fresh and sleek as ever.

Auden, as was hardly surprising, felt tired and ill. The tea and warm rice-wine, which we now drank on empty stomachs, were altogether too much for him. When the orderlies brought supper he rushed out of doors to be sick. Throughout the meal he sat pale and shuddering, with eyes averted from a dish of small, blanched, slippery creatures which stood in the middle of the table. 'It's those dreadful *efts*,' he muttered. 'I daren't look at them, or I shall do it again.' The General, unaware of what was wrong, repeatedly pressed Auden to taste the 'efts'. Auden, with a smile of polite agony, refused to do so. He spent the rest of supper with a handkerchief stuffed into his mouth.

After the meal we were all eager for bed. But, as we were undressing, A. W. Kao came to announce that the 'Anti-Japanese Corpse' of Siaofeng had arrived to give us details of the Japanese atrocities in their town. So we struggled wearily into our clothes and went out to greet them—six men and a woman, all wearing their best clothes, and lined up, as Auden said, like a village choir.

Siaofeng had been occupied by the Japanese three times: in December, in February, and in March. When the regular Chinese troops had been forced to retire the local anti-Japanese corps had remained. Apparently harmless

216

farmers and peasants, they were, in reality, dangerous enemies of the invader. They had a highly-organized intelligence service, which co-operated with the Chinese General Staff. At night the Japanese were sniped at (for the irregulars had hidden stores of arms), bridges were blown up, cars were damaged. The Japanese, of course, had made terrible reprisals. Whole villages had been burnt. There had been mass-executions of men, women, and children.

When the Siaofeng delegates went on to speak of the decay of Japanese morale they were less convincing. Here, as elsewhere, we had the impression that the Chinese were merely saying what they themselves wished to believe. Ten Japanese soldiers had committed suicide in a temple. No doubt. But suicide proves nothing. It is the national reaction to all life's troubles—an officer's reprimand, a love-affair gone wrong, a quarrel, a snub. Twenty Japs had been seen by a peasant sitting round a fire in a wood. 'They looked very sad, and one of them said: "I am tired of this war." ' But were there ever any soldiers anywhere who didn't grumble, since the days of Julius Caesar?

While we were listening, Fleming passed me a piece of paper. It was a memorandum, drawn up in the best Foreign Office style, tactfully suggesting that our expedition should be split up into two parties—those who wished to push on to Meiki and reach the front as quickly as possible, and those who were more interested in investigating the civilian problems in the rear. By this means Fleming hoped to save the faces of T. Y. Liu and Ching, and to speed up our march. We all signed the memorandum and agreed that it should be shown to the others as soon as the meeting was over.

But the memorandum wasn't altogether a success. T. Y. Liu was offended. Nothing, he protested, would induce him to forget his 'Chinese Duty' of accompanying Auden and myself, if necessary, into the jaws of death. A. W. Kao was catty. (He still continued, despite our protests, to address Fleming as 'Mr. Framing' and myself as 'Mr. Isherman'—which, for some obscure psychological reason, annoyed me enormously.) Ching was in frank despair. He claimed that he had a weak heart, and ought never to have come, but he wouldn't agree to travel more slowly than the rest of us. Perhaps he feared that the news of his failure would somehow reach Hankow. Only Shien, as ever, remained placid and cheerful. He was the youngest member of the party, and had a gay, charming disposition. He spoke very little but giggled quietly to himself.

Our camp-beds were left behind in the car at Tien-mu-shan. Tonight we had to sleep on planks. Auden and I soon settled down uncomfortably enough, but, for Fleming, the day wasn't over. Opening his typewriter, he started work on a long dispatch. We fell asleep to the tireless rattle of the keys.

The first light woke us, striking down into the courtyard round which we were sleeping. Somewhere in the woods behind the temple a bird mockingly repeated four distinct notes. Auden said that they meant 'All men are fools.' He was still feeling tired and unwell.

Fleming (whom we now addressed, with the brand of humour only permissible on walking-tours, as 'Frame-Up') had taken Ching aside for a short but firm talk. He now announced to us all: 'Mr. Ching has been very heroically concealing a weak heart. I have persuaded him, much against his will, to return to Tien-mu-shan. We all sympathize with him in his disappointment, knowing how keen he was to get to the front.' So honour was satisfied. Mr. Ching started off up the pass, accompanied by one of the chairs. The rest of us walked into the village, where extra horses and chairs were waiting. In Ching's place, an officer from headquarters was to accompany us to the front. An elderly, cheerful man, he was referred to, somewhat cryptically, as 'the Business Master'. As we set off, Fleming told us: 'I have a bullet for the woman in the shape of a bottle of whisky.'

Walking and riding along the valley we reached Siaofeng. Outside the town the Mayor was waiting to receive us. The local ambulance corps lined the road and stood to attention as we passed. The Mayor led us through street after street of ruins; a wilderness of brick-heaps and rubbish, as hopeless as an unsolved jig-saw puzzle. The streets were crowded, now, to welcome our party, and everybody seemed lively and gay. Business was being carried on as usual. All around the little town the fields were being cultivated; the fertile countryside was in strange contrast to the desolation within. The Mayor told us that the Japanese had special burning-squads, who carried out their work carefully and systematically. Perhaps for this reason there were few actual signs of fire. The buildings simply looked smashed.

After a second breakfast we pushed on again along what looked like an unfinished motor-road, now overgrown with grass. At a booth near the city an old woman was selling food, tea, and cigarettes. T. Y. Liu warned us against a certain brand of cigarettes called *Pirates*. Some consignments of them were said to have been poisoned by the Japanese. Auden, the ever-inquisitive, immediately bought a packet. We both smoked them but neither suf-

219

fered any bad results. (The poisoning story was probably
nonsense, anyway. But we had already heard, on much
better authority, that the Japanese had poisoned several
junk-loads of salt, destined for a district near the south-
eastern front.)

Ti-pu, our next stopping-place, was more badly damaged, even, than Siaofeng. Nevertheless, I was able to buy
a pair of socks. My feet, by this time, were covered with
blisters, and I was glad when my turn came to ride one of
the fat, obstinate little horses. The horses knew what was
before them, it seemed. Nothing would induce them to
hurry. They were saving their strength.

Beyond Ti-pu the road shrank to a narrow flagged path
winding through rice-fields and dense bamboo groves.
Thin rain began to fall. Strings of peasants passed us in
single file, heavily burdened with their household goods,
making their slow way back towards safety. Now and
then we met wounded, carried on rough bamboo litters,
who regarded us with bloodshot incurious eyes. We began
to have that ominous, oppressive feeling experienced by
travellers who are going alone in the wrong, unpopular
direction—towards a glacier or a desert. I strained my
ears for the first sound of the guns.

But we were still a long way from the lines. At four
o'clock we reached Anchi. Here hardly more than a dozen
houses remained standing. In one of them the Mayor received us. We sat in his bedroom drinking Chinese gin.
The gin was of terrific strength. It was exactly what we
needed to get us over the last lap of our day's journey, for
the rain was now falling in torrents.

At five o'clock we set out again. I rode ahead, with
A. W. Kao, Shien, and the 'Business Master'. Drunk and
drenched to the skin, we shouted to each other, sang, and

joked. Later, turning maudlin, I sentimentally embraced my horse and told it, in German, the story of my life. In no time, it seemed, we were crossing the slippery, high-arched pack-bridge which spans the river just outside Meiki.

On the outskirts of the town a little group of people stood waiting under umbrellas in the downpour. They were supporting a banner on which was printed the English word 'Welcome'. Like deliverers we rode slowly down the waterlogged street. Meiki seemed comparatively undamaged. The population crowded in the doorways, grinned and stared. Many saluted.

We were shown upstairs to a candle-lit room, with a charcoal brazier, round which we could strip and get dry. Later, we were told, uniforms would be brought into which we could change. Meanwhile, the steam from our clothes and naked bodies made the atmosphere as thick as a Turkish bath. Presently Auden and Fleming arrived. They had walked the whole way, deep in an argument about Soviet Russia. They were in the highest of spirits and muddy from head to foot. In fact, everybody was cheerful except T. Y. Liu, who had ridden in a covered chair and hadn't got wet at all. We made a mock fuss of him but failed to brighten him up. He sat curled on a stool, pouting and groaning.

The news was vague and bad. The divisional commander was too busy to see us. He would try to come round later. He had telephoned through to Anchi that afternoon, only to find that we had started an hour before. He had wished to prevent our leaving Anchi, for Meiki was already in danger. The Japanese had suddenly attacked from the direction of Hu-chow, and heavy fighting was going on only twenty-five *li* away.

We waited. At last the commander himself appeared. Although very polite he couldn't conceal his dismay at our presence. We were tiresomely notorious foreigners, who might add to his responsibilities by getting killed. Our proper place was on a platform in London—not here, amongst exhausted and overworked officers and officials. We might have to leave, he warned us, in the middle of the night. The evacuation of the civilian population had started already. Touched, and rather ashamed of myself, I thought of those men and women who had wasted their last precious hours of safety, waiting to welcome us with their banner in the rain. The promised uniforms never arrived, and our luggage was too wet to unpack. A soldier brought blankets. We threw ourselves on to the plank beds and tried to sleep, while soldiers installed a field-telephone in case headquarters had to warn us of an emergency.

Soon after midnight I was startled out of an uneasy, drunken doze to see three of these soldiers disappearing into the room where Fleming was lying. When they came out again a moment later I was too fuddled to be certain whether or not Peter was with them. The bastard, I thought soggily, he's sneaking off to visit the front without telling us. Or maybe the Japs are here. Anyhow, I was too lazy to care. So I dozed off again to the sound of falling rain, the creaking of the old wooden house, the endless gossiping murmur of soldiers round the fire in the neighbouring room.

When I woke again about 4 a.m., it was still pitch dark. The Chinese were getting up. The brazier had gone out. Paddling across the wet floor we searched wretchedly by candle- and match-light for our clothes. My trousers were still soaked, my shirt had a large burn on the front—it had lain too near the coals—my shoes were shrunken and stiff with mud. The others were no better off, though the Chinese had plenty of dry clothes to change into, and their hairless faces looked fresh and clean beside our own dirty stubble beards. Auden stole A. W. Kao's stockings. Peter doggedly prised open his drenched suède shoes. Slightly hysterical after this, our third night of insufficient sleep, we laughed and joked at the doleful T. Y.'s expense. 'T. Y., art tha sleeping there below?' A. W. Kao, meanwhile, was telephoning to divisional headquarters. After grinding at the instrument for some minutes like a coffee-machine, he extracted a few grains of the blackest possible news. The general couldn't see us. He was too busy to make any statement. We were to leave immediately.

'Not without our breakfasts,' said Fleming firmly. To Auden and myself he whispered that such delaying tactics gave us our only possible chance of seeing anything at all. T. Y. Liu announced that he would leave Meiki at once by chair. He hadn't slept for a fortnight. He was very ill indeed.

But was there any breakfast to be had? The whole house seemed to have gone suddenly dead. Only a couple of orderlies, fidgeting at the door, remained unwillingly at our disposal. Following Peter's cue, we continued to demand food, and an interview with some responsible staff officer, until even A. W. Kao, who was certainly no coward, began to look a trifle green. Divisional headquarters, he told us, would soon be retiring to Anchi: we could speak to the general there. The Japanese were now only ten *li* away from the town. They would probably attack as soon as it got light.

It did get light. Still we dawdled. I began to feel exceedingly uncomfortable. T. Y. Liu had already left, and there was a rumour that all the horses and chairs had followed him. At half-past seven a little food was reluctantly brought: we ate it with obstinate deliberation. Meanwhile Peter held forth, for the benefit of A. W. Kao, on the waste of his valuable time, *The Times*'s time, in visiting this front, where one saw nothing and where all information was withheld. A. W. was only too easily drawn by this kind of teasing; he controlled his temper and his impatience with difficulty. I wondered what would have happened, by this evening, to the handsome furniture of the upper rooms, and discussed, with Auden, the ethics of pocketing a pair of jade animals to save them from the fate worse than death.

By eight o'clock we had finished eating. There was nothing to do but leave. It was a grey, lowering morning. My feet were so painful that I could barely hobble along the streets: despite the evacuation order there were plenty of people still about. They regarded our bedraggled departure quietly. I felt like the last, lame, ship-deserting rat. A few civilians tried to propitiate Fleming with a promise of some 'unofficial information'—but this consisted only in showing him a couple of soaked newspapers on a ruined wall.

The chairs and horses had waited for us after all. I got on to my little brown pony, which seemed nearly as tired as I was, and away we plodded, along the muddy, straggling field-paths. The whole countryside was sodden like a sponge. The clouds were low over the hills, with occasional streaks of sunshine. It was stuffy and warm. Away behind Meiki, we heard sudden bursts of gunfire. The atmosphere of retreat, coupled with our hangovers, depressed us all—all except Peter, who marched indefatigably ahead, with his tireless, springy stride, puffing at his pipe. He was smoking a cheap brand of Chinese tobacco which smelt, as he himself said, like the burning hair of an old actor's wig.

A. W. Kao had insisted, with some show of reason, that the fall of Meiki—if Meiki did fall—would be unimportant and even strategically advisable: the Japs were to be lured down into the valley and destroyed there by the time-honoured pincer-movement. But nowhere along the whole route did we see any evidences of serious military preparation. We met hardly any troops, except city guards and the wounded.

We got to Anchi about ten o'clock. T. Y. Liu had already arrived. A. W. Kao had proposed staying there to await developments, but it now appeared that the authorities, although most hospitable, were anxious to pass us still further back. The divisional commander had telephoned from Meiki, requesting our immediate evacuation. Our whole party was against this. A. W. Kao pointed out that we couldn't ask the coolies to go on. They had stayed up the whole night, having been warned that we might wish to start at any moment. T. Y. Liu was even more emphatic. If he didn't get some rest, he said, he would be seriously ill, and he curled up to sleep on somebody else's bed.

A. W. had now become very portentous and secretive. He had long conferences with the Mayor. It was evident that he was getting information which he wouldn't transmit. Peter retaliated with semi-humorous bullying: 'All this reticence is creating a most deplorable impression, Mr. Liu. It's quite obvious that the Chinese have been defeated.' 'No, not defeated,' A. W. pedantically insisted. 'This is a strategic withdrawal.'

The authorities now played a new card. The weather,

225

they pointed out, was clearing; the Japanese aeroplanes were therefore to be expected, and the municipal offices —clearly visible as one of the few buildings left standing among the ruins—would almost certainly be bombed. Immediately a party was formed—headed by T. Y. Liu— demanding instant evacuation. Peter teased them, re- minding T. Y. of his exhaustion and A. W. of his solicitude for the coolies' comfort. The coolies, needless to say, were roused at once. So off we started, after saying good-bye to the heroically placid Mayor, who was quietly awaiting yet another occupation of his town, and the probable destruction of its few remaining houses.

Auden and I now relapsed into the chairs. Fleming, with the flattering brutality of a born leader, had ex- tracted T. Y. from one of them and had even persuaded him to march at his side. We advanced by a shorter route through the lonely countryside. The coolies strode along, relieving each other with trained adroitness. We gazed at their bulging calves and straining thighs, and rehearsed every dishonest excuse for allowing ourselves to be carried by human beings: they are used to it, it's giving them employment, they don't feel. Oh no, they don't feel—but the lump on the back of that man's neck wasn't raised by drinking champagne, and his sweat remarkably resembles my own. Never mind, my feet hurt. I'm paying him, aren't I? Three times as much, in fact, as he'd get from a Chinese. Sentimentality helps no one. Why don't you walk? I can't, I tell you. You bloody well would if you'd got no cash. But I *have* got cash. Oh, dear. I'm so heavy.... Our coolies, unaware of these qualms, seemed to bear us no ill-will, however. At the road-side halts they even brought us cups of tea.

We arrived in Siaofeng well before dark, and were welcomed as warmly as on the previous morning. T. Y. Liu was very cocky: 'You see,' he told us, 'I am stronger than you!' A. W. Kao was full of excitement about an anecdote he had heard on the road: a woman had brewed tea and had sent out her little son to offer it, free, to passing soldiers. As Peter commented, it was significant of the former Chinese attitude to soldiers that this action should still be considered so remarkable.

After supper we were asked to address the Government employees and civilian volunteers on our impressions of the war zone. The audience stood to attention while we spoke. A. W. Kao translated.

The day ended with an argument about our future route. T. Y. wanted to get back to the road-head by the way we had come; A. W. wanted to make a detour which would involve a further three days' march. This time Peter and I supported T. Y. We got our own way—much to the relief of my own swollen feet.

Next morning we were told that Meiki had fallen. The Japanese had occupied it less than twelve hours after our departure.

We started at six in far higher spirits. Everybody had slept reasonably well, the weather was fine, and our horses could be urged into a smart trot. As they approached Pao Fu Chun (which they perhaps misguidedly believed to be the end of their day's journey) they even had bursts of cantering. There was the necessary spice of ill-feeling, *en route*, because T. Y. Liu had taken one of the chairs after we had offered them to a party of wounded soldiers.

At the temple we stopped for lessons. Or rather, we sat sulkily while A. W. Kao, the prize scholar, received private tuition—most of which, he told us loftily, he wasn't al-

227

lowed to pass on. He had met a colleague from his own paper, and the clique-atmosphere thickened. When our hosts offered us breakfast A. W. refused it without consulting us, and was rebuked by Peter. 'Surely', A. W. retorted, 'it is a matter of common sense that one does not require two breakfasts?' We protested that we did. A. W. said nothing, but went away for a specially private conference with a staff officer. Presently he returned. 'Is there any news?' Fleming asked. 'There is one piece of news', replied A. W., with a spiteful smile, 'which will interest you greatly: milk is being prepared, and some eggs.'

We started at ten o'clock for the long toil up the pass. I had bought some Chinese shoes in Pao Fu Chun which carried me like magic, and I set off on foot to overtake Peter, whom I found, at last, bathing his feet in the stream. Auden, he told me, was far ahead. Obeying some Nordic *Excelsior*-urge, he was racing, stripped to the waist, for the summit. He awaited us there, amidst a crowd of coolies, who were carrying boxes of ammunition over the mountain, down to Pao Fu Chun. The size and weight of the ammunition-boxes appalled us, but the coolies, with the worst half of their journey behind them, still seemed comparatively fresh. They greeted us gaily with friendly gestures and smiles. It was only later, when we had reached the first farmhouse on the other side of the pass, and were drinking tea, that A. W. Kao told us that the coolies had asked him whether we were Italians or White Russians. If so, they said, they would follow and arrest us. A. W. added, with some satisfaction, that T. Y. Liu had taken another route, a much more difficult one, on the advice of his chair-bearers, and had disappeared. Quite probably he had been robbed and murdered. We expressed more than mere polite concern at this news, for our coats and rucksacks were in the bottom of T. Y.'s chair.

My feet now collapsed utterly. The Chinese shoes had been too small, and I must have bruised my big toe on the rocks, for the toe-nail had turned quite black. I should have to take a chair down to the road-head. This was explained to the bearers (there were only two of them today) and they agreed, although passengers are not usually carried down the upper part of the path, which is narrow and very steep. What followed was quite absurdly alarming. The chair hung poised, for enormous moments, on. the strength of the front man's ankles. A cough or a sneeze, it seemed, would send all three of us headlong over the precipice. But my bearers had the balance of trained acrobats, and we got down to Tien-mu-shan without accident. On arrival I made them a speech of thanks, through A. W. Kao, and gave them a bonus. They seemed pleased and genuinely surprised.

The cars took us to Yü-tsien, a grubby, noisy little town, with a rat's nest of an hotel, where Mr. Ching, in a kimono, had been nursing his heart, and Major Yang his war-wounds and his complicated sense of honour. There was an air-raid alarm, to which nobody paid the least attention, and a crowded supper-party in our bedroom, where hatchets were buried in bowls of rice. T. Y. Liu, neither robbed nor murdered, cleared his reputation at enormous length: he hadn't taken the wounded soldiers' chairs, they had refused them; and he had walked *all* the way over the mountain. 'So you see', he concluded, 'I am not cruel at all.' T. Y. addressed A. W. as 'My dear brother'. Toasts were drunk. A. W. was thanked for his efficiency, Shien for his endurance, Peter for his leadership:

the examination results were published, and everybody came out equal top.

After supper Fleming, Auden, and I explained to A. W. Kao our views on Chinese propaganda. Atrocity stories, we told him, would make little impression on the West—people had heard too many of them already. And the decay of Japanese morale was a subject which was better left alone. A. W. listened carefully and thanked us. He seemed really anxious to get advice. We felt warmly towards him this evening. Whatever might be said against his manners he was certainly a person whom one could admire and respect. We said good night in a friendly spirit.

Good night, but not to sleep. A hand-drum operated by a night-watchman was followed by a mating cat, Mahjongg clatter, a rain-storm, door-slamming, a baby, a dog, and power-diving mosquitoes. In the morning I found that my underlip had swollen into a great flap of hard, hanging flesh. I amused myself by twisting it grotesquely to scare children who peeped through the door, but they only laughed at me. Auden had been bitten, too. We both reproached our Chief, who had promised, on the word of an explorer, that there would be no insects.

We left for Tunki at a fairly civilized hour. The hotel-boy who packed our things had solemnly poured the last drops from a cognac bottle over the bed, as though performing some magical rite. The journey was uneventful. T. Y. Liu, in wonderful spirits, told us: 'I am never sorry.' He spoke too soon, for presently he was sick. We stopped to get petrol near a restaurant where they were cooking bamboo in all its forms—including the strips used for making chairs. That, I thought, is so typical of this country. Nothing is specifically either eatable or uneatable. You could begin munching a hat, or bite a mouthful out of a wall; equally, you could build a hut with the food provided at lunch. Everything is everything.

We arrived at Tunki about midday. Our chief object in returning there had been to interview General Ku, but we couldn't. He had gone away, and no other member of the staff was available. The newspapers, we found, made no reference to the fall of Meiki.

At supper we drank cognac and began an argument on the meaning of the word Civilization. Had China anything to learn from the West? Peter thought not. 'The Chinese', he kept repeating, 'have got everything taped.' 'Surely', I protested, 'you can't pretend that the coolie is well off, in his present condition? Isn't he ever to hear Beethoven? Or see your wife act?' 'Oh,' said Peter airily, 'he's got them both pretty well taped.' Auden was more for providing the coolies with meals from a really good French restaurant. He had decided, finally, against Chinese food.

T. Y. Liu, Yang, Fleming, Auden, and I left Tunki early next morning for Kin-hwa. It had stopped raining, but the road was very soft and treacherous; the rivers we had to cross were all swollen. When we reached the last of them the ferrymen refused altogether to take the car over, so we had to make a detour which brought us into Kin-hwa on foot. It wasn't very far. Just outside the town there was a little amateur ferry over some flood-water, operated by small boys, who punted us in circles until some of the passengers snatched the poles from their hands and helped themselves.

Meanwhile T. Y. had run the whole gamut of his moods. Pre-vomitory sadness (Fleming and Auden had had undecided bets on whether he or Yang would be sick first) was followed by promises and apologies: 'I have tried to satisfy you. I will do everything possible to help you. It is my Chinese duty.' After we had passed the provincial border into Che-kiang he became rather haughty and showed us his seal with the official chop. But the walk from the ferry was too much for him: he relapsed into the blackest of sulks.

Peter, to our great regret, left Kin-hwa by train that same evening, for Nanchang. We had all three enjoyed our expedition together. As Auden said, summing it up: 'Well, we've been on a journey with Fleming in China, and now we're real travellers for ever and ever. We need never go farther than Brighton again.'

Two days later—this was May 20th—we were able to leave Kin-hwa by bus for Wenchow. The alternative route was closed because it seemed likely that the Japanese were about to attempt a landing near Ningpo. The municipal government, hospitable to the last, had arranged that the chief of police should accompany us. A soldier was sent to buy our tickets and reserve our seats on the bus.

At the bus station we said good-bye to Chiang and to T. Y. Liu. Chiang was returning to Hankow with a handsomely-worded testimonial in his pocket: it recommended him to all who wished to make a tour of the Chinese war-areas. T. Y. we presented with our three volumes of Motley, suitably inscribed. 'God bless you, my dear friends!' were his parting words.

The journey was unexciting. Ten miles out from Kin-hwa a Japanese aeroplane appeared, but showed no interest in our bus. At Lishui we were told that we should have to stop the night; a bridge farther down the road had been broken by floods and wouldn't be repaired till morning. We called on the Chief of Police, the city Governor, and the Canadian Catholic Mission. The Canadian Bishop, Monseigneur McGrath, gave us a copy of his book on mission-work in Che-kiang Province, *The Dragon at Close Range.*

The Catholic Fathers at Lishui had no hospital, only a dispensary and a school. There had been no serious air-raids here, they told us, so far; though the Japanese sometimes bombed the air-field. Once they had machine-gunned and killed a dog. On the whole life at the mission-station seemed very happy and pleasant. The countryside was beautiful: the younger and more athletic Fathers toured it on their bicycles. All of them were fond of a day's fishing. In the evenings they listened to the gramophone or played darts. They gave us whisky from Shanghai and American cigarettes.

It was interesting to notice, here as elsewhere, how the missionaries had modified their attitude since the war towards Communism and Communists in China. Two years ago, the Fathers themselves admitted, they had regarded the Communists simply as bandits—or, at best, as Robin Hoods, who robbed the rich to feed the poor. Now they were beginning to take the movement seriously, and to recognize the part it might play in determining the future development of the country.

One of the Fathers told us an extraordinary insect-story. A Chinese boy employed at the Mission had been stung by a centipede and was very ill. The Fathers could do nothing for him until their Chinese catechist produced a certain kind of spider which he had found crawling about the roof. This spider, he told them, would suck the poison from the boy's wound. And it did. When the spider had finished sucking, the catechist put it into a bowl of water so that it could eject the poison from its own body. The boy recovered immediately.

We stayed in Wenchow two days, on board the steamer which was to take us to Shanghai. Although Wenchow itself was still in Chinese hands the mouth of its river was guarded by the Japanese, and only vessels of friendly nationality were allowed to pass in and out unmolested. So the Chinese steamers had taken on foreign officers and got themselves denaturalized: some German, some Italian, some Portuguese. Our ship had been built in Hongkong and had certainly never been outside the China Seas: nevertheless, she was registered at Trieste, had acquired a new Italian name, and had exchanged her Norwegian captain for an Italian. The old captain remained on board, however, and continued to navigate in the tricky channels of the river mouths. He wore civilian clothes and was, officially, a passenger.

A cabin port-hole is a picture-frame. No sooner had we arrived on board than the brass-encircled view became romantic and false. The brown river in the rain, the boatmen in their dark bat-wing capes, the tree-crowned pagodas on the foreshore, the mountains scarved in mist—these were no longer features of the beautiful, prosaic country we had just left behind us; they were the scenery of the traveller's dream; they were the mysterious, *l'Extrême Orient*. Memory in the years to come would prefer this simple theatrical picture to all the subtle and chaotic impressions of the past months. This, I thought—despite all we have seen, heard, experienced—is how I shall finally remember China.

The time passed slowly and agreeably. Released from the tyranny of our journey, we indulged the minor vices, over-eating and over-sleeping. It was a luxury to allow oneself to feel mildly ill. Lounging against the rail we watched children playing on the wharf below. We amused ourselves by dropping coins and ten-cent notes on to the quayside, and waiting to see how long it would be before they were noticed and picked up. It was remarkable that hardly any of the children and dock-labourers who found the money looked up to see where it had come from— either because they feared it might be reclaimed, or from a natural piety which accepted all Heaven's gifts without question. One coin landed near a very dirty little boy of four or five years old—so near that it seemed certain he must have seen it. But, for a long time, he made absolutely no move, except to glance furtively to left and right. Then, very slowly, without ever looking downward, he worked the coin over the ground with his toe into a position from which he could pick it up. Having pocketed it he rose to his feet and toddled off with an air of extreme unconcern. The perfection of his technique—so matter-of-fact that it wasn't even sly—was one of the most shocking things I have ever seen in my life. It told the whole story of the coolie's animal struggle for existence.

The Norwegian ex-captain told us yarns of Spitsbergen, where he had once navigated the ice-breaker *Krassin*, and of his fights with Chinese pirates, as a customs officer, in Bias Bay. He and the Italian officers got on very well together. He played operatic airs on the piano in the saloon, and the Italian captain sang in a fine fruity tenor. He could also give a really marvellous imitation of a hen laying an egg. The Italian captain was one of those handsome, hook-nosed men who talk about women as if they were a kind of wine, or a choice brand of cigar.

On May 23rd we sailed down the river soon after lunch, but it was already dusk when we passed out of the estuary, skirting between the bald, lonely islands, behind which an armed Japanese transport-steamer was lurking, like a highway robber. The Japs signalled to us to ask where we were going. 'If they tell us to stop', said the Captain, 'I shall refuse.' 'But won't they fire on you?' Auden asked. The Italian laughed: 'I'd like to see the bastards try it! I should wireless to one of our warships. She could be here in two hours—and she'd send planes ahead of her.'

Somewhat to our regret, however, the Japanese allowed us to pass without further inquiry.

Two days later, when we had finished breakfast and come up on to the bridge, the ship was already steaming up the Whangpoo River. The Norwegian pointed out to us the ruins at Woosung, where the first fighting took place after the Japanese had made their landing. It was strange and shocking to see lorry-loads of Japanese soldiers moving along the river-bank, and to pass Japanese freighters and ferry-boats plying with the peaceful self-assurance of an enemy who had come to stay. The blood-spot flag, which we had last seen lying disgraced on the ground amidst the war-trophies at Tunki, now hit the eye brazenly from every angle, as it fluttered from the poles of buildings and ships. A Japanese aeroplane passed overhead, and it seemed unnatural and wrong that we didn't have to scamper for cover. In half an hour we should have reached Shanghai.

10

Shanghai. May 25–June 12

Seen from the river, towering above their couchant guardian warships, the semi-skyscrapers of the Bund present, impressively, the façade of a great city. But it is only a façade. The spirit which dumped them upon this unhealthy mud-bank, thousands of miles from their kind, has been too purely and brutally competitive. The biggest animals have pushed their way down to the brink of the water; behind them is a sordid and shabby mob of smaller buildings. Nowhere a fine avenue, a spacious park, an imposing central square. Nowhere anything civic at all.

Nevertheless the tired or lustful business man will find here everything to gratify his desires. You can buy an electric razor, or a French dinner, or a well-cut suit. You can dance at the Tower Restaurant on the roof of the Cathay Hotel, and gossip with Freddy Kaufmann, its charming manager, about the European aristocracy or pre-Hitler Berlin. You can attend race-meetings, baseball games, football matches. You can see the latest American films. If you want girls, or boys, you can have them, at all prices, in the bath-houses and the brothels. If you want opium you can smoke it in the best company, served on a tray, like afternoon tea. Good wine is difficult to obtain in this climate, but there is enough whisky and gin to float a fleet of battleships. The jeweller and the antique-dealer await

237

your orders, and their charges will make you imagine yourself back on Fifth Avenue or in Bond Street. Finally, if you ever repent, there are churches and chapels of all denominations.

We ourselves have alighted on one of the topmost branches of the social tree: we are staying at the British Ambassador's private villa in the French Concession. This villa is the property of an important shipping firm. It is known as their Number One House. Cream-coloured and eminently proconsular, with cool solid Corinthian porticoes, it stands calmly in a big garden of shaven lawns and Empire Exhibition flower-beds. Everything is in perfect working-order and modelled to scale. There is a limousine full of petrol in the garage, complete with a real live chauffeur, wearing white cotton gloves. There are Settlement police to guard the front gate, correctly equipped down to the last detail. There are Chinese servants who can say 'Your Excellency', and bow from the waist. On special occasions they wear coats of lemon-coloured silk. All the doors open and shut, the telephone rings, and the bath-taps turn on and off.

The Ambassador and Lady Kerr are, like ourselves, perfect strangers in this life-size doll's house. It will continue to function years after we are all dead. Nevertheless, they play up splendidly—returning the salutes of the guards at the gate, changing their clothes at the right hours, accepting the food and the service with fine nonchalance. It is only occasionally that one takes them unawares, resting for a moment in the lemon and cream drawing-room amidst the vases and lacquered screens, between tea with the Dutch Ambassador and dinner with the Naval Attaché, and realizes that they are an ordinary married couple, tired and not always in the best of health, who rely profoundly upon each other's intuitions and moods. Lady Kerr reads detective stories. Sir Archibald owns thirty-two pipes. They are the only objects in this vast museum which seem really and intimately to belong to him.

It is the Ambassador's turn to give an official garden-party. The preparations are elaborate. They require the co-operation of the ladies of the British colony, the Seaforth Highlanders, the Embassy staff. Invitations are sent out. The drinks and the cold buffet are organized. The portico is decorated with flags. Bowing deeply, the doll-butlers usher in their national enemies, the bandy-legged, hissing Japanese generals. Everybody is present, including the journalists. Next morning, the local newspapers will carry photographs of the most distinguished guests. Out on the lawn the Scottish pipers play their airs.

Everything goes off like clockwork. It is a beautifully-contrived charade, the perfect image of another kind of life—projected, at considerable expense, from its source on the opposite side of the earth. Such functions, no doubt, are well worth the money they cost, for here and there, amidst the regulation small-talk, a serious word is exchanged, a delicate but pointed hint is dropped. This afternoon certain minute but important readjustments have been made in the exquisite balance of international relationships. At any rate, thank goodness, it hasn't rained.

But gaily as the charade-players laugh, and loudly as they chatter, they cannot altogether ignore those other, most undiplomatic sounds which reach us, at intervals, from beyond the garden trees. Somewhere out in the suburbs, machine-guns are rattling. You can hear them all day long. Everybody in the Settlement knows what they mean—the Chinese guerrilla units are still active here in the enemy's stronghold. But if you are so tactless as to call the attention of the Japanese officers to these noises they will reply that you are mistaken—it is only their own troops at firing-practice.

The International Settlement and the French Concession form an island, an oasis in the midst of the stark, frightful wilderness which was once the Chinese city. Your car crosses the Soochow Creek: on one side are streets and houses, swarming with life; on the other is a cratered and barren moon-landscape, intersected by empty, clean-swept roads. Here and there a Japanese sentry stands on guard, or a party of soldiers hunts among the ruins for scrap-iron. Further out, the buildings are not so badly damaged, but every Chinese or foreign property has been looted—and no kind of wild animal could have made half the mess. At Medhurst College, once a mission-school in the Ling-Ping Road, books and pictures have been torn up, electric-light bulbs smashed, wash-basins wrecked. On the fringes of the city civilians are still living; one hears many stories of their ill-treatment at the hands of the Japanese. Out driving one day we noticed two soldiers with drawn bayonets prodding at a crowd of women and children. We stopped. Here, we thought, was a chance of witnessing an atrocity at first hand. Then we saw a third soldier, holding a basket. The Japanese, in their own inimitably ungracious way, were distributing food.

Like formidable, excluded watchdogs, the real masters of Shanghai inhabit the dark, deserted Japanese Concession, or roam the lunar wilderness of Chapei, looking hungrily in upon the lighted populous international town. On Garden Bridge their surly sentries force every Chinese foot-passenger to raise his hat in salute. Incidents are of weekly occurrence: a foreign lady is insulted, an innocent naturalist is arrested as a spy. Representations are made 'through the proper channels'; apologies are gravely offered and accepted.

Inside the Settlement, too, an underground, deadly political struggle is going on. The Japanese never cease their intrigues to form a puppet-government which is, one day, to rule China under their orders. Blackmail and bribes coerce or tempt a few prominent Chinese to negotiate with the enemy, but the would-be traitors seldom live long enough to be of much use to their new masters, for patriotic terrorists are always on the alert. Going into the Cathay Hotel one morning for a cup of coffee, we found a little crowd round the entrance gazing at a pool of blood. A Chinese business man, notorious for his pro-Japanese sympathies, had been leaving the building when he was fired at by gunmen: his White Russian bodyguard had shot back, and a battle followed, in which several people were killed. The business man himself had been badly wounded in the throat. Next time, most probably, he won't escape alive.

The perimeter of the international town is guarded by a mixed force of foreign troops. The defence sector allotted to the Seaforth Highlanders runs north from Soo-chow Creek to the railway station; going round their pill-boxes and sentry-posts one gets some idea of the extraordinary position in which the British troops found themselves last winter during the attack on Shanghai. The direct line of advance lay through the international zone, and neither the Japanese nor the Chinese would believe that the British weren't going to let the enemy cross it to turn their flank. So they opened fire on each other across the corners of the defence sector, and the British soldiers, right in the line of the shooting, were often unable to leave their pill-boxes for twenty-four hours at a stretch. The walls of all the posts are dented with bullet-marks.

The Shanghai fighting culminated in the rearguard action fought by the 'Doomed Battalion', which was occupying the Chinese Mint Godown, to the west of the Thibet Road bridge. The British General, Telfer-Smollett, saw that if the Chinese persisted in holding the Godown some of the Japanese shells were certain to explode across the creek, in Soochow Road and beyond, so he urged their evacuation. The Chinese commander replied that he could evacuate only under direct orders from the Generalissimo himself. Madame Chiang was first approached. 'No,' she said, 'they must die that China may live.' But General Telfer-Smollett persisted, and the Generalissimo at length agreed that the battalion should be withdrawn. The Japanese were also willing, for the Mint Godown commanded their flank, and its resistance was holding up their advance.

A night was fixed for the withdrawal of the Chinese troops into the International Concession. The telephone lines to the Godown and to the Japanese headquarters had not been broken, so Telfer-Smollett was able to keep in constant communication with both sides. At the last moment the Japanese rang up to say that they refused to guarantee the safe passage of the battalion: they were angry because the Chinese had continued to fire all through the afternoon and had inflicted serious losses. So they trained their machine-guns and searchlights down the Thibet road, which the evacuating troops would have to cross to reach the international zone. At the end of the road, beside the bridge, stood a British pill-box, directly in the line of fire.

General Telfer-Smollett came, with his staff, to superintend the withdrawal personally. He was taking cover behind the Bank of China Godown on the opposite side of the road, and here he received the Chinese, as they dashed across into safety. The Japanese fired all their machine-guns at once: the Chinese got their chance of escape while the guns were being reloaded. Eventually the entire battalion was able to withdraw, bringing its weapons and ammunition, with the loss of only seven men. Some people will tell you that the British troops in their pill-box, tired of being shot at, returned the Japanese fire, and even put a machine-gun out of action. This is officially denied. Anyhow, the Japanese, in the darkness and confusion, could hardly be certain where the bullets were coming from. The battalion, in accordance with a previous agreement, was interned in the International Settlement and will remain there until the end of the war.

Here we were, sitting down to lunch with four Japanese civilians in the dining-room of the Shanghai Club. This lunch had been arranged for us by a prominent British business man—and, of course, we agreed in advance, we should do nothing to embarrass or compromise our host. We would both be very tactful indeed. To make any reference, however indirect, to the war would, we felt, be positively indecent.

Fortified by a drink at the Long Bar (needless to say, it proved to be far shorter than we had expected) we advanced to meet our fellow-guests. The four Japanese were all distinguished personages—a consular official, a business man, a banker, and a railway director. The consular official was smooth-faced, and looked rather Chinese; the others gave us the collective impression of being stumpy, dark brown, bespectacled, moustached, grinning and very neat.

The Japanese, evidently, did not share our scruples: 'You have been travelling in China?' asked one of them, straight away. 'How interesting. . . . I hope you had no inconvenience?' 'Only from your aeroplanes,' I replied, forgetting our resolutions. The Japanese laughed heartily: this was a great joke. 'But surely', they persisted, 'you must have found the transport and living conditions very primitive, very inefficient?' 'On the contrary,' we assured them, 'extremely efficient. Kindness and politeness everywhere. Everybody was charming.' 'Oh yes,' the consular official agreed in an indulgent tone, 'the Chinese are certainly charming. Such nice people. What a pity. . . .' 'Yes, what a pity!' the others chimed in: 'This war could so easily have been avoided. Our demands were very reasonable. In the past we were always able to negotiate these problems amicably. The statesmen of the old school—you could deal with *them*, they understood the art of compromise. But these younger men, they're dreadfully hotheaded. Most unfortunate—' 'You know,' continued the consular official, 'we really love the Chinese. That is the nice thing about this war. There is no bitterness. We in Japan feel absolutely no bitterness towards the Chinese People.' This was really a little too much. The last remnants of our prearranged politeness disappeared. It was hardly surprising, we retorted, with some heat, that the Japanese didn't feel bitter. Why should they? Had they ever had their towns burnt and their women raped? Had they ever been bombed? Our four gentlemen had no answer ready. They merely blinked. They didn't appear in the least offended, however. Then one of them said: 'That is certainly a most interesting point of view.'

They wanted to know about the morale in Hankow. Was there much enthusiasm? Enormous enthusiasm, we replied. What chances were there of a negotiated peace? None, we declared, with spiteful relish—Chiang would continue to resist, if necessary, to the borders of Thibet. The Japanese shook their heads sadly, and drew in their breath with a sharp disappointed hiss. It was a pity . . . a great pity. . . . And then—as we had been expecting—out came the Bolshevik Bogey. Japan was really fighting on China's side—to save her from herself, to protect her from the red menace. 'And from Western trade competition,' we might have added, but it wasn't necessary. For, at this moment, through the dining-room window which overlooked the river, the gun-turrets of H.M.S. *Birmingham* slid quietly into view, moving upstream. In this city the visual statements of power-politics are more brutal than any words. The Japanese had followed the direction of our eyes. Lunch ended in a moment of thoughtful and slightly embarrassed silence.

Mr. Rewi Alley is a factory inspector and official of the Public Works Department—a stocky New Zealander with light cropped ginger hair and a short rugged nose. For seven years he has been working to improve conditions in the hundreds of Chinese factories around Hongkew—and now everything is wrecked. The Japanese have destroyed seventy per cent of China's industry. Some of the luckier concerns have been able to crowd into the International Settlement, and reopen there. Most of these factories are very small—two or three rooms crammed with machinery and operatives. The majority of the operatives

245

are young boys who have been bought from their parents outright for twenty dollars: they work from twelve to fourteen hours a day. Their only wages are their food, and a sleeping-space in a loft above the work-room. There are no precautions whatever against accident or injury to health. In the accumulator factories, half the children have already the blue line in their gums which is a symptom of lead-poisoning. Few of them will survive longer than a year or eighteen months. In scissors factories you can see arms and legs developing chromium-holes. There are silk-winding mills so full of steam that the fingers of the mill-girls are white with fungus growths. If the children slacken in their work the overseers often plunge their elbows into the boiling water as a punishment. There is a cotton mill where the dust in the air makes T.B. almost a certainty. Alley has had its owner into court three times but he has always managed to square the judge. Accidents are invariably found to be due to the carelessness of the workers involved. There is no compensation and no insurance.

Before the war industrial conditions, though still very bad, were slowly improving. Now the destruction of so much plant has created enormous supplies of surplus labour. (In the silk factory, for example, women's wages have fallen from thirty to twenty cents a day.) The Japanese, in Alley's opinion, will exploit the Shanghai workers even more brutally than the Chinese owners have exploited them in the past. They will flood the markets with cheap goods and so gradually lower working-class standards of living all over the world.

If you tire of inspecting one kind of misery there are plenty of others. Refugee camps, for instance—triple tiers of shelves under a straw roof. These hovels would disgrace the dirtiest Chinese village. On each shelf lives, cooks, eats, and sleeps an entire family. A single hut will hold about five hundred people. There is often only one source of water-supply for a whole camp, a fire-hose main in the street: the queue to it reaches into dozens all day long.

Since the Japanese occupation of the outer city, the International Settlement has been dangerously overcrowded. There is no restriction on sub-letting: the minimum sleeping-space on a floor may cost one dollar sixty cents a month. When the British wished to clear a single street a hundred yards long for defensive purposes they were told that this would mean evicting fourteen thousand people. Under present conditions Alley estimates that forty thousand refugee children must die during the next twelve months from under-nourishment and epidemics. Cholera has started in Shanghai already.

Then there is the problem of the rickshaw-coolies. Their standard of life is hardly better than that of the refugees themselves. The profession is recruited chiefly from the country boys who leave their homes and come to Shanghai because they have been told that it is a 'gold- and silver-making place'. The number of rickshaws in the International Settlement is limited to ten thousand. You can buy a rickshaw for fifty to seventy dollars. Then you must register it. The registration-plate costs, officially, five dollars. But these plates, being limited in number and absolutely essential, change hands many times, always at a profit. They have been known to fetch five hundred dollars apiece. The rickshaw-owner hires out his machines to the coolies at the rate of seventy cents a day. (Often a rickshaw is operated by two coolies working on alternate days.) The war has hit the rickshaw trade severely. The midnight curfew has reduced the number of business hours, and the Japanese occupation has restricted the area of traffic—for no rickshaw can now pass the limits of the international zone. The coolie may expect a profit of from thirty to sixty cents: this, if he is sharing his rickshaw, must keep him alive for two days. Often he is unlucky; his registration-plate or his pawn-tickets are stolen or he gets into trouble with the police over some traffic regulation and is fined. Having no reserves it is nearly impossible for him to make good these losses. So he sinks further and further into debt. As one coolie told a Chinese worker who was taking us round the slums: 'Our life seems to be fastened down with live hooks.'

During the past few years, however, something has been done to help the coolies. Four rickshaw-pullers' mutual aid centres have been started in Shanghai. At these centres they can rest, drink tea, have a bath and get medical attention. They are run by the Municipal Council. Each coolie pays five cents a day for his membership. He gives the money to his rickshaw-owner, from whom the Council collects it.

Tucked away in unobtrusive corners, unnoticed and almost forgotten, are the crippled remains of the soldiers who fought to defend Shanghai. We have visited one such hospital with Alley: all its patients have lost an arm or a leg. They are being taught simple trades—soap-making, stocking-knitting, or the manufacture of crude artificial limbs; but the chief doctor, a missionary, doesn't approve of education and tries to get them sent away before they can learn much. Most of them, if they recover, have no future but begging. All day long the unfortunate patients are pestered by Chinese evangelists, who lecture them, lay hands upon them, and try to persuade them to sing hymns. Without much success, however. The other day, we are told, the patients went on strike and tore up all their Bibles.

The soldiers were astonishingly cheerful, and all anxious to be photographed. One boy was a remarkable artist. He drew portraits and caricatures. He had fought in the 'Doomed Battalion'. His younger brother, he told us, had been eaten alive in Shan-si Province by a wolf.

The hospital authorities have circulated a questionnaire among the patients to discover their reasons for joining the army. The results are as follows:

Economic reasons	36
Economic reasons + admiration of military career	26
Patriotism	23
Family difficulties	23
Conscription	16
Homeless	9
Wish to suppress local bandits	7
Deceived by promises of reward	1
Vanity	1

Alley is convinced that China cannot hope to win this war unless she develops an industrial co-operative movement in the interior of the country. During the past thirty years Chinese industry has been concentrated in the coastal area, but the coast towns and the big river ports are now all occupied or threatened by the Japanese. Sooner or later, all China's industrial plant will fall into the enemy's hands unless it is removed in time to the inner provinces.

Japan is planning the economic colonization of China, nothing less. Already she has published schemes for the building of new canals, railways, cotton and silk mills. In Hongkew and the other occupied districts of Shanghai she is reopening her factories. Of the 130,000 operatives now employed in Shanghai ninety per cent are working for the Japanese.

The flight into the international zone is no solution of China's economic problems. Even if the Chinese in the Settlement retain some measure of political freedom their operations can only strengthen the Shanghai area as an economic base for the Japanese war-machine. Their communications with the interior are becoming increasingly difficult and may soon be cut off altogether. And yet, during the first four months of 1938, over 400 new Chinese factories were established in the western district of the Settlement, while less than fifty industrialists moved their plants elsewhere.

The Chinese Government, as Alley points out, has had great success in developing the agricultural co-operative movement—consumers, marketing, and credit co-operatives. It has thereby strengthened the rural purchasing power. In addition to this the local market has been automatically protected as a result of the blockade enforced by war conditions on the import of foreign goods.

The peasants of the interior are therefore able to buy manufactured articles as never before. But there is little or nothing to buy. The enormously reduced Chinese industrial production is quite unable to meet this increased demand. What is now urgently needed is the reorganization of industry on the same basis as the successfully reorganized agriculture. China requires 30,000 industrial co-operatives.

The planners of the industrial co-operative movement propose the establishment of three 'zones of economic de-

250

fence'. First, the big static units—the heavy industries, equipped with elaborate machinery and employing many workers. These will be engaged chiefly in making munitions. Because of their size they cannot easily be moved, so they should be located far out of reach of the enemy, in the extreme western provinces. Secondly, the medium-sized units, situated between the front and the rear. These should be semi-mobile, and equipped with machine-tools. Thirdly, the 'guerrilla' units. These co-operatives should use only light, easily portable tools. Their function would be to provide articles of immediate necessity to the military forces.

Since the Japanese army strikes only along easy lines of communication—a highroad, a railway, or a river—it should be possible for the 'guerrilla' units to operate around and even behind the enemy's positions. If the Japanese have occupied a large town, Chinese industrial co-operatives could still function in the neighbouring villages, providing manufactured articles necessary for the farming population. They would thus prevent areas adjacent to the Japanese garrisons from becoming economically colonized by Japanese goods. Their value, as centres of patriotic propaganda, would therefore be enormous.

Industrial co-operatives would also solve the refugee problem. They could absorb thousands of homeless and workless peasants, and divert the millions of dollars now being spent on refugee camps in the occupied areas, where destitute Chinese are merely kept alive until such time as the Japanese wish to exploit their labour power.

The difficulties in carrying out this scheme are, of course, immense. Chinese industry can only be transplanted and decentralized with the fullest co-operation of the industrialists and the workers themselves. The Chinese are no fonder of moving than anybody else. Many will have to leave their homes and even their families behind them, and set off on a roundabout journey to distant parts of the country, where their native dialect is unintelligible, and where they feel themselves as isolated as an Italian farmer in Wales. In many cases the Government will have to carry out its projects by force: plant, tools, and the means of transport will have to be commandeered. The propaganda-drive for industrial migration will have to be redoubled. Above all, money will be needed—money for transport, money for compensation, money to buy portable machinery, Delco-plants, and charcoal-burning engines. The organizers of the movement plan to appeal to the League of Nations, and to the labour parties of friendly foreign States, for technical and financial aid. We only hope that they won't be disappointed by the results.

In this city —conquered, yet unoccupied by its conquerors—the mechanism of the old life is still ticking, but seems doomed to stop, like a watch dropped in the desert. In this city the gulf between society's two halves is too grossly wide for any bridge. There can be no compromise here. And we ourselves though we wear out our shoes walking the slums, though we take notes, though we are genuinely shocked and indignant, belong, unescapably, to the other world. We return, always, to Number One House for lunch.

In our world, there are the garden-parties and the night-clubs, the hot baths and the cocktails, the singsong girls and the Ambassador's cook. In our world, European business men write to the local newspapers, complaining that the Chinese are cruel to pigs, and saying that the refugees should be turned out of the Settlement because they are beginning to smell. In our world 'the only decent Japanese' (as all the British agree in describing him) defends the wholesale bombing of Canton on the ground that it is more humane than a military occupation of the city. In our world, an Englishman quite seriously suggests that the Japanese should be asked to drive the Chinese farmers from a plot of land enclosing a grave-mound which spoils the appearance of the garden.

And the well-meaning tourist, the liberal and humanitarian intellectual, can only wring his hands over all this and exclaim: 'Oh dear, things are so awful here—so complicated. One doesn't know where to start.'

'I know where *I* should start,' says Mr. Alley, with a ferocious snort. 'They were starting quite nicely in 1927.'

PICTURE COMMENTARY

Madame

The Chiangs

UNITED FRONT

Li Tsung-jen (from the south)

Feng Yü-hsiang (from the north)

UNITED FRONT

Du Yueh-seng (capitalist)

Chou En-lai (communist)

Sian PROVINCIAL GOVERNORS Kiang-si

Staff Officer

Divisional Commander (Chang Tschen)

SOLDIERS AND CIVILIANS

Officer (Major Yang)

Men

SOLDIERS AND CIVILIANS

With legs

Without

CHILDREN IN UNIFORM

SOLDIERS AND CIVILIANS

Railway Engineer (Shang-kui)

City Mayor (Canton)

Chauffeur

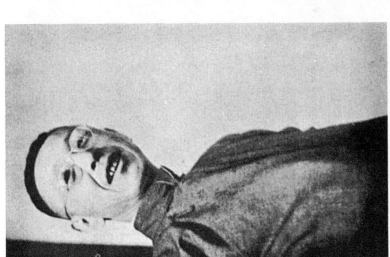

Press Bureau

REPORTERS

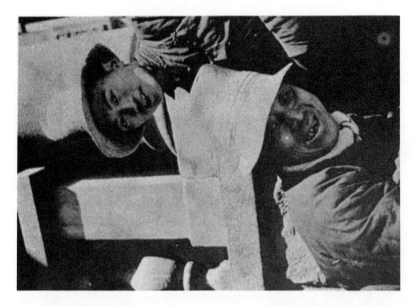

Coolies

Intellectual (C. C. Yeh)

Adviser (W. H. Donald)

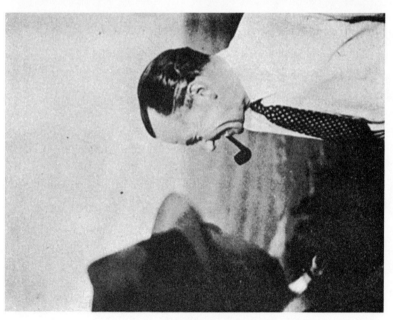

Ambassador (Sir Archibald Clark Kerr)

SOLDIERS AND CIVILIANS

Press Photographer (Capa)

Special Correspondent (Peter Fleming)

Shanghai Business Man

White Russian Restaurant Proprietor

Protestant

MISSIONARIES

Catholic

Swiss (Dr. Mooser)

Canadian (Dr. Brown)

DOCTORS

SOLDIERS AND CIVILIANS

Italian Captain

British Sailor

Japanese sentry

Japanese prisoner

WAR ZONE

IN THE TRENCHES

Temple in front line

Japanese front line

WAR ZONE

Enemy planes overhead

Chiang

WAR ZONE

The Innocent

The Guilty

WAR ZONE

Dynamited Railway Bridge

Houses (Chapei in Shanghai)

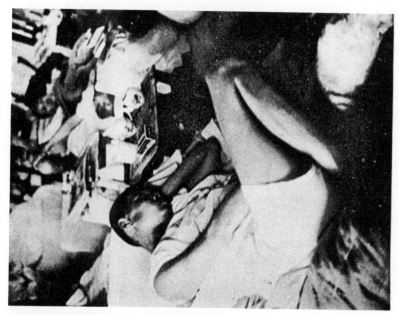

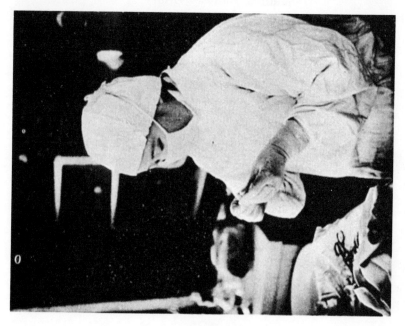

In Hospital

WAR ZONE

Refugees en route

Refugees in camp

WAR ZONE

Accident

Delay

Passengers

Car-boy

WAR ZONE

Train Parasites

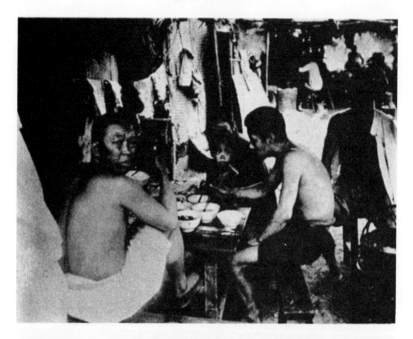

La Condition Humaine

Stills from *Fight to the Last*

Unknown Soldier

IN TIME OF WAR

A Sonnet Sequence
with a verse commentary

I

So from the years the gifts were showered; each
Ran off with his at once into his life:
Bee took the politics that make a hive,
Fish swam as fish, peach settled into peach.

And were successful at the first endeavour;
The hour of birth their only time at college,
They were content with their precocious knowledge,
And knew their station and were good for ever.

Till finally there came a childish creature
On whom the years could model any feature,
And fake with ease a leopard or a dove;

Who by the lightest wind was changed and shaken,
And looked for truth and was continually mistaken,
And envied his few friends and chose his love.

II

They wondered why the fruit had been forbidden;
It taught them nothing new. They hid their pride,
But did not listen much when they were chidden;
They knew exactly what to do outside.

They left: immediately the memory faded
Of all they'd learnt; they could not understand
The dogs now who, before, had always aided;
The stream was dumb with whom they'd always planned.

They wept and quarrelled: freedom was so wild.
In front, maturity, as he ascended,
Retired like a horizon from the child;

The dangers and the punishments grew greater;
And the way back by angels was defended
Against the poet and the legislator.

A SONNET SEQUENCE

III

Only a smell had feelings to make known,
Only an eye could point in a direction;
The fountain's utterance was itself alone;
The bird meant nothing: that was his projection

Who named it as he hunted it for food.
He felt the interest in his throat, and found
That he could send his sérvant to the wood,
Or kiss his bride to rapture with a sound.

They bred like locusts till they hid the green
And edges of the world: and he was abject,
And to his own creation became subject;

And shook with hate for things he'd never seen,
And knew of love without love's proper object,
And was oppressed as he had never been.

IV

He stayed: and was imprisoned in possession.
The seasons stood like guards about his ways,
The mountains chose the mother of his children,
And like a conscience the sun ruled his days.

Beyond him his young cousins in the city
Pursued their rapid and unnatural course,
Believed in nothing but were easy-going,
And treated strangers like a favourite horse.

And he changed little,
But took his colour from the earth,
And grew in likeness to his sheep and cattle.

The townsman thought him miserly and simple,
The poet wept and saw in him the truth,
And the oppressor held him up as an example.

V

His generous bearing was a new invention:
For life was slow; earth needed to be careless:
With horse and sword he drew the girls' attention;
He was the Rich, the Bountiful, the Fearless.

And to the young he came as a salvation;
They needed him to free them from their mothers,
And grew sharp-witted in the long migration,
And round his camp fires learnt all men are brothers.

But suddenly the earth was full: he was not wanted.
And he became the shabby and demented,
And took to drink to screw his nerves to murder;

Or sat in offices and stole,
And spoke approvingly of Law and Order,
And hated life with all his soul.

VI

He watched the stars and noted birds in flight;
The rivers flooded or the Empire fell:
He made predictions and was sometimes right;
His lucky guesses were rewarded well.

And fell in love with Truth before he knew her,
And rode into imaginary lands,
With solitude and fasting hoped to woo her,
And mocked at those who served her with their hands.

But her he never wanted to despise,
But listened always for her voice; and when
She beckoned to him, he obeyed in meekness,

And followed her and looked into her eyes;
Saw there reflected every human weakness,
And saw himself as one of many men.

VII

He was their servant—some say he was blind—
And moved among their faces and their things;
Their feeling gathered in him like a wind
And sang: they cried—'It is a God that sings'—

And worshipped him and set him up apart,
And made him vain, till he mistook for song
The little tremors of his mind and heart
At each domestic wrong.

Songs came no more: he had to make them.
With what precision was each strophe planned.
He hugged his sorrow like a plot of land,

And walked like an assassin through the town,
And looked at men and did not like them,
But trembled if one passed him with a frown.

VIII

He turned his field into a meeting-place,
And grew the tolerant ironic eye,
And formed the mobile money-changer's face,
And found the notion of equality.

And strangers were as brothers to his clocks,
And with his spires he made a human sky;
Museums stored his learning like a box,
And paper watched his money like a spy.

It grew so fast his life was overgrown,
And he forgot what once it had been made for,
And gathered into crowds and was alone,

And lived expensively and did without,
And could not find the earth which he had paid for,
Nor feel the love that he knew all about.

IX

They died and entered the closed life like nuns:
Even the very poor lost something; oppression
Was no more a fact; and the self-centred ones
Took up an even more extreme position.

And the kingly and the saintly also were
Distributed among the woods and oceans,
And touch our open sorrow everywhere,
Airs, waters, places, round our sex and reasons;

Are what we feed on as we make our choice.
We bring them back with promises to free them,
But as ourselves continually betray them:

They hear their deaths lamented in our voice,
But in our knowledge know we could restore them;
They could return to freedom; they would rejoice.

IN TIME OF WAR

X

As a young child the wisest could adore him;
He felt familiar to them like their wives:
The very poor saved up their pennies for him,
And martyrs brought him presents of their lives.

But who could sit and play with him all day?
Their other needs were pressing, work, and bed:
The beautiful stone courts were built where they
Could leave him to be worshipped and well fed.

But he escaped. They were too blind to tell
That it was he who came with them to labour,
And talked and grew up with them like a neighbour:

To fear and greed those courts became a centre;
The poor saw there the tyrant's citadel,
And martyrs the lost face of the tormentor.

XI

He looked in all His wisdom from the throne
Down on the humble boy who kept the sheep,
And sent a dove; the dove returned alone:
Youth liked the music, but soon fell asleep.

But He had planned such future for the youth:
Surely His duty now was to compel;
For later he would come to love the truth,
And own his gratitude. The eagle fell.

It did not work: his conversation bored
The boy who yawned and whistled and made faces,
And wriggled free from fatherly embraces;

But with the eagle he was always willing
To go where it suggested, and adored
And learnt from it the many ways of killing.

XII

And the age ended, and the last deliverer died
In bed, grown idle and unhappy; they were safe:
The sudden shadow of the giant's enormous calf
Would fall no more at dusk across the lawn outside.

They slept in peace: in marshes here and there no doubt
A sterile dragon lingered to a natural death,
But in a year the spoor had vanished from the heath;
The kobold's knocking in the mountain petered out.

Only the sculptors and the poets were half sad,
And the pert retinue from the magician's house
Grumbled and went elsewhere. The vanquished powers
    were glad

To be invisible and free: without remorse
Struck down the sons who strayed into their course,
And ravished the daughters, and drove the fathers mad.

XIII

Certainly praise: let the song mount again and again
For life as it blossoms out in a jar or a face,
For the vegetable patience, the animal grace;
Some people have been happy; there have been great
    men.

But hear the morning's injured weeping, and know why:
Cities and men have fallen; the will of the Unjust
Has never lost its power; still, all princes must
Employ the Fairly-Noble unifying Lie.

History opposes its grief to our buoyant song:
The Good Place has not been; our star has warmed to
    birth
A race of promise that has never proved its worth;

The quick new West is false; and prodigious, but wrong
This passive flower-like people who for so long
In the Eighteen Provinces have constructed the earth.

IN TIME OF WAR

XIV

Yes, we are going to suffer, now; the sky
Throbs like a feverish forehead; pain is real;
The groping searchlights suddenly reveal
The little natures that will make us cry,

Who never quite believed they could exist,
Not where we were. They take us by surprise
Like ugly long-forgotten memories,
And like a conscience all the guns resist.

Behind each sociable home-loving eye
The private massacres are taking place;
All Women, Jews, the Rich, the Human Race.

The mountains cannot judge us when we lie:
We dwell upon the earth; the earth obeys
The intelligent and evil till they die.

XV

Engines bear them through the sky: they're free
And isolated like the very rich;
Remote like savants, they can only see
The breathing city as a target which

Requires their skill; will never see how flying
Is the creation of ideas they hate,
Nor how their own machines are always trying
To push through into life. They chose a fate

The islands where they live did not compel.
Though earth may teach our proper discipline,
At any time it will be possible

To turn away from freedom and become
Bound like the heiress in her mother's womb,
And helpless as the poor have always been.

XVI

Here war is simple like a monument:
A telephone is speaking to a man;
Flags on a map assert that troops were sent;
A boy brings milk in bowls. There is a plan

For living men in terror of their lives,
Who thirst at nine who were to thirst at noon,
And can be lost and are, and miss their wives,
And, unlike an idea, can die too soon.

But ideas can be true although men die,
And we can watch a thousand faces
Made active by one lie:

And maps can really point to places
Where life is evil now:
Nanking; Dachau.

XVII

They are and suffer; that is all they do:
A bandage hides the place where each is living,
His knowledge of the world restricted to
The treatment that the instruments are giving.

And lie apart like epochs from each other
—Truth in their sense is how much they can bear;
It is not talk like ours, but groans they smother—
And are remote as plants; we stand elsewhere.

For who when healthy can become a foot?
Even a scratch we can't recall when cured,
But are boist'rous in a moment and believe

In the common world of the uninjured, and cannot
Imagine isolation. Only happiness is shared,
And anger, and the idea of love.

XVIII

Far from the heart of culture he was used:
Abandoned by his general and his lice,
Under a padded quilt he closed his eyes
And vanished. He will not be introduced

When this campaign is tidied into books:
No vital knowledge perished in his skull;
His jokes were stale; like wartime, he was dull;
His name is lost for ever like his looks.

He neither knew nor chose the Good, but taught us,
And added meaning like a comma, when
He turned to dust in China that our daughters

Be fit to love the earth, and not again
Disgraced before the dogs; that, where are waters,
Mountains and houses, may be also men.

XIX

But in the evening the oppression lifted;
The peaks came into focus; it had rained:
Across the lawns and cultured flowers drifted
The conversation of the highly trained.

The gardeners watched them pass and priced their shoes;
A chauffeur waited, reading in the drive,
For them to finish their exchange of views;
It seemed a picture of the private life.

Far off, no matter what good they intended,
The armies waited for a verbal error
With all the instruments for causing pain:

And on the issue of their charm depended
A land laid waste, with all its young men slain,
The women weeping, and the towns in terror.

XX

They carry terror with them like a purse,
And flinch from the horizon like a gun;
And all the rivers and the railways run
Away from Neighbourhood as from a curse.

They cling and huddle in the new disaster
Like children sent to school, and cry in turn;
For Space has rules they cannot hope to learn,
Time speaks a language they will never master.

We live here. We lie in the Present's unopened
Sorrow; its limits are what we are.
The prisoner ought never to pardon his cell.

Can future ages ever escape so far,
Yet feel derived from everything that happened,
Even from us, that even this was well?

XXI

The life of man is never quite completed;
The daring and the chatter will go on:
But, as an artist feels his power gone,
These walk the earth and know themselves defeated.

Some could not bear nor break the young and mourn for
The wounded myths that once made nations good,
Some lost a world they never understood,
Some saw too clearly all that man was born for.

Loss is their shadow-wife, Anxiety
Receives them like a grand hotel; but where
They may regret they must; their life, to hear

The call of the forbidden cities, see
The stranger watch them with a happy stare,
And Freedom hostile in each home and tree.

XXII

Simple like all dream wishes, they employ
The elementary language of the heart,
And speak to muscles of the need for joy:
The dying and the lovers soon to part

Hear them and have to whistle. Always new,
They mirror every change in our position;
They are our evidence of what we do;
They speak directly to our lost condition.

Think in this year what pleased the dancers best:
When Austria died and China was forsaken,
Shanghai in flames and Teruel retaken,

France put her case before the world; 'Partout
Il y a de la joie.' America addressed
The earth: 'Do you love me as I love you?'

A SONNET SEQUENCE

XXIII

When all the apparatus of report
Confirms the triumph of our enemies;
Our bastion pierced, our army in retreat,
Violence successful like a new disease,

And Wrong a charmer everywhere invited;
When we regret that we were ever born:
Let us remember all who seemed deserted.
To-night in China let me think of one,

Who through ten years of silence worked and waited,
Until in Muzot all his powers spoke,
And everything was given once for all:

And with the gratitude of the Completed
He went out in the winter night to stroke
That little tower like a great animal.

XXIV

No, not their names. It was the others who built
Each great coercive avenue and square,
Where men can only recollect and stare,
The really lonely with the sense of guilt

Who wanted to persist like that for ever;
The unloved had to leave material traces:
But these need nothing but our better faces,
And dwell in them, and know that we shall never

Remember who we are nor why we're needed.
Earth grew them as a bay grows fishermen
Or hills a shepherd; they grew ripe and seeded;

And the seeds clung to us; even our blood
Was able to revive them; and they grew again;
Happy their wish and mild to flower and flood.

XXV

Nothing is given: we must find our law.
Great buildings jostle in the sun for domination;
Behind them stretch like sorry vegetation
The low recessive houses of the poor.

We have no destiny assigned us:
Nothing is certain but the body; we plan
To better ourselves; the hospitals alone remind us
Of the equality of man.

Children are really loved here, even by police:
They speak of years before the big were lonely,
And will be lost.

And only
The brass bands throbbing in the parks foretell
Some future reign of happiness and peace.

We learn to pity and rebel.

XXVI

Always far from the centre of our names,
The little workshop of love: yes, but how wrong
We were about the old manors and the long
Abandoned Folly and the children's games.

Only the acquisitive expects a quaint
Unsaleable product, something to please
An artistic girl; it's the selfish who sees
In every impractical beggar a saint.

We can't believe that we ourselves designed it,
A minor item of our daring plan
That caused no trouble; we took no notice of it.

Disaster comes, and we're amazed to find it
The single project that since work began
Through all the cycle showed a steady profit.

XXVII

Wandering lost upon the mountains of our choice,
Again and again we sigh for an ancient South,
For the warm nude ages of instinctive poise,
For the taste of joy in the innocent mouth.

Asleep in our huts, how we dream of a part
In the glorious balls of the future; each intricate maze
Has a plan, and the disciplined movements of the heart
Can follow for ever and ever its harmless ways.

We envy streams and houses that are sure:
But we are articled to error; we
Were never nude and calm like a great door,

And never will be perfect like the fountains;
We live in freedom by necessity,
A mountain people dwelling among mountains.

COMMENTARY

Season inherits legally from dying season;
Protected by the wide peace of the sun, the planets
Continue their circulations; and the galaxy

Is free for ever to revolve like an enormous biscuit:
With all his engines round him and the summer flowers,
Little upon his little earth, man contemplates

The universe of which he is both judge and victim;
A rarity in an uncommon corner, gazes
On the great trackways where his tribe and truth are
    nothing.

Certainly the growth of the fore-brain has been a success:
He has not got lost in a backwater like the lampshell
Or the limpet; he has not died out like the super-lizards.

His boneless worm-like ancestors would be amazed
At the upright position, the breasts, the four-chambered
    heart,
The clandestine evolution in the mother's shadow.

'Sweet is it', say the doomed, 'to be alive though
    wretched,'
And the young emerging from the closed parental circle,
To whose uncertainty the certain years present

COMMENTARY

Their syllabus of limitless anxiety and labour,
At first feel nothing but the gladness of their freedom,
Are happy in the new embraces and the open talk.

But liberty to be and weep has never been sufficient;
The winds surround our griefs, the unfenced sky
To all our failures is a taciturn unsmiling witness.

And not least here, among this humorous and hairless
    people
Who like a cereal have inherited these valleys:
Tarim nursed them; Thibet was the tall rock of their
    protection,

And where the Yellow River shifts its course, they
    learnt
How to live well, though ruin threatened often.
For centuries they looked in fear towards the northern
    defiles,

But now must turn and gather like a fist to strike
Wrong coming from the sea, from those whose paper
    houses
Tell of their origin among the coral islands;

Who even to themselves deny a human freedom,
And dwell in the estranging tyrant's vision of the earth
In a calm stupor under their blood-spotted flag.

Here danger works a civil reconciliation,
Interior hatreds are resolved upon this foreign foe,
And will-power to resist is growing like a prosperous
    city.

COMMENTARY

For the invader now is deadly and impartial as a judge:
Down country footpaths, from each civic sky,
His anger blows alike upon the rich, and all

Who dwell within the crevices of destitution,
On those with a laborious lifetime to recall, and those,
The innocent and short whose dreams contain no children.

While in an international and undamaged quarter,
Casting our European shadows on Shanghai,
Walking unhurt among the banks, apparently immune

Below the monuments of an acquisitive society,
With friends and books and money and the traveller's
    freedom,
We are compelled to realize that our refuge is a sham.

For this material contest that has made Hongkew
A terror and a silence, and Chapei a howling desert,
Is but the local variant of a struggle in which all,

The elderly, the amorous, the young, the handy and the
    thoughtful,
Those to whom feeling is a science, those to whom study
Of all that can be added and compared is a consuming
    love,

With those whose brains are empty as a school in August,
And those in whom the urge to action is so strong
They cannot read a letter without whispering, all

In cities, deserts, ships, in lodgings near the port,
Discovering the past of strangers in a library,
Creating their own future on a bed, each with his treasure,

COMMENTARY

Self-confident among the laughter and the *petits verres*,
Or motionless and lonely like a moping cormorant,
In all their living are profoundly implicated.

This is one sector and one movement of the general war
Between the dead and the unborn, the Real and the
    Pretended,
Which for the creature who creates, communicates, and
    chooses,

The only animal aware of lack of finish,
In essence is eternal. When we emerged from holes
And blinked in the warm sunshine of the Laufen Ice
    Retreat,

Thinking of Nature as a close and loyal kinsman,
On every acre the opponents faced each other,
And we were far within the zone where casualties begin.

Now in a world that has no localized events,
Where not a tribe exists without its dossier,
And the machine has taught us how, to the Non-Human,

That unprogressive blind society that knows
No argument except the absolute and violent veto,
Our colours, creeds and sexes are identical,

The issue is the same. Some uniforms are new,
Some have changed sides; but the campaign continues:
Still unachieved is *Jen*, the Truly Human.

This is the epoch of the Third Great Disappointment:
The First was the collapse of that slave-owning empire
Whose yawning magistrate asked, 'What is truth?'

COMMENTARY

Upon its ruins rose the Universal Churches:
Men camped like tourists under their tremendous
    shadows,
United by a common sense of human failure,

Their certain knowledge only of the timeless fields
Where the Unchanging Happiness received the faithful,
And the Eternal Nightmare waited to devour the wicked.

In which a host of workers, famous and obscure,
Meaning to do no more than use their eyes,
Not knowing what they did, then sapped belief;

Put in its place a neutral dying star,
Where Justice could not visit. Self was the one city,
The cell where each must find his comfort and his pain,

The body nothing but a useful favourite machine
To go upon errands of love and to run the house,
While the mind in its study spoke with its private God.

But now that wave which already was washing the heart,
When the cruel Turk stormed the gates of Constantine's
    city,
When Galileo muttered to himself, '*sed movet*',

And Descartes thought, 'I am because I think',
Today, all spent, is silently withdrawing itself:
Unhappy he or she who after it is sucked.

Never before was the Intelligence so fertile,
The Heart more stunted. The human field became
Hostile to brotherhood and feeling like a forest.

COMMENTARY

Machines devised by harmless clergymen and boys
Attracted men like magnets from the marl and clay
Into towns on the coal-measures, to a kind of freedom,

Where the abstinent with the landless drove a bitter
    bargain,
But sowed in that act the seeds of an experienced
    hatred,
Which, germinating long in tenement and gas-lit cellar,

Is choking now the aqueducts of our affection.
Knowledge of their colonial suffering has cut off
The Hundred Families like an attack of shyness;

The apprehensive rich pace up and down
Their narrow compound of success; in every body
The ways of living are disturbed; intrusive as a sill,

Fear builds enormous ranges casting shadows,
Heavy, bird-silencing, upon the outer world,
Hills that our grief sighs over like a Shelley, parting

All that we feel from all that we perceive,
Desire from Data; and the Thirteen gay Companions
Grow sullen now and quarrelsome as mountain tribes.

We wander on the earth, or err from bed to bed
In search of home, and fail, and weep for the lost ages
Before Because became As If, or rigid Certainty

The Chances Are. The base hear us, and the violent
Who long to calm our guilt with murder, and already
Have not been slow to turn our wish to their advantage.

COMMENTARY

On every side they make their brazen offer:
Now in that Catholic country with the shape of Cornwall,
Where Europe first became a term of pride,

North of the Alps where dark hair turns to blonde,
In Germany now loudest, land without a centre
Where the sad plains are like a sounding rostrum,

And on these tidy and volcanic summits near us now,
From which the Black Stream hides the Tuscarora
    Deep,
The voice is quieter but the more inhuman and
    triumphant.

By wire and wireless, in a score of bad translations,
They give their simple message to the world of man:
'Man can have Unity if Man will give up Freedom.

The State is real, the Individual is wicked;
Violence shall synchronize your movements like a tune,
And Terror like a frost shall halt the flood of thinking.

Barrack and bivouac shall be your friendly refuge,
And racial pride shall tower like a public column
And confiscate for safety every private sorrow.

Leave Truth to the police and us; we know the Good;
We build the Perfect City time shall never alter;
Our Law shall guard you always like a cirque of mountains,

Your Ignorance keep off evil like a dangerous sea;
You shall be consummated in the General Will,
Your children innocent and charming as the beasts.'

COMMENTARY

All the great conquerors sit upon their platform,
Lending their sombre weight of practical experience:
Ch'in Shih Huang Ti who burnt the scholars' books,

Chaka the mad who segregated the two sexes,
And *Genghis Khan* who thought mankind should be
    destroyed,
And *Diocletian* the administrator make impassioned
    speeches.

Napoleon claps who found religion useful,
And all who passed deception of the People, or who said
Like Little *Frederick*, 'I shall see that it is done.'

While many famous clerks support their programme:
Plato the good, despairing of the average man.
With sad misgiving signs their manifesto;

Shang-tzu approves their principle of Nothing Private;
The author of The Prince will heckle; *Hobbes* will
    canvass,
With generalizing *Hegel* and quiet *Bosanquet.*

And every family and every heart is tempted:
The earth debates; the Fertile Crescent argues;
Even the little towns upon the way to somewhere,

Those desert flowers the aeroplane now fertilizes,
Quarrel on this; in England far away,
Behind the high tides and the navigable estuaries;

In the Far West, in absolutely free America,
In melancholy Hungary, and clever France
Where ridicule has acted a historic role,

COMMENTARY

And here where the rice-grain nourishes these patient
    households
The ethic of the feudal citadel has impregnated,
Thousands believe, and millions are half-way to a
    conviction.

While others have accepted *Pascal*'s wager and resolve
To take whatever happens as the will of God,
Or with *Spinoza* vote that evil be unreal.

Nor do our leaders help; we know them now
For humbugs full of vain dexterity, invoking
A gallery of ancestors, pursuing still the mirage

Of long dead grandeurs whence the interest has
    absconded,
As Fahrenheit in an odd corner of great Celsius'
    kingdom
Might mumble of the summers measured once by him.

Yet all the same we have our faithful sworn supporters
Who never lost their faith in knowledge or in man,
But worked so eagerly that they forgot their food

And never noticed death or old age coming on,
Prepared for freedom as *Kuo Hsi* for inspiration,
Waiting it calmly like the coming of an honoured guest.

Some looked at falsehood with the candid eyes of
    children,
Some had a woman's ear to catch injustice,
Some took Necessity, and knew her, and she brought
    forth Freedom.

COMMENTARY

Some of our dead are famous, but they would not care:
Evil is always personal and spectacular,
But goodness needs the evidence of all our lives,

And, even to exist, it must be shared as truth,
As freedom or as happiness. (For what is happiness
If not to witness joy upon the features of another?)

They did not live to be remembered specially as noble,
Like those who cultivated only cucumbers and melons
To prove that they were rich; and when we praise their
    names,

They shake their heads in warning, chiding us to give
Our gratitude to the Invisible College of the Humble,
Who through the ages have accomplished everything
    essential.

And stretch around our struggle as the normal landscape,
And mingle, fluent with our living, like the winds and
    waters,
The dust of all the dead that reddens every sunset;

Giving us courage to confront our enemies,
Not only on the Grand Canal, or in Madrid,
Across the campus of a university city,

But aid us everywhere, that in the lovers' bedroom,
The white laboratory, the school, the public meeting,
The enemies of life may be more passionately attacked.

And, if we care to listen, we can always hear them:
'*Men are not innocent as beasts and never can be,*
Man can improve himself but never will be perfect,

COMMENTARY

Only the free have disposition to be truthful,
Only the truthful have the interest to be just,
Only the just possess the will-power to be free.

For common justice can determine private freedom,
As a clear sky can tempt men to astronomy,
Or a peninsula persuade them to be sailors.

You talked of Liberty, but were not just; and now
Your enemies have called your bluff; for in your city,
Only the man behind the rifle had free-will.

One wish is common to you both, the wish to build
A world united as that Europe was in which
The flint-faced exile wrote his three-act comedy.

Lament not its decay; that shell was too constricting:
The years of private isolation had their lesson,
And in the interest of intelligence were necessary.

Now in the clutch of crisis and the bloody hour
You must defeat your enemies or perish, but remember,
Only by those who reverence it can life be mastered;

Only a whole and happy conscience can stand up
And answer their bleak lie; among the just,
And only there, is Unity compatible with Freedom.'

Night falls on China; the great arc of travelling shadow
Moves over land and ocean, altering life:
Thibet already silent, the packed Indias cooling,

COMMENTARY

Inert in the paralysis of caste. And though in Africa
The vegetation still grows fiercely like the young,
And in the cities that receive the slanting radiations

The lucky are at work, and most still know they suffer,
The dark will touch them soon: night's tiny noises
Will echo vivid in the owl's developed ear,

Vague in the anxious sentry's; and the moon look down
On battlefields and dead men lying, heaped like treasure,
On lovers ruined in a brief embrace, on ships

Where exiles watch the sea: and in the silence
The cry that streams out into the indifferent spaces,
And never stops or slackens, may be heard more clearly,

Above the everlasting murmur of the woods and rivers,
And more insistent than the lulling answer of the
     waltzes,
Or hum of printing-presses turning forests into lies;

As now I hear it, rising round me from Shanghai,
And mingling with the distant mutter of guerrilla
     fighting,
The voice of Man: '*O teach me to outgrow my madness.*

It's better to be sane than mad, or liked than dreaded;
It's better to sit down to nice meals than to nasty;
It's better to sleep two than single; it's better to be happy.

Ruffle the perfect manners of the frozen heart,
And once again compel it to be awkward and alive,
To all it suffered once a weeping witness.

COMMENTARY

Clear from the head the masses of impressive rubbish;
Rally the lost and trembling forces of the will,
Gather them up and let them loose upon the earth,

Till they construct at last a human justice,
The contribution of our star, within the shadow
Of which uplifting, loving, and constraining power
All other reasons may rejoice and operate.'

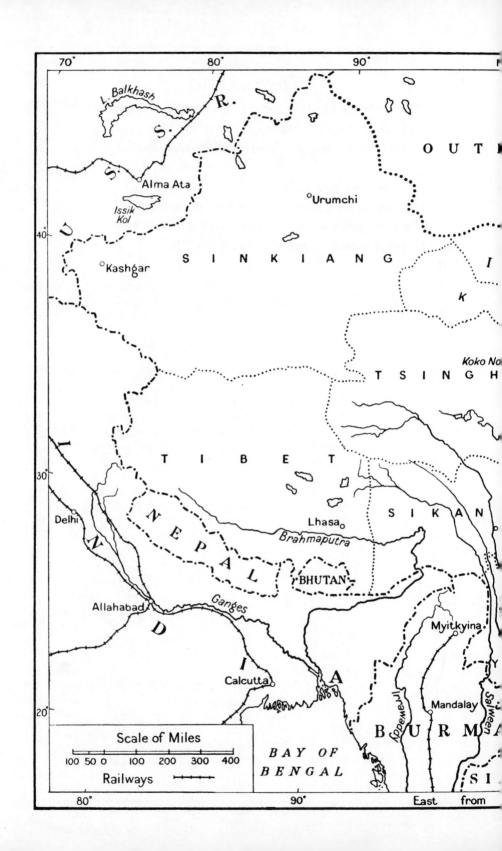